MANAGING INFORMATION
HOW INFORMATION SYSTEMS IMPACT ORGANIZATIONAL STRATEGY

THE BUSINESS ONE IRWIN/APICS LIBRARY OF INTEGRATED MANAGEMENT

Customers and Products

   Marketing for the Manufacturer *J. Paul Peter*
   Field Service Management: An Integrated Approach to Increasing Customer Satisfaction *Arthur V. Hill*
   Effective Product Design and Development: How to Cut Lead Time and Increase Customer Satisfaction *Stephen R. Rosenthal*

Logistics

   Integrated Production and Inventory Management: Revitalizing the Manufacturing Enterprise *Thomas E. Vollmann, William L. Berry, and D. Clay Whybark*
   Purchasing: Continued Improvement through Integration *Joseph Carter*
   Integrated Distribution Management: Competing on Customer Service, Time and Cost *Christopher Gopal and Harold Cypress*

Manufacturing Processes

   Integrative Facilities Management *John M. Burnham*
   Integrated Process Design and Development *Dan L. Shunk*
   Integrative Manufacturing: Transforming the Organization through People, Process and Technology *Scott Flaig*

Support Functions

   Managing Information: How Information Systems Impact Organizational Strategy *Gordon B. Davis and Thomas R. Hoffman*
   Managing Human Resources: Integrating People and Business Strategy *Lloyd Baird*
   Managing for Quality: Integrating Quality and Business Strategy *V. Daniel Hunt*
   World-Class Accounting and Finance *Carol J. McNair*

MANAGING INFORMATION
HOW INFORMATION SYSTEMS IMPACT ORGANIZATIONAL STRATEGY

Gordon B. Davis

Scott Hamilton

BUSINESS ONE IRWIN
Homewood, Illinois 60430

© RICHARD D. IRWIN, INC, 1993

All rights reserved. No part of this publication may be reproduced, stored in a retrieval systems, or transmitted, in any form or by any means, electronic, mechanical, photocopying, recording, or otherwise, without the prior written permission of the publisher.

This publication is designed to provide accurate and authoritative information in regard to the subject matter covered. It is sold with the understanding that neither the author nor the publisher is engaged in rendering legal, accounting, or other professional service. If legal advice or other expert assistance is required, the services of a competent professional person should be sought.

From a Declaration of Principles jointly adapted by a Committee of the American Bar Association and a Committee of Publishers.

Editor-in-chief: Jeffrey A. Krames
Project editor: Karen J. Nelson
Production manager: Diane Palmer
Designer: Jeanne M. Rivera
Art coordinator: Heather Burbridge
Typeface: 10.5/12 Times Roman
Printer: Book Press, Inc.

Library of Congress Cataloging-in-Publication Data

Davis, Gordon Bitter.
   Managing information : how information systems impact organizational strategy / Gordon B. Davis, Scott Hamilton.
     p.   cm.
   Includes bibliographical references and index.
   ISBN 1-55623-768-5
    1. Strategic planning—Data processing. 2. Information technology—Management. 3. Industrial management—Data processing.
I. Hamilton, Scott. II. Title.
HD30.28.D387   1993
658.4'012'028—dc20   92-36284

Printed in the United States of America
1 2 3 4 5 6 7 8 9 0 BP 0 9 8 7 6 5 4 3

FOREWORD

Managing Information: How Information Systems Impact Organizational Strategy is one book in a series that addresses the most critical issue facing manufacturing companies today: integration—the identification and solution of problems that cross organizational and company boundaries—and, perhaps more important, the continuous search for ways to solve these problems faster and more effectively! The genesis for the series is the commitment to integration made by the American Production and Inventory Control Society (APICS). I attended several brainstorming sessions a few years ago in which the primary topic of discussion was, "What jobs will exist in manufacturing companies in the future—not at the very top of the enterprise and not at the bottom, but in between?" The prognostications included:

- The absolute number of jobs will decrease, as will the layers of management. Manufacturing organizations will adopt flatter organizational forms with less emphasis on hierarchy and less distinction between white collars and blue collars.
- Functional "silos" will become obsolete. The classical functions of marketing, manufacturing, engineering, finance, and personnel will be less important in defining work. More people will take on "project" work focused on continuous improvement of one kind or another.
- Fundamental restructuring, meaning much more than financial restructuring, will become a way of life in manufacturing enterprises. The primary focal points will be a new market-driven emphasis on creating value with customers, as well as greatly increased flexibility, a new business-driven attack on global markets which includes new deployment of information technology, and fundamentally new jobs.
- Work will become much more integrated in its orientation. The payoffs will increasingly be made through connections across organizational and company boundaries. Included are customer and vendor partnerships, with an overall focus on improving the value-added chain.
- New measurements that focus on the new strategic directions will be required. Metrics will be developed, similar to the cost of quality metric, that incorporate the most important dimensions of the environ-

ment. Similar metrics and semantics will be developed to support the new uses of information technology.
- New "people management" approaches will be developed. Teamwork will be critical to organizational success. Human resource management will become less of a "staff" function and more closely integrated with the basic work.

Many of these prognostications are already a reality. APICS has made the commitment to *leading* the way in all of these change areas. The decision was both courageous and intelligent. There is no future for a professional society not committed to leading-edge education for its members. Based on the Society's past experience with the Certification in Production and Inventory Management (CPIM) program, the natural thrust of APICS was to develop a new certification program focusing on integration. The result, Certification in Integrated Resource Management (CIRM) is a program composed of 13 building block areas which have been combined into four examination modules, as follows:

Customers and products
    Marketing and sales
    Field service
    Product design and development

Manufacturing processes
    Industrial facilities management
    Process design and development
    Manufacturing (production)

Logistics
    Production and inventory control
    Procurement
    Distribution

Support functions
    Total quality management
    Human resources
    Finance and accounting
    Information systems

As can be seen from this topical list, one objective in the CIRM program is to develop educational breadth. Managers increasingly *must* know the underlying basics in each area of the business: who are the people who work there, what are day-to-day *and* strategic problems, what is state-of-the-art practice, what are the expected improvement areas, and what is happening with technology? This basic breadth of knowledge is an absolute prerequisite to understanding the potential linkages and joint improvements.

But it is the linkages, relationships, and integration that are even more important. Each examination devotes approximately 40 percent of the questions to the connections *among* the 13 building block areas. In fact, after a candidate has successfully completed the four examination modules, he or she must take a fifth examination (Integrated Enterprise Management), which focuses solely on the interrelationships among all functional areas of an enterprise.

The CIRM program has been the most exciting activity on which I have worked in a professional organization. Increasingly, manufacturing companies face the alternative of either proactive restructuring to deal with today's competitive realities, or just sliding away—giving up market share and industry leadership. Education must play a key role in making the necessary changes. People working in manufacturing companies need to learn many new things and "unlearn" many old ones.

There were very limited educational materials available to support CIRM. There were textbooks in which basic concepts were covered and bits and pieces which dealt with integration, but there simply was no coordinated set of materials available for this program. That has been the job of the CIRM series authors, and it has been my distinct pleasure as a series editor to help develop the ideas and facilitate our joint learning. All of us have learned a great deal, and I am delighted with every book in the series.

Thomas E. Vollmann
Series Editor

PREFACE

The development and writing of this book is the result of collaboration between an academic with strong ties to both scholarship and practice in information systems and a scholarly practitioner with extensive experience in developing and implementing manufacturing information systems and acting as a consultant to companies making decisions about such systems. The result is a book designed to achieve a balance between completeness of explanation suited to academic study and emphasis that reflects business practices.

A key framework for the book is one in which the business architecture with its organization and business processes interacts with an information system architecture with its infrastructure and information processing applications. It is this two way interaction that provides the basis for strategic uses of information technology and redesign of business processes to use the technology effectively.

The book presents a combination of concepts for understanding the use of information technology in organizations, overviews of the key technologies, and development and implementation processes. There is an emphasis on understanding design, development, and use alternatives and their key differences. The discussion covers both large company systems and systems for smaller companies. Manufacturing and distribution are frequently used as examples, but other types of activities are also employed to illustrate concepts and practices.

There are selected references for additional reading at the end of some chapters. The focus of the references is on concepts and managerial implications rather than technical coverage.

A number of companies gave permission to use their experiences as illustrations. We appreciate their willingness to share them. Some parts of the book draw on excerpts and figures from Gordon B. Davis and Margrethe H. Olson, *Management Information Systems: Conceptual Foundations, Structure, and Development*, McGraw-Hill Book Company, New York, 1985. These are used with the permission of McGraw Hill Book Company. They are not individually referenced. Quotations, figures, or ideas from other authors or books are referenced where used.

Gordon B. Davis
Scott Hamilton

CONTENTS IN BRIEF

CHAPTER 1	INFORMATION TECHNOLOGY IN BUSINESS STRATEGY	1
CHAPTER 2	THE VALUE OF INFORMATION TECHNOLOGY TO AN ORGANIZATION AND THE INDIVIDUAL WORKER	24
CHAPTER 3	BUSINESS AND INFORMATION SYSTEM ARCHITECTURES	45
CHAPTER 4	TYPES OF APPLICATIONS IN AN INFORMATION SYSTEM	65
CHAPTER 5	COMPUTER HARDWARE SYSTEMS	88
CHAPTER 6	COMMUNICATIONS TECHNOLOGY	110
CHAPTER 7	COMPUTER SOFTWARE	131
CHAPTER 8	APPLICATION DEVELOPMENT AND IMPLEMENTATION	156
CHAPTER 9	ACHIEVING CORRECT AND COMPLETE REQUIREMENTS	180
CHAPTER 10	MODELING DATA REQUIREMENTS AND USING DATABASES	199
CHAPTER 11	ORGANIZATION AND OPERATION OF THE INFORMATION MANAGEMENT FUNCTION	224
CHAPTER 12	INFORMATION SYSTEMS AND INTEGRATED RESOURCES MANAGEMENT	253
	INDEX	277

CONTENTS

CHAPTER 1 INFORMATION TECHNOLOGY IN BUSINESS STRATEGY 1

Strategy and Information Technology Applications, 1
- *Interaction of Business Strategy, Information Technology, and Business Processes,* 2
- *Information Technology in Support of Basic Strategies,* 4
- *Information Technology and Changes in Strategy,* 4
- *Information Technology Innovations and Sustainable Competitive Advantage,* 5

Information Technology and Business Processes, 6
- *Problems with Business Processes,* 6
- *A Traditional Approach to Business Processes,* 7
- *Software Packages as an Alternative Approach to Business Processes,* 7

Information Technology and Organizational Downsizing, 9
- *The Advantages of Decentralizing and Downsizing the Organization,* 9
- *Decentralizing and Downsizing Information Systems,* 9

Information Technology and Customer-Oriented Strategy, 11

Information Technology and Just In Time (JIT), 15

Information Technology and Computer Integrated Manufacturing, 17

Complexity of Information System Development and Implementation, 18

Reengineering Business Processes, 19
- *No Business Process Change but Add Information Technology,* 19
- *Streamlining Business Process to Incorporate Improved Information Technology,* 20
- *Reengineering Business Processes,* 20

Information Management Terminology, 21

Lessons for Managers, 22

Selected References for Additional Reading, 23

CHAPTER 2 THE VALUE OF INFORMATION TECHNOLOGY TO AN ORGANIZATION AND THE INDIVIDUAL WORKER 24

The Societal Benefits from Information Technology Investments, 25
   The Measurement and Definition Problem, 25
   Variety and Customization Effects, 26
The Organizational Benefits of Information Technology Investments, 27
   The Organizational Benefits of Manufacturing Resource Planning (MRP), 28
   Quantifiable Benefits from an MRP Systems, 29
   MRP System Benefits on the Balance Sheet, 30
   MRP Benefits on the Income Statement, 31
   MRP Impact on Key Financial Ratios, 32
   MRP Impact on Stock Price, 35
The Integrative Effects of MRP Information System, 35
   Effects on Accounting, 35
   Effects on Product and Process Design, 36
   Effects on Production and Materials Management, 36
   Effects on Sales, 37
   Effects on the MIS Function, 37
Value of Individual Competence in Information Management, 37
   Value in Interacting with the Information Systems Function, 38
   Value in Projects for Planning and Developing Large Applications, 38
   Value in Using Applications Developed by Others, 39
   Value in Developing and Managing One's Own Applications and Databases, 39
   Value of Competence in Industry- or Function-Specific Information Systems, 40
The Value Of Individual Competence in Selected Knowledge Work Software, 40
   Knowledge Work, 40
   Value of Competence in a Basic Software Toolkit, 40
   Value of Competence in a Domain Software Toolkit, 44
Lessons for Managers, 44

CHAPTER 3   BUSINESS AND INFORMATION SYSTEM ARCHITECTURES   45

Concept of Business Architecture and Information System Architecture, 45
   Business Architecture, 46
   Information System Architecture, 47

Functions and Activities in Business Operations, 49
- Business Planning, 49
- Sales Planning, 50
- Sales Order Processing, 51
- Production Planning/Master Scheduling, 51
- Capacity Planning, 51
- Material Planning, 51
- Procurement, 52
- Production Activity Control, 52
- Accounting, 52
- Examples of Unique Requirements, 52

Alternatives for Business and Information Architecture, 53
- Extent of Integration, 54
- Location and Control of Data and Facilities, 54
- Directions in Business and Information System Architecture, 55

Non-Integrated Systems in a Single Business Unit, 55

Integrated Systems within a Single Business Unit, 57
- Centralized Shared Computer, 57
- Distributed Approach Using a Client Server System, 57

Integration across Multiple Business Units, 58
- Consolidation of Financial Results, 59
- Standardized Bills of Material, 59
- Product Costs, 60
- Centralized Master Scheduling, 60
- Centralized Purchasing, 60
- Centralized Payables and Cash Management, 61
- Centralized Invoicing and/or Receivables, 61
- Centralized Order Entry and Distribution Requirements Planning (DRP), 61

Lessons for Managers, 62

Selected References for Additional Reading, 64

CHAPTER 4 TYPES OF APPLICATIONS IN AN INFORMATION SYSTEM 65

Overview of Types of Applications in an Information System, 65
- Concepts of Data and Information, 66
- The Definition of an Information System Based on Essential Characteristics, 66
- Information Systems Based on Type of Application, 67

Information Systems as Subsystems for Organizational Functions, 68
Transaction Processing Applications, 69
Management Reporting Applications, 71
Executive Information Systems (EIS), 72
  The Need for an EIS, 73
  The Costs and Benefits of an EIS, 74
Decision Support Systems, 75
Collaborative Work Systems, 77
  Electronic Meeting Systems, 79
  Collaborative Work Electronic Mail Systems, 80
Knowledge Work Applications, 80
Knowledge-Based Systems, 82
  Knowledge-Based Expert Systems, 82
  Data-Based Neural Networks, 85
Lessons for Managers, 85
Selected References for Additional Reading, 86

CHAPTER 5 COMPUTER HARDWARE SYSTEMS   88

Microelectronics, 88
  Logic and Memory Chips, 88
  Boards and Buses, 89
  Microcode and Machine-Language Instructions, 90
Computer Hardware System for Information Processing, 92
  Hardware for Direct Data Entry or Data Input, 93
  Hardware for the Central Processing Unit (CPU), 93
  Hardware for Secondary Storage, 95
  Hardware for Output, 96
Classes of Computer Systems, 96
Operating System Software, 97
Data Representation for Computers, 99
  The Binary Code for Alphanumeric Data, 100
  Binary Coding of Numeric Data for Calculations, 100
  Representing Images in Storage, 101
Input and Output Devices, 101
  Individual Data Entry Devices, 101
  Readers for Encoded Data, 102
  Individual Output Devices, 103

Print and Graphics Output Devices, 104
Storage Devices, 104
  Direct Access Devices, 104
  Serial Access Devices, 106
  Optical Storage, 107
A User View of Interaction with Computer Hardware Systems, 107
  Batch System Use, 107
  Online System Use, 108
  Microcomputer Use, 108
Lessons for Managers, 109

CHAPTER 6 COMMUNICATIONS TECHNOLOGY 110
Basic Communications Facilities, 110
  Model of a Communications System, 110
  Transmission Media for Communications Channels, 113
  Front-End Processors, 115
Communication Networks, 115
  Need for Communication Networks, 116
  Concept of a Communication Network, 117
  Local Area Network (LAN), 118
  Wide Area Network, 120
  Protocols, 120
Distributed Systems, 121
  Distributed Computing, 121
  Client Server Systems, 122
Communication Applications, 124
  Voice Mail, 124
  Electronic Mail (E-Mail), 125
  Facsimile Transmission (Fax or Telefax), 126
  Electronic Data Interchange (EDI), 127
  Integrated Services Digital Networks (ISDN), 128
  Other Telephone Services Useful in Business Systems, 128
Lessons for Managers, 130

CHAPTER 7 COMPUTER SOFTWARE 131
The Role of Software, 131
The Technology Platform for Application Software, 132
  The Hardware/Software Platform for Applications, 132
  The Hardware and Operating System, 134

User Interface Software, 134
Communications Software, 135
Database Management Software, 135
Application Development Tools, 135
Choices for Application Software Acquisition or Development, 136
The Application Software Package Approach, 136
Advantages and Disadvantages of Application Packages, 136
Use Application Package without Change, 138
Customizing Application Package with Input/Output Changes, 138
Customizing Application Package with Unique Features, 138
The Application Generator Package Approach, 139
Issues in Software Package Acquisition and Use, 140
Portability, 140
Individual versus Company Package Decisions, 141
Freeware, Shareware, and Pirate Software, 142
The Programming Language Approach to Application Development, 142
The Programming Process, 143
Assembly Language, 144
Procedure-Oriented Languages, 144
Problem-Oriented Programming Facilities, 145
Very High Level Languages (4GLs), 145
Object-Oriented Languages, 147
The Structure of Computer Programs, 147
Dealing with Program Complexity, 148
Some Program Definitions, 148
Structured Program Design, 149
Routines and Subroutines, 150
Introduction to Some Commonly Used Programming Languages, 151
C and C++, 151
Common Business Oriented Language (COBOL), 152
Algorithmic Programming Languages, 152
Structured Query Language (SQL), 154
Lessons for Managers, 154

CHAPTER 8   APPLICATION DEVELOPMENT AND IMPLEMENTATION   156
Application Development Methodologies and Strategies, 156
Development Methodology and Development Strategy, 157

Methodology Perspectives, 157

Four Development Strategies, 158

Traditional Approach to Application Development, 158

Stage 1: Definition, 160

Stage 2: Development, 162

Stage 3: Installation and Operation, 166

Prototyping Approach to Application System Development, 167

A Model of the Prototyping Process, 167

Evaluation of the Prototyping Approach, 170

Software Package Approach to Application Development, 170

Identifying and Selecting a Package, 171

Implementation of a Software Package, 172

Simplified Development Approach for End-User Computing, 172

Application Development Methods and Tools, 174

Selection of Methods, 174

The Use of CASE Tools, 175

Implementation of Information Systems as an Organizational Change Process, 175

Approaches to Overcoming Resistance, 176

Sociotechnical Approach to System Design and Implementation, 176

Evaluating Quality of an Application System, 177

Lessons for Managers, 178

CHAPTER 9 ACHIEVING CORRECT AND COMPLETE REQUIREMENTS 180

The Three Levels of Information Requirements, 180

Organization-Level Information Requirements, 181

Database Requirements, 181

Application-Level Information Requirements, 181

Why Determination of Information Requirements Can Be Difficult, 182

The Effect of Complexity on Information Requirements Determination, 182

Constraints on Humans in Information Requirements Determination, 183

Strategies for Determining Information Requirements, 184

Asking Directly, 186

Deriving from an Existing Information System, 186

Synthesis from Characteristics of Business Processes, 187

Discovering from Experimentation with an Evolving Information System, 188

Selecting a Strategy for Determining Information Requirements, 188

Determining Organizational Information Requirements, 191

Requirements from the Strategic Alignment Stage, 192

Performing the Organizational Information Requirements Stage, 193

Application Requirements, 194

The Selection of an Application Requirements Strategy, 194

User Interface Requirements, 194

Lessons for Managers, 197

CHAPTER 10 MODELING DATA REQUIREMENTS AND USING DATABASES 199

Data Concepts, 200

Entities, Attributes, and Relationships, 200

Files, Records, and Data Items, 202

Sequencing of Data, 203

Traditional Types of Files, 203

Databases, 204

Data Modeling, 206

Logical and Physical Data Models, 206

Formalisms for Logical Data Modeling, 208

Preparing a Data Model, 209

Conceptual Database Organizations, 211

Hierarchical Database Model, 211

Network Database Model, 212

Relational Database Model, 213

Object-Oriented Database Model, 214

Issues of a Physical Database Model, 215

Physical Database Organization, 216

Concerns in Database Organization, 217

Sequential Access Method, 217

Hashed Access Method, 218

Indexed Access Method, 218

Multiattribute Access Method, 218

Issues in Enterprise Databases, 219

Other Kinds of Databases, 220
   Text Databases, 220
   Graphics, Picture, and Document Image Databases, 221
   Voice and Multimedia Databases, 221
   Modelbases, 221
Online Databases from External Suppliers, 221
Lessons for Managers, 222

CHAPTER 11 ORGANIZATION AND OPERATION OF THE INFORMATION MANAGEMENT FUNCTION   224

The Information Management Function, 224
   The Evolution of the Information Management Function in Medium to Large Organizations, 224
   The Evolution of the Information Management Function in Small Organizations, 226
   Why Organizations Have a Separate MIS Function, 227
Organizing the Information Management Function, 227
   Activities within the Information Management Function, 228
   Organization Structure, 228
   MIS Positions in a Large Organization, 232
   MIS Positions in a Small Company, 233
   Major Alternatives in Centralization/Decentralization, 233
   Alternatives for System Operations, 234
   Centralization-Decentralization of Application Development, 236
Organization and Management of End-User Computing, 236
The Information System Master Plan, 238
   Information System Goals, Objectives, and Architecture, 239
   Current Capabilities, 239
   Forecast of Developments Affecting the Plan, 239
   The Specific Plan, 240
   Maintenance of the Master Plan, 240
Allocating Scarce Information System Resources, 240
   Central Authority for Resource Allocation, 241
   Decentralized Authority for Resource Allocation, 241
Information Management Operations, 242
   Facility Operations, 242
   Customer Service, 243
   Capacity Planning and Technology Acquisition, 244

Information System Security, 245
Managing Information Processing Costs, 245
   Data Center Hardware Cost Management, 245
   Application Software Cost Management, 246
   Personnel Cost Reductions, 246
   Outsourcing, 247
Assessment of the Information Management Function, 247
   The Context for Information Systems, 248
   An Overview of an Information Systems Assessment, 248
Assessment of Information System Effectiveness, 251
Lessons for Managers, 251

CHAPTER 12 INFORMATION SYSTEMS AND INTEGRATED RESOURCES MANAGEMENT   **253**

Sources of Corporate Integration through the Information Systems Function, 253
   Integration from an Information System Strategy and Architecture, 254
   Integration from Corporate Data Modeling and Corporate Databases, 254
   Integration from Communication and Coordination Technologies, 256
   Integration from Interaction of Business Processes and Information Processes, 257
   Integration from Use of Analytical and Decision Making Tools, 257
   Integration through Support to Business Functions, 258
Marketing and Sales and Information Systems, 259
   Integrated Use of Marketing and Sales Information, 259
   Expanded Information Use by Marketing and Sales through Information Systems, 260
   Applications of Information Technology to Marketing and Sales Activities, 261
Field Service and Information Systems, 261
   Integrated Use of Field Service Information, 262
   Expanded Information Use by Field Service through Information Systems, 262
   Applications of Information Technology to Field Service Activities, 262
Product Design and Development and Information Systems, 263

Integrated Use of Product Design and Development Information, 263

Expanded Information Use by Product Design and Development through Information Systems, 263

Applications of Information Technology to Product Design and Development Activities, 263

Production and Inventory Control and Information Systems, 264

Integrated Use of Production and Inventory Control Information, 264

Expanded Information Use by Production and Inventory Control through Information Systems, 264

Applications of Information Technology to Production and Inventory Control Activities, 265

Procurement and Information Systems, 265

Integrated Use of Procurement Information, 265

Expanded Information Use by Procurement through Information Systems, 265

Applications of Information Technology to Procurement Activities, 266

Distribution and Information Systems, 266

Integrated Use of Distribution Information, 266

Expanded Information Use by Distribution through Information Systems, 267

Applications of Information Technology to Distribution Activities, 267

Industrial Facilities Management, 267

Integrated Use of Industrial Facilities Management Information, 268

Expanded Information Use by Industrial Facilities through Information Systems, 268

Applications of Information Technology to Facilities Management Activities, 268

Process Design and Development and Information Systems, 268

Integrated Use of Process Design and Development Information, 269

Expanded Information Use by Process Design and Development through Information Systems, 269

Applications of Information Technology to Process Design and Development Activities, 269

Manufacturing and Information Systems, 269

Integrated Use of Manufacturing Information, 269

Expanded Information Use by Manufacturing through Information Systems, 270

Applications of Information Technology to Manufacturing Activities, 270

Human Resources and Information Systems, 271

Integrated Use of Human Resources Information, 271

Expanded Information Use by Human Resources through Information Systems, 271

Applications of Information Technology to Human Resources Activities, 271

Accounting and Finance and Information Systems, 272

Integrated Use of Accounting and Finance Information, 272

Expanded Information Use by Accounting and Finance through Information Systems, 272

Applications of Information Technology to Accounting and Finance Activities, 273

Quality Management and Information Systems, 273

Integrated Use of Quality Management Information, 273

Expanded Information Use by Quality Management through Information Systems, 274

Applications of Information Technology to Quality Management Activities, 274

Information Technology Applied to the Information Systems Function, 274

Integrated Use of Information Systems Information, 274

Expanded Information Use by Information Systems through Information Systems, 275

Applications of Information Technology to Information System Activities, 275

Lessons for Managers, 276

INDEX 277

CHAPTER 1

INFORMATION TECHNOLOGY IN BUSINESS STRATEGY

Organizational strategy defines the broad directions and approaches an organization is taking or will take in carrying out its mission. Information technology is important to strategy because it can affect what an organization does, how it operates, how it interacts with its customers, and its competitive position.

Implementation of strategy often involves design of new business processes or redesign of old ones. Information technology is important to this effort, since it is incorporated in a broad range of business and organizational processes.

As a terminology note, the terms information systems and information technology are often used somewhat interchangeably. Information technology is a broader term with respect to technology because it can encompass the use of the technology in products or services, but information systems is a broader term with respect to business systems because it includes people, data, and procedures as well as technology. Since the dominant use of information technology in organizations is in information systems, the two terms may be considered as referring roughly to the same organizational phenomenon.

This chapter will focus attention on opportunities for using information technology to improve organizational competitiveness and performance. It will explain the role of technology in business processes. It will describe how information technology is a vital element in competitive changes such as downsizing of organizations, customer-oriented strategies, just in time manufacturing, and reengineering of business processes. There will be a short terminology review as preparation for the remainder of the book.

STRATEGY AND INFORMATION TECHNOLOGY APPLICATIONS

Information systems and information technology innovations interact with strategic planning and strategic decisions. They can support basic competitive strategies. They can also interact with strategic decision making by suggesting new ways of competing and ways to strengthen the organization's competitive position. An important consideration in using information technology in competitive strategy is to achieve a sustainable competitive advantage rather than a momentary change. These considerations will be described in this section. An important source of sustainable competitive advantage is in business processes; this strategic use of information technology will be explained in the next section.

Interaction of Business Strategy, Information Technology, and Business Processes

In order to achieve the full range of potential from information technology, strategic planning should follow an approach that emphasizes the interaction of strategy with information technology and the interaction of business processes with information technology (Figure 1-1). The business strategy and business process planning are iterative. The logic of the iterative approach follows.

- Develop a business strategy using information technology as an important element in the conditions on which strategy is decided and as a significant way to achieve competitive advantage. Consider how business processes (also using information technology) can be part of the competitive strategy. The process is iterative because strategy considerations may suggest information technology uses and information technology uses may suggest changes in strategy. Strategy decisions lead to requirements for business processes, but innovative processes may suggest changes in strategy.
- Develop (or redesign) business processes using information technology and information systems. The business process needs suggest the applications of the technology, but technology innovations may suggest new or redesigned business processes.

Five examples illustrate how information technology can influence strategy and business processes. The implications of the examples will be explained in the chapter.

> *Example.* An organization is discussing downsizing as a part of the business strategy. This will have effects on the business structure and business processes. The technology options suggest that downsizing will be facilitated by the ability to downsize the information systems that support business units. In fact, the technology options suggest further changes in the downsized organization structure.

> *Example.* In planning the business processes to support the business strategy, the company has the option of building them from their specifications or using

FIGURE 1-1
Business Strategy, Business Processes, and Information Technology

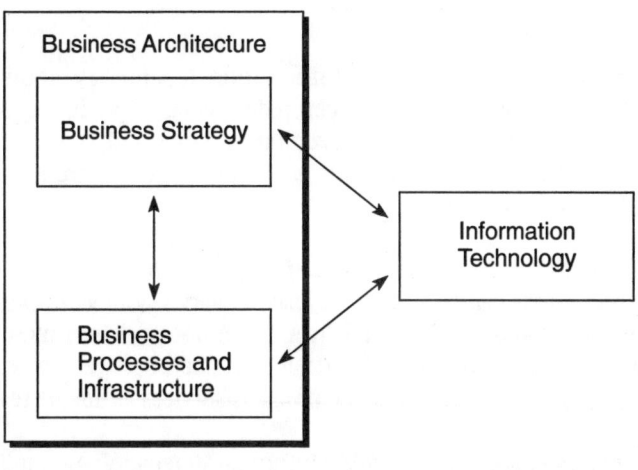

a commercially available software package. The use of the application package will structure the business processes. In other words, the information technology as contained in the package establishes the framework for the rest of the business processes.

Example. New production strategies such as the quick response just in time (JIT) strategy require a new view of business processes and business infrastructure. They directly affect the use of information technology in business processes. They simplify business processes and eliminate the need for many traditional applications.

Example. A customer-oriented strategy is enabled by information technology. Without the technology, many ideas for improved customer service would not be possible. Also, the technology suggests possibilities for service that might not have been considered.

Example. Applications of information technology have been developed in manufacturing that do not communicate with each other. These "islands of automation" are generally employed within a specific function. A computer-aided design system, for example, coordinates design engineering efforts to create product specifications and drawings. Many firms are making significant capital outlays to link these islands via Computer Integrated Manufacturing (CIM). Implementing CIM requires changes in both manufacturing strategies and in the design and integration of business processes.

Information Technology in Support of Basic Strategies

Information technology can be used to support and enhance the strategy of an organization. For each of the following basic strategies, there are related information technology applications.

Being a low cost producer. Information technology applications can help analyze costs of products/services, reduce costs of producing or delivering the products/services, improve utilization of plant and equipment, increase efficiency in the use of labor and materials, and reduce current assets such as receivables and inventory.

Differentiating products/services from competition. Information technology applications can be used to reduce delivery leadtime, improve ability to make delivery promises (and then deliver as promised), deliver more customized products/services, or produce higher quality products/services. Information technology itself may be embedded in the products/services as unique features.

Focusing on a market niche. Information technology applications can be used to identify and track the niche market (e.g., through market analysis and lead tracking) and deliver products/services to the market.

Growth in terms of product offerings or business units. Information technology applications increase the ability of an organization to plan and control larger numbers of end-items and options/features in product families and to coordinate multiple business functions and autonomous business units.

Innovation in products and processes. Information technology applications can help reduce development/production cycle time for new products (e.g., using CAD/CAM systems) and support new business processes such as JIT and TQM (Total Quality Management).

Alliances with customers and suppliers. Information technology applications are vital in the communication and coordination for effective alliances. For example, information systems can support communication and coordination for customer requirements (e.g., sales forecasts and orders) and supplier deliveries (e.g., vendor schedules). Time delays can be reduced by communication technologies combined with computer processing.

Information Technology and Changes in Strategy

In the discussion above, the emphasis was on information technology and information systems as support for strategies that the organization had selected.

This may be an aggressive use of information technology capabilities, but it is passive with respect to changes in strategy. A more active use of information technology is to use it to change strategies. In other words, the existence of powerful information technology possibilities should cause changes in strategic thinking about how to do business, how to deal with customers, how to achieve sustainable competitive advantage, and so forth. Some examples illustrate this idea.

Build in switching costs. Information technology applications may be used in ways to make it costly and unattractive for customers to switch to a competitor. For example, transaction costs may be reduced or services provided by systems that are not available if the customer switches to competitors.

Change the basis of competition. Information technology may be used to provide new features or services not previously offered.

Build barriers to new entrants. Information technology applications may be used to increase the cost and difficulty for new competitors to enter the market.

Enhance supplier relationships. Information technology applications may strengthen supplier relationships and reduce transaction costs.

These ideas suggest how the strategic applications of information technology can change the fundamental nature of an industry by changing the nature of the products/services, the markets served, and the economics of production.

The discussion has suggested an aggressive, first mover strategy. In many cases, an organization may have a very successful strategy of following competitor innovations. The company may wait until competitors introduce new information technology and then move aggressively to improve upon what they have done.

When competitors innovate with information technology, an organization may not have a choice about adopting similar technology changes. It may be necessary in order to remain competitive. For example, a bank must offer automatic teller machines (ATMs) for 24-hour customer cash withdrawals and deposits. Once the machines had been introduced and accepted by customers, they became a required business process.

Information Technology Innovations and Sustainable Competitive Advantage

With any innovative applications of information technology, an issue is the sustainability of competitive advantages that are obtained. Computer hardware is not unique; software functionality can be duplicated and competitors can respond with similar systems. In the manufacturing industry, for example, application software packages (such as computer aided design, manufacturing resource planning, and statistical process control) can be purchased by any firm.

Any application, viewed simply as technology, is probably easy to copy. The key to sustainable competitive advantage with information technology applications is integration with the competitive strategy and business processes of the organization. When applications are embedded in a company's strategy and business processes, the advantages of the information technology are very difficult to duplicate. In the manufacturing industry, for example, it is estimated that only 10% to 15% of firms achieve Class A status by using manufacturing resource planning systems effectively in their business processes.

INFORMATION TECHNOLOGY AND BUSINESS PROCESSES

Planning and implementation of strategic applications of information technology should always include a strong focus on the basic business processes and operations. Every organization has "mission critical" applications that must work or the firm's operation shuts down. These should be examined very carefully for innovative uses of information technology. Doing these systems well can provide significant competitive advantages that are difficult for competitors to duplicate because system success is not just technology-based. Successful systems involve a combination of well-designed processes, information technology, trained personnel, forms and procedures, and organizational culture.

Significant structural changes to business processes are typically required to use information systems and technology effectively. For example, in a manufacturing organization, using information systems in business processes means that functional areas must standardize and integrate their procedures to maintain a common database and work from a common plan. A company-wide vision must be diffused and professional skills enhanced through employee training. There will be changes in business structure, such as changes in assignment of responsibilities, procedures, feedback loops, and flow of information across organizational boundaries.

Problems with Business Processes

Business processes are a vital part of the operational effectiveness and competitive behavior of organizations. There is a tendency to make frequent minor modifications so that, over time, the processes increase in efficiency. However, the minor modifications may obscure the fact that the processes have become obsolete and non-competitive due to changes in the business, technology, and competitive environments.

Using manufacturing companies as an example, business processes have had to respond to changes in the competitive environment. Procedures for managing engineering, operations, accounting, and preparing timely management reports have tended to become overwhelmed by increased volumes of transactions and data. Difficulties in coordinating functional areas, especially in communicating changes (e.g., in product design or customer demands), have led to poor resource management. These problems are reflected in parts shortages, excessive expediting, excess/obsolete inventories, production disruptions, end-of-month production rushes, long receivables, late shipments, cash shortages, and delayed financial reports.

A Traditional Approach to Business Processes

The traditional approach (Figure 1-2) has been to design or redesign business processes and incorporate information technology within them. There are many advantages to this traditional approach. Company strategy, policies, customs, and innovations may be built into the processes and information systems. Given sufficient time, system design expertise, and resources, the traditional approach has a comparative advantage. However, there are problems with the traditional approach.

One problem is that there may be a tendency in the traditional approach to replicate existing practices. Existing practices seem a logical point for defining requirements. However, many managers have a functional bias (e.g., toward engineering, production, quality, purchasing, sales, cost accounting) and lack training and experience with integrated systems. This limits their understanding of a companywide information system and their ability to specify the requirements for improved systems. The complexity of current practices, rather than being reviewed and simplified, can become "requirements" in a new system. Unnecessary requirements may be included because they existed in the old system. For example, detailed production tracking systems become unnecessary when cycle times are reduced from weeks to hours.

Changes in strategy and accompanying systems often run counter to existing management methods and business practices. It may require looking at the world differently. Approaches to business process design can incorporate new thinking; it requires a significant management effort to ensure that it does.

Software Packages as an Alternative Approach to Business Processes

The availability of software packages for major business processes has introduced an alternative approach to the design of these processes. In the traditional approach, the business process is designed first and the software is then developed or a package selected. The alternative is to use commercially

FIGURE 1-2
Two Approaches to Business Processes

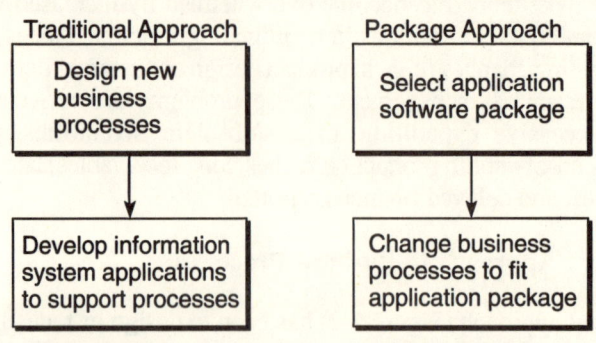

available information system application packages as the basis for business process design or redesign.

Standard application packages are more common in some parts of the organization than in others. For example, accounting application packages have been quite successful in such areas as sales order processing, receivables, payables, and general ledger. The adoption of these packages was aided by standard accounting practices and the procedural discipline common to accountants. The packages frequently caused a change in accounting procedures when they were introduced.

The application software package approach is especially attractive in three situations. The first is in a situation where the expertise and resources to design or redesign systems are not present. This situation often applies to small companies. The second is where there is a need for rapid change and package use will reduce the time required to implement the change. The third is when the package is innovative; it is essentially a way of introducing innovations that might otherwise require significant efforts to duplicate in house.

The inherent advantage of application packages is in the expertise and effort required to produce a commercially viable package. This often results in software that incorporates the best thinking and the best procedural discipline. Industry standards and best practices are included. These advantages are somewhat offset by the generality that must be built into commercial packages so that the user must adapt to the package. The packages have options to customize for the individual user, but even after selecting customizing options, the user's business processes must change to use the package effectively.

The use of an application package essentially reverses the traditional approach to business process design or redesign. The software package is selected first and this is used as the basis for structural and procedural changes in the organization. The application causes the organization to break with old methods and thinking. Training requirements follow both from the application software and from the revised structures and procedures.

How can competitive advantage be achieved if commercially available packages are used as the basis for business processes? The answer lies in the overall business system that is built. The software may provide a good framework for the business process, but the competitive advantage lies in using it well and innovating in the rest of the system.

INFORMATION TECHNOLOGY AND ORGANIZATIONAL DOWNSIZING

There appears to be a trend away from very large, centrally managed organizations. Many companies are forming small, autonomous business units out of larger enterprises. These thrusts to "demassify" the organization have been coupled with efforts to push decision making down in the organization, empower individual employees, reduce corporate staff, and eliminate layers of management. Associated with this general trend is decentralization of the MIS function.

The Advantages of Decentralizing and Downsizing the Organization

The movement to smaller plants has an objective of fostering an entrepreneurial spirit and "ownership" within the plant management and employees. The smaller size reduces bureaucracy. Decisions are delegated to personnel who best understand the manufacturing processes and can create the best solutions to problems in the shortest time. It helps middle managers become profit-oriented. Good management rests on decentralization with coordinated control. Both centralization and decentralization have advantages and disadvantages. From centralized coordination, there are efficiencies and economies. From decentralization, benefits are initiative, responsibility, development of personnel, and decisions close to the facts. These are qualities needed if an organization is to adapt to new conditions.

Decentralizing and Downsizing Information Systems

The effect of decentralization and downsizing on information systems occurs in both the hardware and software and in the information systems function. Relative to information system applications and the hardware/software on which they run, decentralization and downsizing have been followed by a process of migrating application functions from centralized mainframes to networks of smaller decentralized systems. In the information system function, decentralizing and downsizing are associated with moving some MIS responsibilities into functional units. The downsized MIS organization is able to exploit the technologies of the 1990s to reduce MIS costs, improve user access, and provide greater flexibility.

The effect of small plants on the MIS function is to reduce MIS staff (along with other corporate staff). In some cases, operations personnel initiate the efforts to downsize MIS because they have found support from centralized corporate MIS to be inadequate. They also question the costs of mainframe services (if there is a chargeout system or if they are involved with the corporate MIS budget).

PC-based applications have accelerated the movement to downsize. Compared to mainframe centralized applications, they can be implemented faster (perhaps in a fourth or fifth of the time) and at less cost. PC-based packages designed with end users in mind, such as spreadsheets and database management systems, reduce the need for MIS staff to develop applications for analysis or ad hoc reporting.

Decentralized systems address problems associated with a centralized MIS system. Decentralization and downsizing centralized MIS system may complicate the acquisition or divestiture of businesses units. With a centralized MIS system, a newly acquired unit must convert from an existing information system to a system that meets central specifications. Divesting a business unit may change the overhead allocations and pricing for services from the central MIS. With decentralized units and MIS, the MIS changes in a newly acquired unit can be less severe and take place over a longer period.

> *Example.* Eastman Kodak has over 250 manufacturing plants located around the world. Until a short time ago, all of the Kodak Apparatus Division plants were centrally controlled and served by a large mainframe system located in Rochester, New York. The centralized MIS did not provide the response, flexibility, and cost benefit that was required. Plant managers were upset that they could not control all of the resources required to do their jobs efficiently and effectively. Corporate manufacturing executives were troubled when, because of centralized information system failings, they could not hold local managers responsible for plant performance.
>
> Using a decentralized PC/LAN-based manufacturing resource planning (MRP) system, Kodak significantly reduced MIS costs (from $1.2 million annually to $250,000) and increased inventory turns, customer service, and quality at each plant. Many benefits have been intangible, such as having employees "own" and run the manufacturing systems themselves. Working together in a small business unit within a large corporation has improved employee morale, strengthened communications, and achieved large cost savings. The general manager of each Kodak facility has more autonomy and can close the books one or two days after the end of a fiscal period. It took 10 to 12 days with the centralized approach because of the number and levels of personnel

involved in the process. Information is now more current and gives local managers the opportunity to take timely corrective action to control the manufacturing process. Kodak has also seen significant reductions in the product development cycle.

Example. At a disk drive subsidiary of a computer company, MIS costs were a large percentage of manufacturing costs. Replacing their use of a centralized mainframe system with a PC/LAN-based MRP system required 5.5 months to implement from start to finish. MIS costs were reduced by $500,000 per year. Other benefits included inventory reductions from 7.5 weeks to 3.5 weeks during a period when sales volume was increasing. Strong feelings of local ownership and control also enabled the development of reports that met the requirements of local managers.

INFORMATION TECHNOLOGY AND CUSTOMER-ORIENTED STRATEGY

The strategy of a world class organization is to serve its customers. If the competitive strategy of the organization is built around differentiation of its goods and services, a key issue is whether or not the customer perceives the differentiation. What makes a customer perceive your products/services as more valuable and differentiated from the competition? In other words, a company that emphasizes the customer must provide products and services that are perceived to be sufficiently differentiated that customers are willing to pay a premium for them and will hesitate to switch to competitors. A customer-oriented strategy thus is tied to a competitive differentiation strategy.

Customer service begins with the customer's initial contact with the firm. It continues through product acquisition and upgrades and ends when the customer terminates product usage. The steps in the customer relationship follow a predictable pattern. They can be characterized by a life cycle of how customers acquire and use a firm's products/services (or resources). This has been termed the Customer Resource Life Cycle. Differentiation of goods and services can occur at one or more of the steps in the cycle.

Information technology applications potentially can be used in every step of the Customer Resource Life Cycle[1] to differentiate interactions with the customer and services provided (Figure 1-3). In other words, for every step the customer must take, the company looks for ways to use information technology to assist, support, or simplify what the customer must do. The aid may be customer support applications, sharing of company data, allowing the customer to interact with company systems, and so forth. If this customer assis-

---

[1] B. Ives and G. P. Learmonth, "The Information System as a Competitive Weapon," Communications of the ACM, Volume 27, Number 12, December 1984, pp. 1193-1201.

TABLE 1–1
The Life Cycle of How Customers Acquire/Use Resources (Products and Services) and the Use of Information Technology Applications by Supplying Firm

Customer Does This Step	Supplying Firm Can Aid/Support Customer Step by
Initial Contact To identify potential resources	Lead tracking system
Establish Requirements and Attributes To determine how much of a resource is required and estimate future needs	Sales forecasting system supplied to customer Job estimating system supplied to customer Decision support system supplied to customer Customer requirements analysis supplied to customer
Select Source To locate an appropriate source for the required resource	Online product catalog accessible by customer Approved vendor system with cross references for substitute products Check availability of goods to promise, especially at other distributors
Order To place an order for the resource	Order entry system with pricebook and allocation capabilities accessible by customers Electronic transfer of orders and advanced shipping notices (via Electronic Data Interchange)
Authorize and Pay for To authorize the expenditure and pay for the resource (or arrange for payment)	Credit checking online to reduce approval delay Handling various payment methods (e.g., cash, credit card, money transfers, prepayments) to reduce customer effort Invoicing and accounts receivable electronically to reduce customer effort

TABLE 1–1 (*concluded*)

Customer Does This Step	Supplying Firm Can Aid/Support Customer Step by
	Calculate appropriate taxes (American, Canadian, VAT) Electronically handle various currencies and currency conversions
Acquire To deliver the resource	Use transportation management and shipping system and supply customer data electronically
Test and Accept To verify acceptability of a resource	Supply customer with quality control data on products shipped and provide software for customer to use in inspection
Integrate To integrate the resource into inventory (or capacity) and manage its usage	Support inventory control of items stored on-site for the customer

Monitor
To ensure the resource's use and behavior remains acceptable while in customer inventory
	Support customers with:
	  Lot traceability system (with lot expiration and retest capabilities)
	  Customer support system (especially telephone support per contract)

Upgrade/Maintain
To repair the resource and keep it in good operating condition
To upgrade the resource when changes occur in customer requirements or in the resource capabilities
	Provide customer with suggestions and analysis from:
	  Maintenance management system
	  Product tracking system
	  Field service scheduling system

Transfer or Dispose
To handle returns, transfers, or disposal of the resource by the customer
	Share with customers data from:
	  Product tracking system
	  Warranty and returned goods system
	  Hazardous waste disposal system
	  Rental/lease tracking system

Account for To track where and how much money is spent by the customer on the resource	Provide customized billing and usage reports

FIGURE 1-3
Assisting and Supporting Customers in Acquisition and Use of Company Products and Services

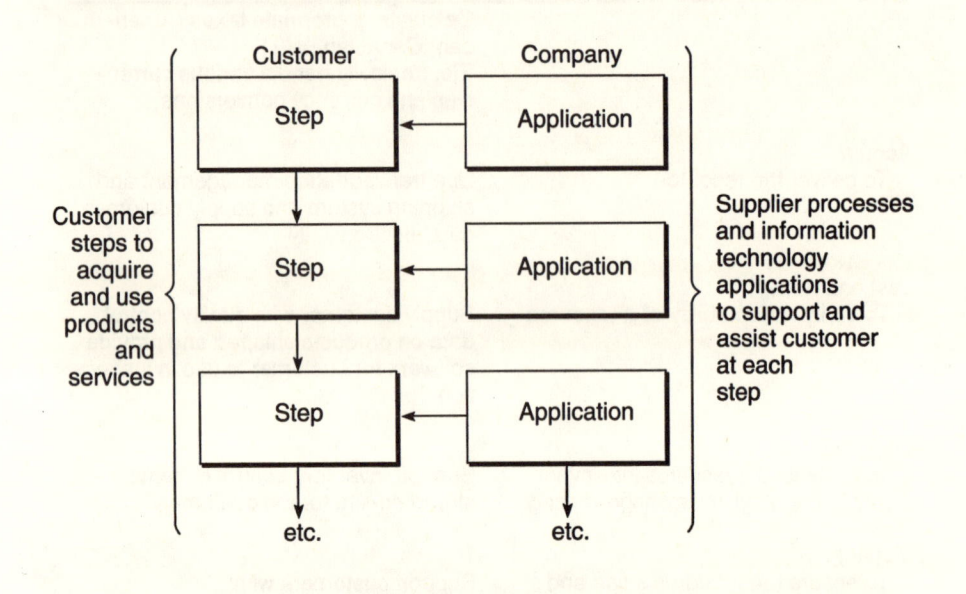

```
                    Customer          Company
                   ┌────────┐       ┌───────────┐
                   │  Step  │ ◄──── │Application│
                   └────────┘       └───────────┘
                        │
                        ▼
Customer           ┌────────┐       ┌───────────┐     Supplier processes
steps to           │  Step  │ ◄──── │Application│     and information
acquire            └────────┘       └───────────┘     technology
and use                                                applications
products                │                              to support and
and                     ▼                              assist customer
services           ┌────────┐       ┌───────────┐     at each
                   │  Step  │ ◄──── │Application│     step
                   └────────┘       └───────────┘
                        │                 │
                        ▼                 ▼
                      etc.              etc.
```

tance is done well, it differentiates the company as a supplier and provides competitive advantage. In Table 1-1, the steps in the cycle are presented along with examples from the manufacturing industry that illustrate how information technology can be applied. Note that some information technology applications support more than one step in the cycle.

Innovative uses of information technology illustrate how some of the uses noted in Table 1-1 can increase the level of customer service and differentiate its goods and services.

Example. Handheld or laptop computers make it feasible for a salesperson, field service representative, or analyst to use customer sales applications during face-to-face meetings for quick responses without waiting until they are "back at the office."

Example. Providing customers with direct access to supplier applications (such as direct order placement into an order entry system or inquiry into bulletin boards of product information) can eliminate intermediaries while offering "no hassle" immediate information to customers.

Example. Electronic communication of orders, shipments and payments with the customer can reduce paperwork and communication errors/costs and provide improved customer service.

A customer-oriented strategy can also be employed when the customer and supplier are closely linked in a JIT partner relationship. In a JIT environment (described in the next section), the customer benefits from improved customer service (responding to exact customer demand), a steady, reliable source of supply, and possibly lower costs. Lower costs may be achieved because of cost efficiencies. These benefits are achieved by long-term commitments expressed in extended contracts and a stable production plan (allowing for mix changes and responses to economic conditions) that the customer will honor. When the customer sources a family of parts to the supplier, it facilitates handling of mix changes and minimizes communication with multiple suppliers.

INFORMATION TECHNOLOGY AND JUST IN TIME (JIT)

A just in time (JIT) manufacturing operations strategy is based on values different from those in traditional manufacturing business practices. The result of JIT should simplify operations and eliminate waste. Implementing JIT requires changing business processes and information technology applications.

The JIT strategy promotes a flexible manufacturing organization that can produce to exact customer demand. In other words, the goal is to quickly respond to customer requirements. In order to reduce and process slack for contingencies, the processes are designed with total quality management (TQM). This means making perfect parts every time, holding the operator responsible for producing those parts, recognizing the chain of internal customers, utilizing process control (not inspection) and problem-solving methods, stopping out-of-control processes for immediate fixes, employing visible management techniques to easily identify potential problems, and performing preventive maintenance to ensure machines are always ready. Overall, JIT emphasizes continuous improvement, respect for and empowerment of people, and a long-term perspective.

To be successful, JIT requires several changes in business structure, responsibility, and processes. As will be explained later, it also requires changes in information systems.

• Changes in corporate culture, management policies and practices, and worker capabilities and attitudes. This involves overcoming old values (e.g., about large lot sizes, long runs, and inventory buffers) and instilling new ones.

- Changes in organizational structure. Increasing responsibilities of production personnel, reducing staff support functions (such as industrial engineering, production control, and quality control), and eliminating layers of management.
- Possible changes to factory layout. These changes are to simplify material flow (e.g., by dedicating a "focused factory" to each product family and employing group technology for a family of similar parts).
- Changes to the product design process. Product design is changed from a sequential, segmented approach of hand-offs (from marketing to design engineering to manufacturing engineering to purchasing and production) to simultaneous engineering by an interdisciplinary team.
- Eliminates jobs and changes responsibilities. It eliminates inspectors, alters the master scheduler's job, and transforms the buyer responsibilities.
- Changes in transportation practices. Transportation is changed to support JIT practices.

As part of the basic thrust to simplify processes and eliminate waste, JIT also requires changes to the information systems. These changes eliminate some information system applications and add or enhance others. Some traditional applications are unnecessary. JIT eliminates detailed shop floor tracking (because of short cycle times), detailed labor reporting, and dispatch lists for coordinating production (since JIT uses synchronized replenishment signals). JIT replaces manufacturing orders with rate-based schedules and tracks costs by period (not by order). It replaces individual purchase orders with blanket orders and vendor schedules. It replaces customer orders with long-term contracts and customer schedules. Eliminating unnecessary transaction processing and reports simplifies the information systems and focuses worker effort on productive activities.

For JIT, some new applications must be developed and some existing applications enhanced. Applications are needed for statistical process control and preventive maintenance. Scheduling must account for smaller time increments (hours rather than weeks or days) and shop calendars must apply to workcenters, suppliers, and customers. Transportation scheduling must account for days (and hours) of possible shipments.

Current MRP information systems provide the integrated database and many of the functions needed in a JIT environment. The MRP system can provide bills of material and resources, product costing, planning bills, production planning and capacity planning, sales order processing (and available-to-promise information), final assembly scheduling, planned orders (e.g., for supplier scheduling), and integrated financial applications. In the transition period to JIT, a hybrid information system that uses traditional MRP approaches may be needed.

INFORMATION TECHNOLOGY AND COMPUTER INTEGRATED MANUFACTURING

Individual stand-alone applications of information technology to structured tasks have been reasonably easy to justify and implement in a specific functional area. Some examples are a Computer-Aided Design (CAD) system in design engineering, an automated assembly system or flexible manufacturing system in manufacturing, and an automated material handling system in distribution. Efforts to link these stand alone applications are termed Computer Integrated Manufacturing (CIM).

The MRP planning and control system forms the heart of CIM since it provides integration across functional areas, coordination of functional activities to meet top management's strategic plans, and integration of activities between the firm and its customers and suppliers. Many of the stand-alone CIM applications can be integrated through links to the MRP system. The relationship between CIM and information processing is demonstrated by examples of data exchanges that loosely couple the parts of the system:

- Computer-aided design applications require item data from MRP and provide item and bill of material data to MRP.
- Shop floor data collection applications require information about manufacturing orders and routings from MRP; they provide event reporting to MRP (such as unit completions and labor hours by operation).
- Automated material handling systems require information about shipping schedules from MRP and provide material movement data to MRP.
- Automated assembly systems and flexible manufacturing systems require MRP information about the manufacturing schedule and product/process design (such as routing details, tools, component parts and identification of numerically controlled machine programs); they provide information about manufacturing events (such as units completed and scrap).

CIM generally fits manufacturers that sell engineer-to-order products. Customers are attracted to a manufacturer that has an integrated manufacturing process that reduces the risks associated with design and manufacturing of an ill-defined product. As firms adopt the CIM philosophy, they add integration. Before undertaking significant capital outlays for this integration, it is critical that business processes be reengineered to fit the concept. The cost and difficulty of implementing CIM increase as integration becomes more extensive.

COMPLEXITY OF INFORMATION SYSTEM DEVELOPMENT AND IMPLEMENTATION

At first glance, using a computer and related information technology in job tasks seems simple. Some data and a few instructions are provided to the computer, the computer follows a program of instructions in retrieving and processing data, and outputs such as instructions, analyses, or reports are provided to users.

To design and implement an application of information technology does not appear complicated. Users provide a set of requirements; developers design and build the programs, screen formats, reports, data files, and data communications to achieve them. In some simple applications, users design and build the application themselves (such as a spreadsheet for analysis).

Reality contradicts these simple, uncomplicated views. Very large differences in the outcomes of information technology applications suggest more complexity. Some organizations achieve competitive advantage from using information technology; others are ineffective. Some departments in an organization are significant users of computers; others have no significant applications. Some work groups enhance their work through information technology; others use it infrequently or poorly. Some individuals improve their performance with information technology; others appear to be less productive. The success rate for new information system applications appears to be less than half.

How can there be such differences in outcomes? The differences arise because information technology applications have technical complexity and they are placed in, support, and interact with complex human systems. The business processes and tasks may be complex. The information system application is used by individuals who have human capabilities and limitations in providing inputs and using outputs. The way the inputs and outputs are structured and presented (the interfaces) will affect comprehension, acceptance, error rates, and usage.

The application may fit within the activities of a work group that has communication, interaction, and performance dynamics. The design of the application and its interfaces will affect these dynamics.

The system is used in an organization that has an explicit or implied strategy, an organizational culture, and organizational lines of authority and divisions of responsibility. There is a mixture of shared and individual ideas about how things should be done and how individuals and organizations should behave. The fit between the design of the information system and these organizational factors affects how it will be used or if it will be used at all.

The information system can affect the way the organization interacts with its suppliers, customers, and suppliers of capital. It affects the types of interaction that are feasible, the information obtained or provided, the speed and accuracy of interactions, the transaction cycle time, and the utilization of feedback.

> *Example.* A very innovative expert system was designed to assist computer sales personnel in configuring each computer system with all components necessary for installation and client operation. Even though the support system was designed to solve significant problems related to configuring the sale and installation, it received very little use. An investigation disclosed that the sales representatives did not perceive configuration to be a problem, they were not evaluated on reducing difficulties and costs of configuration, and there were no incentives for them to spend time dealing with it. In other words, the support system for configuration was technically excellent, but the organizational changes and incentives for use were not implemented along with it.

REENGINEERING BUSINESS PROCESSES

When an opportunity for applying information technology to business processes is identified and a project initiated, one of three approaches is usually employed:

1. Do not change the business process but add information technology or make technology improvements.
2. Streamline or enhance the basic business process to incorporate new or improved information technology.
3. Radically redesign the business process using new or improved information technology in the redesigned system (often termed reengineering).On the surface, it might seem it would always be best to do reengineering, but there are many situations in which the first two approaches may be preferred.

No Business Process Change but Add Information Technology

The introduction of information technology often results in innovations and changes that are not foreseen by the advocates of change. It may not be possible to redesign processes when the technology is first introduced. The major changes emerge during a process of use and innovation.

> *Example.* When microcomputers (personal computers) were first introduced, users programmed applications using an algorithmic programming language. The value of personal computers in most jobs was not clear. The development of spreadsheet software (VisiCalc followed by LOTUS 1-2-3) changed the use of personal computers. Other software followed. Most users no longer employ a programming language but work with software packages designed for types of problems or types of analysis. In this case, the most innovative approach was to

add information technology and let users decide how to apply it to existing processes.

There are limits to the usefulness of such an approach. Although users innovate, they fail to achieve many benefits because old work habits interfere with added productivity gains. The computer changes many aspects of what they do, but the design of workspace, the design of files, the organization of combined physical and computer workspace, and the flow of work are not necessarily changed. The reason is that the incremental nature of the changes does not motivate users to recognize the inefficiencies built into the combination of old business procedure and new technology.

Streamlining Business Process to Incorporate Improved Information Technology

When the basic business process is well defined, works well, and meets basic requirements, it may be desirable to retain the process and only make changes necessary to use new or improved information technology. For example, a well designed payroll system that is accepted by personnel may be streamlined and enhanced by new technology, but the basic system may not need to be redesigned.

Using information technology requires a willingness to follow procedures carefully (a use discipline). Where a use discipline is already established, it may be appropriate to innovate by employing the technology with the existing process rather than adding a new process and new technology at the same time. The cost of radical change may suggest streamlining rather than redesign.

On the other hand, organizational inertia (tendency to want to keep things as they are) may give undue support for this approach. Therefore, the "improve but don't radically change" approach should be questioned in all cases in order to avoid the mistake of rejecting radical change when it is the better solution.

Reengineering Business Processes

A major activity in the ongoing transformation of organizations to achieve greater productivity is the redesign of organizational processes. It has been termed reengineering, business process redesign, and organizational transformation. The rethinking of systems and procedures is not a new concept; the use of information technology gives it new importance and change potential. Three examples illustrate the concept of redesign and reengineering using information technology as the focus of the changes.

Example. Cycle time reduction for an accounts receivable system: An accounts receivable system for an industrial company was built to send a bill for each invoice as soon as the shipping company verified the amount of the freight. Bills were typically sent five days after shipment. Payments received were applied to invoices except when the payments were for multiple invoices. The checks were not deposited until payments were applied. The delay was from one to five days. Rather than applying improved information technology to this old system, an entirely new order entry system was designed to send the invoice the same day as the shipment using an estimated freight charge. When payments were received, an online payment application system applied 90 percent of the checks the day they were received and the other 10 percent the following day. The system performed automatic application for 70 percent of the payments; a human operator with online access applied remaining payments.

Example. Cycle time reduction for processing insurance policy applications and inquiries: An insurance company had the problem of delay in processing insurance applications and responding to inquiries about them. The existing system required the application and associated documents to be passed by several persons before final approval. The natural delays inherent in this serial processing resulted in an unsatisfactory overall response time. Also, if the applicant called to inquire about the status of the application, it could not be found easily. Rather than reducing the processing time at each step by using information technology and streamlined procedures, the organization redesigned the entire application approval process. The application and associated documents were placed on optical storage. With one common electronic copy, all persons having review responsibilities were able to work in parallel. Also, the system kept track of the processing and identified bottlenecks. If there were inquiries, the status and all notes and processing were available to any person to which an inquiry was directed.

Example. Reduction in cycle time for reordering and reduction in costs: A manufacturing company needed to reduce its inventory of purchased materials, supplies, and components. Rather than applying information technology to reduce the time for processing placement of an order with a supplier, there was a rethinking of the process. Using a system designed around electronic communications, vendors who agreed to ship immediately were given blanket orders; the order processing for all standard items was handled semiautomatically. The computer generated an analysis of the orders to be placed. For the items handled in this way, individuals reviewed the orders but did not need to negotiate price or evaluate bids. The result was a dramatic reduction in the lead time for replenishment and an increase in productivity in placing orders.

INFORMATION MANAGEMENT TERMINOLOGY

Five terms will be defined briefly here and the meanings expanded later in the text.

Information technology refers broadly to the technology of computers and electronic communications as applied to processing, transfer, and storage of information. It encompasses computer hardware, data communications, software, and a large variety of input and output devices. Local area and wide area communications networks for information transfer are also included.

Management information system (MIS) and *information system* are often used interchangeably. The MIS or information system of an organization consists of:

- An information technology infrastructure of computers and communications hardware, software, and files and databases.
- Applications using information technology. Application systems are often termed information systems (because they are systems to process information). Some of the purposes for applications are:
  (1) Perform processing in connection with organizational transactions.
  (2) Support communications and coordination.
  (3) Support knowledge work activities such as analysis, decision making, planning, control, and management.
  (4) Incorporate information and information processing in the design and delivery of goods and services.

The concept of an MIS is very comprehensive and includes management reporting, decision support, group support, and executive support. *Information management* is the management of information systems and information resources by an individual, a group, or an organization.

The *information management, MIS,* or *information systems function* is essentially a new business function with responsibility to define organizational information requirements, plan and build an information infrastructure and information system applications, operate the system, and organize, staff, and manage these activities.

LESSONS FOR MANAGERS

The chapter demonstrates that an organization must do integrated resource management to coordinate activities in separate functions and that the information system is a key element in the integration among functions.

The first lesson for managers is the opportunity for using information technology to improve organizational competitiveness and performance. The business architecture with its organizational strategy and business processes interacts with information technology. This interaction causes changes in tactics as strategic uses of information technology are examined. The interaction between information technology and business processes results in business process design or reengineering. Innovations in competitive behavior with information technology should be selected and implemented in such a way as to achieve sustainable competitive advantage.

The second managerial lesson is that significant structural changes to business processes are typically required to use information systems and technology effectively. There will be changes in business structure, such as changes in assignment of responsibilities, procedures, feedback loops, and flow of information across organizational boundaries. The traditional approach has been to design or redesign business processes and incorporate information technology within them. An alternative is to use commercially available information system application packages as the basis for business process design or redesign.

The third lesson for managers is in the explanation of how information technology is a vital element in current competitive changes such as downsizing of organizations, customer-oriented strategy, just in time manufacturing, computer integrated manufacturing, and reengineering of business processes. These are important current business developments affecting business architecture and business strategy, business processes, and the organizational infrastructure. Each of these changes is accompanied by (or even driven by) information technology opportunities and systems.

The chapter concluded with a short terminology review useful for managers as preparation for the remainder of the book. The terms defined were information technology, management information system (MIS), information system, information management, and the information management or information system function.

SELECTED REFERENCES FOR ADDITIONAL READING

Drucker, P. "The Emerging Theory of Manufacturing," *Harvard Business Review*, May-June 1990.

Ives, B., and Learmonth, G. P. "The Information System as a Competitive Weapon," *Communications of the ACM*, 1984.

Johnson, R. N., and Carrico, S. R. "Developing Capabilities to Use Information Strategically," *MIS Quarterly*, 12:1, January 1988, pp. 37-48.

Porter, M. E. *Competitive Strategy: Techniques for Analyzing Industries and Competitors*. New York: The Free Press, 1980.

Porter, M. E., and Millar, V. E. "How Information Gives You Competitive Advantage," *Harvard Business Review*, July-August 1985, pp. 149-160.

Rackoff, N.; Wiseman, C.; and Ullrich, W. A. "Information Systems for Competitive Advantage: Implementation of a Planning Process," *MIS Quarterly*, 9:4, 1985, pp. 285-294.

Scott Morton, M. S. *The Corporation of the 1990s* New York: Oxford University Press, 1991.

Wiseman, C. *Strategic Information Systems*. Homewood, Illinois: Richard D. Irwin, Inc., 1988.

Zuboff, S. *In the Age of the Smart Machine: The Future of Work and Power*. New York: Basic Books, 1988.

CHAPTER 2

THE VALUE OF INFORMATION TECHNOLOGY TO AN ORGANIZATION AND THE INDIVIDUAL WORKER

Why devote time and effort to learning about information technology and information management? There are three broad issues in this question:

- The overall productivity effects of information technology
- The value of information technology to an organization
- The value of an individual being competent in information management

The first issue dealing with the value of information technology is important because of the general concern in society with productivity. A large percentage of societal investment in plant, equipment, and systems is going for information technology. Using traditional methods of economic analysis, the productivity benefits appear to be very low.

The value of information technology to an organization is not just a top management concern. The question is pervasive and may be asked of anyone involved in the design and use of information technology in business systems. Does information technology provide economic value to an organization? Does it improve profitability? Do the benefits differ for different functions and uses? How do information technology applications affect production and distribution?

With regard to the third issue, an individual may believe that information technology provides benefits to an organization, but also believe that personal knowledge and competence about it is not important. Why not leave these matters to technical specialists such as systems analysts and programmers? Isn't information technology like the telephone? A person doesn't need to understand the telephone system technology in order to be an effective user of telephones.

This chapter is directed at all three issues. It describes how information technology applications are valuable to productivity in society. It explains how they are valuable to an organization and suggests how this value may affect profitability. In addition to general concepts, it provides examples drawn from manufacturing and distribution operations. The chapter also explains the value of individual competence in information management. The discussion focuses on what a person needs to be able to do rather than what topics to study. The chapter ends with a discussion of the value of knowing a basic set of knowledge-work software plus software specific to one's own function and industry.

THE SOCIETAL BENEFITS FROM INFORMATION TECHNOLOGY INVESTMENTS

There have been a number of analyses by economists relative to the societal productivity effects of information technology investments. In general, these analyses have not shown productivity improvements. However, there are serious definitional and measurement issues relative to the analyses of economywide economic effects of information technology investments. A major source of societal productivity may have been overlooked.

The Measurement and Definition Problem

The measurement issue is well understood and sometimes acknowledged by those making the arguments about lack of productivity effects. Productivity is a simple concept in the abstract. It reflects the outputs (goods and services) produced by a set of inputs (labor, material, capital). Changes in productivity are most easily understood if the outputs do not change in kind or quality. For example, the hours of labor, materials, and capital to produce a bushel of wheat provide a rather precise measurement of productivity. It becomes difficult to assess changes in productivity if there are changes in quality or features. Does the extra time and material to put an airbag in an automobile reduce the productivity of the automobile industry? It is possible to make adjustments for quality or features, but these adjustments are subject to measurement error.

A more serious deficiency than measurement error is the problem of definition. Productivity is based on physical products or services. The measurement adjustments that are made do not obscure this basic notion. One can make an effective argument at the societal level that information technology has changed the nature of goods and services, and measurements are not recognizing the very real societal value of information technology.

Variety and Customization Effects

In the industrial revolution, in which huge productivity gains were made, there was a change from customized, handcrafted products to mass-produced products. Machines produced standardized goods and reduced the inputs required. The reengineering of work processes produced low unit costs from standardization, assembly lines, and so forth. The benefits of standardizing products and production were related to physical processes, but there were also significant reductions in the costs of marketing, distribution, and accounting. These costs are partly associated with physical activities but are largely information processing costs.

What happens when the cost of information processing is reduced significantly? Some organizations apply the increased power and reduced cost of information technology to increase the variety and customization of their products. When one company in a market opts for increased variety or customization of products, other companies in the market may be forced to follow. From the traditional measurement of productivity, there is no increase in productivity from such increased variety or customization. From the standpoint of customers, the increased variety of goods and services and increased customization have significant value.

> *Example:* Prior to widespread use of computers, airlines had simple fare structures. There was one price for a ticket between two points with no differences for advance purchase, time of week traveled, age, and other factors. There was no advance seat assignment, and the airline did not know anything about a customer in order to customize service (such as vegetarian meals) or reward frequent flyers. Also, the process of confirming space was fragmented and meant that a customer might be told there was no space available when in fact another location selling seats might still have unsold seats.
>
> With online reservation systems, reservations and seat assignments can be made immediately. The airlines keep track of customer needs for specialized services. There are a number of different airfares that reflect the different demands placed on the airlines and the willingness of travelers to fly at off-peak times. In other words, the airlines have created more variety in airfares and a much more customized and responsive reservation system. No airline could survive if it tried to operate without this level of customization. From the standpoint of outputs of reservations per inputs of hours and capital, reservation systems may not reflect any change in productivity, but there is a clear benefit to travelers.
>
> *Example:* Information technology investments have been made in automatic teller machines (ATMs) that accept deposits and dispense cash and provide account information. There are large networks, so that a traveler can obtain cash from machines not only in the same country but in cities in almost any industrialized country. From the standpoint of a banking function of dispensing cash and accepting deposits, it is not clear that the investment in ATMs produced any

reduction in the costs, but the level of service for customers has changed dramatically. The number of "banking" locations has increased a hundredfold. The convenience of accessing funds from locations in different cities and different countries can be described as increasing the customization and variety of service. Assuming the unit cost of dispensing cash and accepting deposits has not changed or even increased, would most banking customers be willing to forgo the ATMs?

Example: A few years ago, when one sent a letter or small package by the post office, it was impossible to locate it if it failed to arrive on time. It was impossible to have reasonable assurance of when the package would be delivered. Federal Express introduced a new type of service that used information technology to track every package. If it did not arrive, it could be located and delivery time predicted. The information technology improved package handling, so that next day delivery could be predicted with an extremely high degree of confidence. The cost of this service, based on information technology, was higher than the standard mail delivery. The customization of the service (so each item could be tracked and located) was a change in the character of service provided. Yet from a productivity standpoint, the delivery output required more inputs. Did society value the new customized service? The market mechanism gave a resounding affirmative answer.

This line of reasoning and the examples suggest that, at the level of the economy, a major productivity effect of information technology is greater customization and variety of goods and services, including personalization of services to reflect individual needs.[1] Some of the customization and variety that was lost in the industrial revolution has returned through the information age capabilities of information technology.

THE ORGANIZATIONAL BENEFITS OF INFORMATION TECHNOLOGY INVESTMENTS

The strategic application of information technology can frequently provide firms with a competitive advantage. It can help a firm become a low-cost producer for a given product/service or differentiate its product offering from its competitors. Strategic applications of information technology can support or shape organizational strategy as the technology itself is used to gain/maintain a competitive advantage or reduce a rival's advantage. The use of information systems to gain a competitive edge may focus on direct benefits to customers or to internal business processes of the organization.

---

[1]The customization effect of information technology is based on a pathbreaking dissertation by Geoffrey M. Brooke, "Information Technology and Productivity: An Economic Analysis of the Effect of Product Differentiation," Unpublished Ph.D. Dissertation, University of Minnesota, 1990.

- For customer benefits, they may support service delivery (such as on-site computer access for electronic order placement), product delivery (such as portable computers to assist field personnel in selling and diagnosing customer needs), or other delivery mechanisms (such as downloading software or data).
- For internal business process benefits, they may support product delivery (such as an integrated manufacturing/distribution system), service delivery (such as expert systems for handling customer questions), or market intelligence delivery (such as integration of internal and external marketing information).

The internal business process benefits are derived from information technology that focuses on internal operations, on automating the basic business processes, and satisfying decision makers' needs for information. There are large benefits from doing the basics well. In the traditional sense, information technology's primary function has been to process predefined transactions to produce standard reports on schedule and to satisfy the information needs of management through query and analysis capabilities. One example of how information technology supports the basic activities and decision areas of an organization is an MRP (Manufacturing Resource Planning) system. As a companywide planning and control system, MRP illustrates how doing the basics in a manufacturing information system can improve communication and coordination. MRP can also be used to illustrate the organizational benefits of information technology investments, especially as they relate to integrated resource management.

The Organizational Benefits of Manufacturing Resource Planning (MRP)

Are there benefits to be gained from improvements in manufacturing resource planning? Will these improvements affect profitability? There are costs associated with implementing an MRP system, but there are significant costs from not doing it. Manufacturers often pay more for the lack of systems than they would have paid for improved systems.

> *Example.* A consumer products manufacturer with $50 million revenues had to write off $10 million in obsolete inventory. A $30 million consumer products manufacturer with 2.5 inventory turns per year calculated they were carrying $6 million in excess inventory. They were also writing off approximately $50,000 after every monthly physical inventory because the costs of goods sold were evaluated incorrectly. An industrial products manufacturer could not react to changes in demand fast enough; during an upturn in the marketplace they experienced stockouts on 35 percent of the orders and lost numerous sales, even though they had excess inventory and unused capacity.

Improved management of resources—material, labor, equipment—is critical to most manufacturers. These resources affect the cost of goods, which typically constitutes 60 to 80 cents of every sales dollar. Investment decisions in these resources are reasonably straightforward. Equipment purchases, for example, are based on quantitative cost/benefit analyses as well as qualitative factors such as flexibility and safety. The expected return on investment for an MRP system provides the cost justification and motivation for investing in information technology. There are quantifiable benefits as well as intangible benefits in the MRP investment decision. The quantifiable benefits have a bottom-line impact on profitability and asset turnover and a potential effect on stock value.

Quantifiable Benefits from MRP Systems

Studies that surveyed manufacturers about the impact of MRP systems on firm performance indicate that company size and industry do not affect the results. Benefits have been indicated for large and small firms, whether they make standard or custom products or are in discrete or process manufacturing environments. The major benefits are explained in this section and typical improvement factors are presented.

Inventory reduction. Typically, improved planning and scheduling practices lead to inventory reductions of 20 percent or better. This provides not only a one-time reduction in assets (and inventory typically constitutes a large proportion of assets), but also provides on-going savings of the inventory carrying costs. The cost of carrying inventory includes not only interest but also the costs of warehousing, handling, obsolescence, insurance, taxes, damage and shrinkage. With interest rates of 10 percent, the carrying costs can be 25 percent to 30 percent.

MRP systems lead to lower inventories because manufacturers can make and buy only what is needed. Time-phased plans are driven by demands rather than demand-insensitive order points. Deliveries can be coordinated to actual need dates; orders for unneeded material can be postponed or canceled. The bills of material ensure matched sets are obtained rather than too much of one item and not enough of another. Planned changes in the bills also prevent inventory build-up of obsolete materials. With fewer part shortages and realistic schedules, manufacturing orders can be processed to completion faster and work-in-process inventories can be reduced. Implementation of just in time (JIT) philosophies can further reduce manufacturing lead times and the corresponding inventories.

Material cost reductions. Improved purchasing practices lead to better vendor negotiations for prices, typically resulting in cost reductions of 5 percent or better. Valid schedules permit purchasing people to focus on vendor negotiations and quality improvement rather than on expediting shortages and getting material inside normal lead times at premium prices. MRP systems provide negotiation information, such as projected material requirements by commodity group and vendor performance statistics. Giving suppliers better visibility of future requirements helps them achieve efficiencies that can be passed on as lower material costs.

Labor cost reductions. Improved manufacturing practices lead to fewer shortages and interruptions, and less rework and overtime. Typical labor savings from successful MRP are a 10 percent reduction in direct and indirect labor costs. By minimizing rush jobs and parts shortages, less time is needed for expediting, material handling, extra setups, disruptions, and tracking split lots or jobs that have been set aside. Production supervisors have better visibility of required work and can schedule capacity or shift loads to meet schedules. Supervisors also have more time for managing, directing and training people; production personnel have more time to develop better methods and improve quality and throughput.

Improved customer service and sales. Improved coordination of sales and production results in better customer service and increased sales. Improvements in making and meeting delivery promises, and shorter order-to-ship lead times, lead to high customer satisfaction and repeat orders. Sales people can focus on selling instead of verifying or apologizing for late deliveries. Taken together, these improvements in customer service can lead to fewer lost sales and actual increases in sales, typically 10 percent or more.

In custom product environments, sales order configurations can be quickly identified and priced, often by order entry or sales personnel rather than technical staff.

MRP systems also provide the ability to react to changes in demand and diagnose delivery problems. Corrective actions, such as determining shipment priorities, notifying customers of changes to promised delivery dates, or altering production schedules to satisfy demand, can be taken early.

Improved accounting controls. Improved collection procedures can reduce the number of days of outstanding receivables, thereby providing additional available cash. Underlying these improvements are fast accurate invoice creation directly from shipment and freight transactions, timely customer statements, and follow through on delinquent accounts. Credit checking during order entry and easy handling of customer inquiries further reduces the number of problem accounts.

Trade credit can also be maximized by taking advantage of supplier discounts and cash planning, and paying only those invoices with matching receipts. This can lead to lower requirements for cash-on-hand.

MRP System Benefits on the Balance Sheet

Benefits from improved business processes and improved information provided by a good MRP system can directly affect the balance sheet of a manufacturer. To illustrate this impact, a simplified balance sheet is shown in

FIGURE 2-1
Summarized Balance Sheet for Sample $10 Million Firm

	Current	Typical Improvement	Benefit
Current Assets			
Cash and Other	$ 500,000		
Accounts Receivable	2,000,000	18%	$356,200
Inventory	3,000,000	20%	600,000
Fixed Assets	3,000,000		
Total Assets	$8,500,000		$956,200
Current Liabilities	xxx,xxx		
Non-Current Liabilities	xxx,xxx		
Stockholder's Equity	xxx,xxx		
Total Liabilities and Equity	xxx,xxx		

Figure 2-1 for a typical manufacturer with annual revenue of $10 million. The biggest impact will be on inventory and accounts receivable.

In the example, the company has $3 million in inventory and $2 million in outstanding accounts receivable. Based on prior research concerning industry averages for improvements, implementation of an MRP system can lead to a 20 percent inventory reduction and an 18 percent receivables reduction.

- **Inventory Reduction.** A 20 percent inventory reduction results in $600,000 less inventory. Improved purchasing practices (that result in reduced material costs) could lower this number even more.

- **Accounts Receivable.** Current accounts receivable represent 73 days of outstanding receivables and an 18 percent reduction (to 60 days' receivables) results in $356,200 of additional cash available for other uses.

MRP Benefits on the Income Statement

A simplified, summary income statement for the same $10 million manufacturer is shown in Figure 2-2. For manufacturers, the cost of sales typically is from 65 to 75 percent of sales (the example will use 75 percent). Using industry averages for each major benefit, the improved business processes and associated information system almost double the current pretax income.

- **Inventory Reduction.** A 20 percent reduction in the current inventory of $3 million results in on-going benefits of lower inventory carrying charges. Using a carrying cost of 25 percent results in $150,000 in lower carrying charges each year, identified here as part of the administrative expenses.
- **Material Cost Reductions.** A 5 percent reduction in material costs because of improved purchasing practices results in annual savings of $225,000.
- **Labor Cost Reductions.** A 10 percent reduction in labor costs because of less overtime and improved productivity results in annual savings of $100,000.
- **Increased Sales.** Improvements in customer service typically lead to a 10 percent sales increase; this is not shown in the figure.

Annual benefits totaling $475,000 in this example almost equals the current pretax income of $500,000.

MRP Impact on Key Financial Ratios

Another way to look at the impact on financial performance of information integration achieved by MRP is through ratio analysis. Three ratios illustrate the effect—two related to liquidity and one to operating performance.

- *Inventory Turnover (Cost of Sales/Inventory).* Low inventory turnover can indicate possible overstocking and obsolescence. It may also indi-

FIGURE 2-2
Summarized Income Statement for Typical $10 Million Firm

		Current	Typical Improvement	Benefit
Sales		$10,000,000	10%	
Cost of Sales		7,500,000		
Material	$4,500,000	60%	5%	$225,000
Labor	1,000,000	13%	10%	$100,000
Overhead	2,000,000	27%		
Administrative Expenses		2,000,000		150,000
Pretax Income		$ 500,000		$475,000

FIGURE 2-3
Worksheet for Calculating Return on Assets

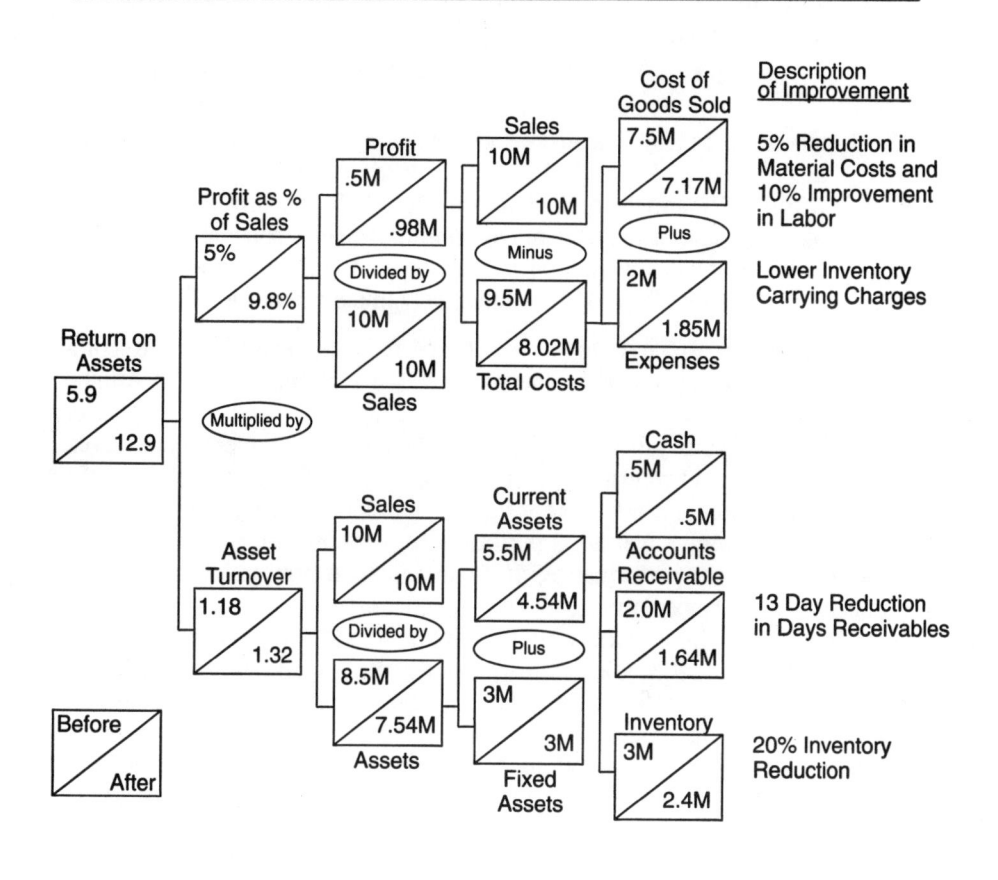

cate deeper problems of too much of the wrong kind of inventory which can create shortages of needed inventory for production and sales. High turnover indicates better liquidity and superior materials management and merchandising. Given the example $10 million company, the current number of inventory turns is 2.5. With a 20 percent inventory reduction, the number of inventory turns increases to 3.1.

- *Days of Receivables (365 * 1/(Sales/Receivables))*. This ratio expresses the average time in days that receivables are outstanding. It is a measure of the management of credit and collections. Generally, the greater the number of days outstanding, the greater the probability of delinquencies in accounts receivable. The lower the number of days, the greater the cash availability. With an 18 percent reduction in receivables, the current days receivable of 73 days can be reduced to 60. This means $356,200 is available for other purposes.

- *Return on Assets (Profit Before Taxes/Total Assets).* This ratio measures the effectiveness of management in employing the resources available to it. Several calculations are necessary to determine the return on assets. The worksheet in Figure 2-3 shows current data as the figures before MRP and the projected data after MRP. The difference between the two sets of data illustrate typical improvements obtainable as applied to the example $10 million manufacturer. The return on assets can be improved from 5.9 to 12.9 by effectively implementing an MRP system.

Another approach to ratio analysis for performance evaluation is to compare one's own company with other firms in the same industry. The Annual Statement Studies[2] provide comparative ratios for this purpose. This use of comparative ratio analysis will use the same three ratios for inventory turnover, days receivable, and return on assets. To perform the analysis, identify the median and upper quartile ratios for firms in the same industry. These roughly correspond to average and good performance. By comparing the ratios with your firm's current performance, you can calculate how much better your company should be performing to be competitive.

Using the inventory turns ratio for the example $10 million manufacturer, assume the Statement Studies indicate that the median and upper quartile are four and six turns for other firms in the same industry. Average performance of four inventory turns translates into an expected inventory of $1.875 million ($7.5 million divided by four). If the example firm had this ratio, it would have had $1.125 million less in inventory. With inventory carrying costs at 25 percent, this would produce savings of $281,250 each year.

For the Days Receivable ratio, assume the Statement Studies indicate that 60 and 50 days are the median and upper quartile. The days receivable in the example $10 million manufacturer is currently 73 days; an improvement to 60 days would reduce receivables by $356,200 (using a daily sales rate of $27,400 and a 13 day reduction). This means that cash is available for other purposes.

Note that the return on assets ratio is 5.9 for the example company as shown in Figure 2-3. Assuming the Statement Studies indicate the return on

---

[2]Robert Morris Associates, the national association of bank loan and credit officers, publishes the Annual Statement Studies. The Statement Studies contain composite financial data on manufacturing industries broken down by four-character Standard Industrial Classification (SIC) codes. For each industry, it displays a common-size balance sheet and income statement, with each item a percentage of total assets or sales, respectively. Ratios are also calculated, and each ratio has three values: the upper quartile, median quartile, and lower quartile.

FIGURE 2-4
Calculating the Potential Stock Appreciation

	Before MRP	After MRP
Before tax profit	$500,000.00	$980,000.00
Earnings per share	$5.00	$9.80
Current stock price	$30.00	$58.80(6 * 9.80)
Multiplier	6	6

assets is 10 and 15 for firms in the same industry at the median and upper quartiles, improving the return on assets to equivalent levels would mean increased profits and/or asset turnover.

MRP Impact on Stock Price

If the integration and improved information of an MRP system results in a better balance sheet and increased profits, these improvements should impact stock price for the company. Although stock price is affected by a variety of factors, the typical effect of improved profits and balance sheet ratios can be estimated. Using the example $10 million manufacturer and typical benefits already described, and assuming 100,000 shares outstanding and an existing stock price of $30.00 per share, Figure 2-4 shows the stock price effects of an effective MRP.

These calculations suggest that MRP systems can lead to significant impacts on financial results, including the balance sheet, income statement, key ratios, and stock price.

THE INTEGRATIVE EFFECTS OF AN MRP INFORMATION SYSTEM

The intangible or nonfinancial benefits of an integrated MRP information system can be viewed from several perspectives. For illustrative purposes, the discussion will focus on the benefits for accounting, product and process design, production, sales, and information system functions. From the overall company standpoint, MRP provides a framework for working effectively together. It provides a consistent plan for action.

Effects on Accounting

With a common database from MRP, accounting no longer requires duplicate files and redundant data entry. Product costing, for example, can be performed using accurate and up-to-date product structures.

Customer invoices can be based on actual shipments (without duplicate data entry), which helps speed invoice processing. Payables can use purchase order and receipt data for three-way matching with supplier invoices.

As manufacturing transactions are recorded, the financial equivalents are automatically generated for updating the general ledger. This provides a complete audit trail from account totals to source documents, ensures accurate and up-to-date financial information, and permits tracking of actual versus budgeted expenses. Detailed transaction activity can also be easily accessed on-line for answering account inquiries.

Differences between actual and standard costs are highlighted as variances. Order-related variances help pinpoint problem areas.

Since manufacturing transactions automatically update the general ledger, time-consuming manual journal entries can be eliminated. Period-end closing procedures can be performed in hours or days, rather than weeks. This improves timeliness of financial reports.

Financial reports can be easily customized to meet the needs of various decision makers. Financial projections can be based on detailed MRP calculations for future requirements. Decision support tools (such as spreadsheets, graphics packages and data managers) can use the financial data maintained in the MRP database.

Effects on Product and Process Design

The product structure database offers engineering much greater control over product and process design, especially in terms of engineering change control. Planned changes can be phased in and emergency changes can be communicated immediately.

MRP systems offer numerous analytical tools for the engineering function. When diagnosing the impact of changes to materials and resources, for example, engineers can check where-used information to identify the affected products.

Effects on Production and Materials Management

MRP systems help establish realistic schedules for production and communicate consistent priorities so that everyone knows the most important job to work on at all times. Visibility of future requirements helps production prepare for capacity problems, and also helps suppliers anticipate and meet your needs. As changes to demands or supplies do occur, MRP helps identify the impact on production and purchasing.

MRP helps eliminate many crisis situations, so people have more time for planning and quality. Buyers can spend more time in vendor negotiation and quality improvement. When the shortage list is no longer used to manage the shop, the quality of working life can improve.

Effects on Sales

Customer service can be improved by making valid delivery promises and then meeting those promises. Custom product quotations can be developed faster and more accurately, which improves job estimating. Delivery leadtimes can be shortened and customer inquiries on order status can be answered immediately.

Effects on the MIS Function

An MRP system implemented as an integrated software package offers several advantages to the MIS function. The software package can offer a growth path from simple to comprehensive applications built on top of a database management system, reduce the development time and cost for software, documentation, and training classes (that would be incurred before the firm can start obtaining the benefit of MRP), and permit the MIS staff to focus their attention on organizational change (as change agents) and servicing user needs for customization and professional assistance.

VALUE OF INDIVIDUAL COMPETENCE IN INFORMATION MANAGEMENT

Individual competence focuses on the knowledge and skill to apply information systems and information management principles to business processes, specifically in one's work. The knowledge includes how to manage information resources in support of individual work, cooperative work, and organizational processes. Individual competence in information management is much more than computer literacy. Computer literacy for an individual is a basic knowledge of computer technology sufficient to support use of a computer terminal or personal computer for simple, well-defined applications. Computer literacy is a required background but insufficient for real competency.

This section explains the value of individual competence in information systems. There are four areas in which your value as an individual is increased: in interacting with the information management function, in projects for planning and developing applications, in using applications developed by others, and in developing and managing your own small applications and databases. Doing your own information management may include redesign of your work. The emphasis on personal competence in information management is consistent with the total quality management concept of empowering individuals. The competence is described in terms of what a person needs to be able to do rather than a list of topics.

Value in Interacting with the Information Systems Function

The information management function has emerged as the corporate function charged with planning, developing, managing, and operating the corporate information systems. It is also responsible for standards, training, and support for functional areas, groups, and individuals in their use of information technology. In interacting with the information systems function, there is value in having some general understanding of what the function does. This is similar to the value of understanding some accounting in order to interact with the accounting/controllership function. There is also value in having knowledge and skills to interact with information systems personnel in defining innovative applications and in making resource allocation decisions for MIS resources.

- *Innovator in defining applications for information technology.* This interaction involves identification of ways in which information technology may be used in improving productivity, redesigning business systems, and achieving competitive advantage.
- *Participant in corporate information management.* At the corporate level, there are management issues that should be understood by all managers and other knowledge workers. These include allocation of resources for information technology, controlling use, evaluating economic benefits, defining an information management strategy, and managing development and operation of information systems.

Value in Projects for Planning and Developing Large Applications

There is value in being able to participate effectively in the development of large corporate information system development projects. These projects tend to cross functional boundaries and require high levels of formal project control and formal development methodologies.

- *Participant in large application development projects.* Information competence includes a project-participant depth of understanding of large scale information system project methods, formal development methodologies, and software development methods.
- *Specifier of information requirements.* There is value in being able to specify the information requirements of tasks, jobs, and functions. This specification is necessary in order to build systems. Information competence includes a knowledge of methods for eliciting correct and complete requirements. The knowledge extends to providing data modeling information for functional area or enterprise-wide applications.

Value in Using Applications Developed by Others

Many applications are in operation, so the major value of information competence is in being a skilled, effective user.

- *Supplier of input data.* Information competence for this role involves basic information system processes and procedures. It provides value because it allows the user to make appropriate decisions about data being collected, stored, and processed.
- *User of information quality assurance procedures.* There is value in assuring accuracy and completeness of input and output, maintaining integrity of databases, and safeguarding files and databases. Effective users understand and apply procedural discipline in information resource use and management.
- *User/evaluator of output from information system applications.* Information competence provides the background for understanding the characteristics and limitations of outputs from applications. This includes knowledge of systems and systems behavior. The value added is the ability to evaluate the quality of data and its appropriateness for a suggested use.
- *Interactive user of applications.* Various applications for analysis, evaluation, and similar tasks are well structured as to procedures but require more than simple input or use of output. The applications have interactive procedures for input based on intermediate results, selection among alternatives, revision of inputs, and so forth. Many standard software packages are of this type. Information competence related to these activities is beneficial because it supports effective use.

Value in Developing and Managing One's Own Applications and Databases

In order to achieve the full benefits of individual productivity, it is often not sufficient for a knowledge worker merely to use information technology. It may be necessary to redesign knowledge work jobs, work space, work habits, information management, and information technology support.

- *Designer of own databases and user of variety of databases.* Information competence includes the knowledge to create and use small databases for individual tasks as well as using enterprise databases and databases from external suppliers. The value is in effective personal use of data resources in analysis and decision making.
- *User/developer of small end-user applications.* At the level of individual or small group applications, the systems are often most effectively designed and built by the person or group that will use them. End-user applications are typically developed using software packages. End-user development processes represent a significant downsizing of processes used in large system develop-

ment, but quality should still be built into the systems. The benefit of this competence is in end-user systems that meet needs and have high quality.

• *Manager of own information resources and participant in group information management.* An individual knowledge worker has significant responsibility for evaluating his or her need for information and the personal systems associated with it. Information processing and communication dominate the time schedule of a knowledge worker, so personal information system design and information management decisions have an impact on work effectiveness and efficiency. The decisions allocate scarce economic resources plus scarce personal resources of time and cognition.

Value of Competence in Industry- or Function-Specific Information Systems

Every function (such as production and inventory control) or industry (such as manufacturing) must deal with unique business systems and information management applications. The value of a person is increased by being competent in both. For example, a person in manufacturing should understand integrated resource management and information technology applications such as MRP systems.

THE VALUE OF INDIVIDUAL COMPETENCE IN SELECTED KNOWLEDGE WORK SOFTWARE

The previous section described what a person should be able to do relative to information management; the knowledge and skills for performing these activities were implied by the nature of the activities. Unanswered by that section was the value of having some competence in software packages. The discussion of software package knowledge and skills will be relative to general knowledge work and to the specific domain of one's work.

Knowledge Work

Knowledge work consists of activities using individual and external knowledge to produce outputs characterized by information content. Typical knowledge work outputs are analyses, reports, decisions, instructions, schedules, directions, and plans. A few examples of jobs that are dominated by knowledge work are managers, analysts, schedulers, and planners.

Value of Competence in a Basic Software Toolkit

Just as any worker may have a standard set of tools (a toolkit) that tend to be necessary for good work, there is a fundamental set of software that applies to knowledge work. These are generic types of software packages that apply to types of problems rather than being brand names. They may be found singly or in combination in commercial software packages.

Information competence with respect to the software toolkit for knowledge work assumes that the knowledge worker understands the domain to which the software is being applied and the underlying techniques being implemented by the software. For example, one of the packages in the knowledge work software toolkit is a statistics package. This assumes a knowledge of statistics sufficient to formulate the problem and use the features in the software. Given this knowledge base, software packages are often useful in eliciting the knowledge of the user and helping the user make good decisions in problem formulation, choice of procedures, and evaluation of results. Using the statistics example, a statistics package can enhance the statistical knowledge of a user by suggesting alternatives, asking questions, and providing help screens at critical decision points.

There are eight software packages that are generally so valuable that they can be termed the universal toolkit:

1. Word processor
2. Spreadsheet processor
3. Statistical software
4. Presentation graphics software
5. Electronic mail software
6. Numerical database management software
7. Text database software
8. Personal computer management software

There are four additional packages for cooperative work and analysis that are recommended as being valuable in a strategy of individual competence.

1. Cooperative work software
2. Financial modeling software
3. Scheduling and project management software
4. Forecasting software

Each package in the software toolkit will be described briefly and the value of individual competence noted.

• *Word processor.* Supports preparation of documents, memoranda, notes, letters. Wide range of capabilities such as moving blocks of text, checking spelling, suggesting alternative words, and formatting.

• *Spreadsheet processor.* Supports analysis. This type of package allows the user to build a computational model with a tabular format of rows and columns. It supports a fundamental way of modeling data. For example, it fits analyses that model changes in data through time and analyses that operate on subclasses or breakdowns of summary figures. Any analysis that might be done manually using a large columnar pad is a natural candidate for a spreadsheet processor.

- *Statistical software.* Supports statistical analysis and inference through statistics. Although descriptive statistics are provided by a spreadsheet processor, more sophisticated statistical analysis requires statistical software. This includes regression to analyze relationships and inferential statistics to analyze sample data, make inferences about the population, and accept or reject hypotheses. Many software packages include help facilities to guide user selection of the appropriate statistical technique and to assist in evaluation of results. This software may include some forecasting and times series analysis described later as forecasting software.
- *Presentation graphics software.* Supports preparation of presentations. Some presentation graphics capabilities are usually part of spreadsheet and statistical software, but there are also specialized presentation graphics software packages. They are used to prepare charts, graphs, and line drawings. They support preparation of slides and overheads containing graphs and drawings.
- *Electronic mail software.* Supports electronic mail communications. An electronic mail system may be internal to an organization, or within a professional organization or group. This also includes accessing bulletin board information.
- *Numerical database management software.* Every knowledge worker has files and databases of numeric data to build, manage, and use. A typical knowledge work task might involve access to databases maintained at a group, departmental, or corporate level. Database management systems support collection, storage, and retrieval of data plus preparation of analyses that present the data in a meaningful way.
- *Text database software.* A knowledge worker may need to build, maintain, and access textual data. In addition to personal files of textual data, a knowledge worker should be able to access external databanks containing textual data. These are library-like databases containing keywords, abstracts, and/or full texts of documents available from information services. A knowledge worker doing research on a topic should understand how to use typical software and procedures for searching the appropriate literature. The online data sources include financial reports, business and financial journals, major newspapers and news journals, and scientific journals.
- *Personal computer management software.* This does not mean an extensive knowledge of the operating systems and system software. Rather, it suggests a user knowledge of basic facilities for managing a personal computer work environment. The software packages aid in operating system use and provide additional system management facilities for management of files, switching between applications, copying files, backing up files, compression of files to

reduce storage space, detection and elimination of software viruses, and so forth. Personal computer and information management software frequently includes some personal work management applications such as a calendar, notes, or a telephone directory.

- *Cooperative work software.* Organizations make significant use of teams or groups. There are problems in participation, decision making, and consensus building in group meetings. There are also problems of coordination when group members are not in the same location. Software for coordination and group meeting support is fairly new, but it can be viewed as part of the basic software support for knowledge work. The software is often termed electronic meeting support or group decision support systems (GDSS).
- *Financial modeling software.* Supports analysis through modeling. Although spreadsheet processors can be used effectively for even moderately complex financial models, more sophisticated problems benefit from financial modeling software. The software provides better documentation of the assumptions in the model because of the modeling language and provides additional capabilities in doing both deterministic and probabilistic "what if" analyses.
- *Scheduling and project management software.* Knowledge workers are often participants in projects in which activities must be carefully planned, scheduled, and tracked. Even with fairly simple projects, the use of scheduling and project management software will be useful. The software supports input of activities, times, completion requirements, resource availability, and activity dependencies. Outputs include feasible schedules, gantt charts, and critical path analyses, and so forth. The tracking facilities identify critical path activities, effect of delays on completion time, and project dependencies. The need for project management, ease of software use, and low cost make this software a useful part of the toolkit.
- *Forecasting software.* Forecasting is required in a number of knowledge work activities. Although specialists may need to be consulted in many cases, most knowledge workers should be able to deal with simple forecasting issues. Forecasting software is useful for both generalist and specialist users. The software identifies patterns in data and suggests the best forecasting model considering trends and non-seasonal or seasonal patterns.

This does not exhaust the list of types of software packages that are useful in knowledge work; it represents the basic toolkit. Looking to the future, a software package that may have general potential for knowledge workers and be added to the toolkit is an expert systems shell. Although some expert systems require significant programming expertise to develop and implement, there are potentially many small rule-based systems that can be built by a user/designer. Building a rule-based system is difficult for a person not skilled in programming. An expert system shell is a package that manages the programming effort for an expert system in much the same way as other packages in the toolkit do for the problems they address.

Value of Competence in a Domain Software Toolkit

Knowledge workers in specific functional areas have software for problems that are part of the function. For example, an engineer may use a computer-aided design (CAD) package, production personnel may use a statistical process control (SPC) application, a master scheduler may use an optimization package, and distribution professionals should have a good knowledge of distribution requirements planning software.

LESSONS FOR MANAGERS

The productivity value of information technology is not just in producing more physical goods at lower cost. Much of the productivity impact of the societal investment in information technology has been increased variety of goods and services. The technology has supported a trend to mass customization. Also, new goods and services have emerged as a result of innovative information technology applications.

Moving from a societal perspective to a view of a single organization, does information technology add any economic value? The chapter explains how the effective application of information technology (using an MRP information system as an example) can improve the bottom line of profitability and provide intangible benefits for different functional areas.

Unlike many technologies used by an organization, information technology has a pervasive effect. There are four areas in which information competence adds value to and empowers an individual working in an organization: in interacting with the information management function, in projects for planning and developing applications, in using applications developed by others, and in developing and managing individual applications and databases. The competence encompasses both general knowledge and skills and specialized knowledge and skills associated with a function or industry.

Individual information management competence includes the ability to select and use an appropriate software package for knowledge work. The software toolkit common to most knowledge workers includes eight basic packages and four recommended extensions. In addition, there are software packages that are important to knowledge workers in a given function or industry.

CHAPTER 3

BUSINESS AND INFORMATION SYSTEM ARCHITECTURES

The information system of an organization is a vital system. It is analogous to the nervous system of the body, because it helps in communication, coordination, and control of activities across functional areas within the firm and between the firm and its business partners.

The business system of an organization can be described in terms of its architecture, e.g., functions, communication between functions, and control structure. Likewise, the information system follows an information architecture. The architecture of the information system should be aligned with and match the architecture of the business. This means that an understanding of business architecture and operations is critical to effective design and implementation of an information system architecture.

This chapter explains the concept of information system architecture and describes common, fundamental architectures for the information system of an organization. The principles of aligning or matching business architecture and information architecture apply across the entire range of profit and non-profit organizations and different types of businesses. As a way of making the concepts more concrete, the illustrations and examples of the chapter will emphasize businesses involved in manufacturing and distribution.

CONCEPT OF BUSINESS ARCHITECTURE AND INFORMATION SYSTEM ARCHITECTURE[1]

Organizations are not natural systems. They are artificial systems built by humans to deal with problems of organizing and managing activities and to

---

[1] This section was influenced by J. A. Zachman, "A Framework for Information Systems Architecture," *IBM Systems Journal*, 26:3, 1987, pp. 276-292, and P. Van der Poel and R. Van Waes, "Framework for Architectures in Information Planning," in E. D. Falkenberg and P. Lindgreen (Editors), *Information Systems Concepts: An In-depth Analysis*. New York: Elsevier Science Publishing Company, 1989, pp. 177-191.

FIGURE 3-1
Business and Information System Architectures

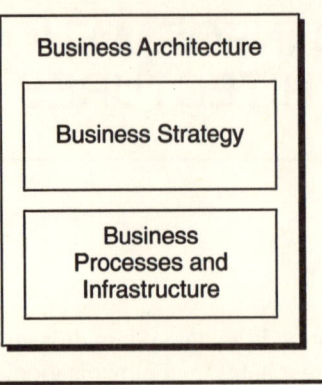

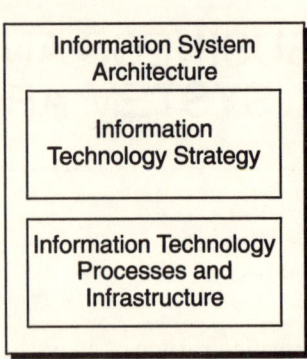

Business Architecture	Information System Architecture
Business Strategy	Information Technology Strategy
Business Processes and Infrastructure	Information Technology Processes and Infrastructure

achieve objectives. There are different organizational designs to match different conditions. In other words, the best organization design depends on conditions such as industry, products, distribution channels, customers, and personnel. Also, the design of the organization may be influenced by how information technology is applied. In turn, the information system of an organization is an artificial system; it can have many structures. The main organizing principle, however, should be that it match, support, align with, and conform to the structure and design of the business (Figure 3-1).

The concept of architecture applied to these two systems is based on the idea that these systems have a structure. The structure reflects the functions to be performed, the need for coordination and communications, the objects that the system deals with, and management and control. By analogy, the architecture of a building (a model) reflects the functions of the building, the need to coordinate these functions (both physically and aesthetically) within the building and with surrounding buildings, and with the people, businesses and events that use the building. Architecture is not the only way of conceptualizing a model of a business and its information system, but it is a very useful approach.

Business Architecture

The business architecture is a model of the business that reflects the business strategy, business processes, and infrastructure. We can segment the business architecture into four factors: business functions, coordination and communication between functions, the objects of interest, and the management control structure.

Factors for Business Architecture	Description
Business functions	The activities that provide products and services; the assignment of responsibilities defines the division and location of work.
Coordination and communications	The coordination of activities within and among business functions, especially at remote locations.
Objects of interest	The vendors, customers, products, sales orders, invoices, and other objects that are involved in performing activities in each business function.
Management and control	The location and assignment structure of responsibility for functions, activities, and decision making. The control structure for supervision and management.

These four factors help define a model of how a business operates. The information system architecture also models how a business operates with respect to information.

Information System Architecture

The information system architecture should reflect the business architecture. The four factors of business architecture (business functions, communication and coordination, objects of interest, and management and control structure) help define the information system architecture since both model how a business operates.

Factors for Business Architecture	Corresponding Factors for Information System Architecture
Business functions	Transaction systems and other applications for supporting the business functions. Applications for management support such as management reporting, executive support systems, and decision support systems.
Coordination and communications	Communication facilities to coordinate activities within and among business functions. Types and location of communication facilities.
Objects of interest	Data model defining entities and attributes. Basis for databases.
Management and control structure	Responsibility and control of information system resources (i.e., hardware, software, databases). Allocation of work among local and centralized functions. Development and planning responsibilities.

Several fundamental decisions significantly influence the nature of the business processes and how they are modeled in the information system architecture. Some decisions are dictated by industry practices, others by business strategy.[2] Some of these fundamental decisions include

1. Does the business bill its customers or accept cash?
2. Does it deliver its product in the future or immediately?
3. Does it know its customers' buying behavior or not?
4. Does it negotiate price for its product or stipulate it?
5. Does it rent/lease its product or sell it?
6. Does it track each product sold or not?
7. Does it make the product to order or provide it from stock?
8. Does it engage in manufacturing or service operations?
9. Does it employ discrete or process operations?
10. Does it utilize repetitive or job shop operations?
11. Does it employ standard or actual cost accounting
12. Does it use project or process accounting?

[2]Based on work of Don Bernstein as reported by M. Carlson in "Business Information Analysis and Integration Technique (BIAIT)," Database, Spring 1979, pp. 3–9.

Answers to these decisions will determine how the business will operate and how to design information systems to model the business.

FUNCTIONS AND ACTIVITIES IN BUSINESS OPERATIONS

The functions and activities of business operations are a starting point for understanding the business and the need for an information system. To illustrate the functions and activities in business operations, it is helpful to focus on a manufacturing operation and the need for integrated resource management applications. The concepts can be easily translated to other types of businesses. The discussion in this section will be centered on major information flows, including the transaction processing and some key management reports involved in a manufacturing business.

Manufacturers have significant similarity in the need for information to manage their resources. They all deal with the basic manufacturing equation: define what resources you plan to make (the master schedule), what resources you need (the bill of material/resources), what resources you have (inventory and capacity), and determine what you need to get (purchasing and production). Figure 3-2 shows the major information flows in manufacturing operations. This top-down model shows how aggregate plans—the business, sales and production plans—are translated into detailed plans for execution by procurement and production. These information flows utilize master files concerning customers, vendors, items/bills of material, workcenters/routings, inventory locations, and general ledger accounts. The figure shows nine business functions and related information flows for a manufacturing organization. The nine functions are described briefly.

Distributors have similar information flows to manufacturers; the major differences are the lack of production activity and the absence of custom product configuration during sales order processing. Production planning (for families of end-items) still applies. The master schedule represents the materials plan for purchasing activity. Capacity planning focuses on different types of resources (such as warehouse space/personnel or capacity of key vendors) and information still flows to accounting.

Business Planning

Business planning defines the business mission of the company, markets, profit objectives, and resources. Business planning results in an annual budget that establishes the baseline for financial planning and measurement purposes. Budget revisions may be developed periodically to reflect contingency planning or anticipated changes. As a result of activities to execute the business plan, actual costs can be compared to budget.

FIGURE 3-2
Simplified Information Flows in a Manufacturing Business

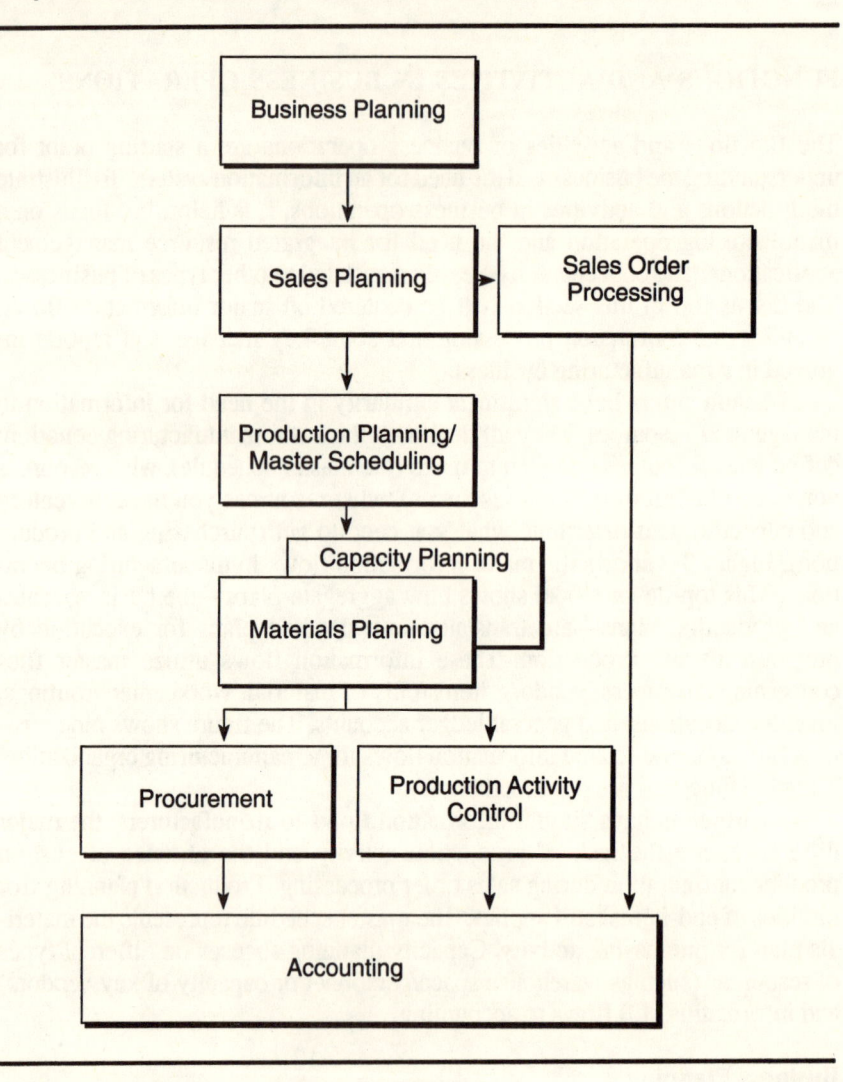

```
                    ┌──────────────────┐
                    │ Business Planning│
                    └────────┬─────────┘
                             │
                             ▼
                    ┌──────────────────┐     ┌──────────────────┐
                    │  Sales Planning  │────▶│   Sales Order    │
                    │                  │     │   Processing     │
                    └────────┬─────────┘     └────────┬─────────┘
                             │                        │
                             ▼                        │
                    ┌──────────────────┐              │
                    │Production Planning/│            │
                    │ Master Scheduling │             │
                    └────────┬─────────┘              │
                             │                        │
                             ▼                        │
                    ┌──────────────────┐              │
                    │ Capacity Planning│              │
                    ├──────────────────┤              │
                    │ Materials Planning│             │
                    └────┬────────┬────┘              │
                         │        │                   │
                         ▼        ▼                   │
                ┌──────────┐  ┌──────────────────┐    │
                │Procurement│  │Production Activity│   │
                │          │  │     Control       │   │
                └────┬─────┘  └────────┬─────────┘    │
                     │                 │              │
                     ▼                 ▼              ▼
                    ┌──────────────────────────────────┐
                    │            Accounting            │
                    └──────────────────────────────────┘
```

Sales Planning

Sales planning defines demands being placed on the firm, both actual customer orders and forecast orders. Analysis of sales history can be used to project future sales. Product families can be used for aggregate planning purposes, where the forecast is expressed in terms of product family and product mix percentage for items within each family. These planning bills may consist of end-items for a family of standard products, the modular options for an assemble-to-order custom product, or resource profiles for make-to-order and engineer-to-order products.

Sales Order Processing

Sales order processing starts with entry of the customer order, where availability should be checked for each item ordered. Sales orders may represent releases against customer schedules and contracts. An item may be shipped immediately if available in inventory or promised for future delivery based on scheduled receipts of purchased or manufactured items. In a custom products environment, the customer order defines what should be built and a quotation (the first step in the sales order processing cycle) of the job cost estimate may need to be developed. Shipment activities require paperwork such as consolidated picklists (for assembling orders), packing lists, and bills of lading. Shipments generate information for the general ledger and invoicing.

Production Planning/Master Scheduling

The production plan identifies the monthly rate of output by product family, whereas the master schedule states daily production for specific family members (e.g., end-items or modular options). The production plan must cover the sales plan and the inventory plan (or backlog plan) when required by seasonal variations in sales. The master schedule and final assembly schedule of customer-specified custom products drive the material/capacity plans and the procurement/production activities.

Capacity Planning

Capacity planning takes the schedules defined by the production plan/master schedule and final assembly schedule, extends them by the routing for each item, and calculates the load on each resource. With infinite loading, load is compared to capacity for bottleneck resources and overloaded periods identified. With finite loading, a level load is calculated for key resources that may result in revisions to the production schedule. Loads can be reduced (by rescheduling) or the capacity increased (by overtime, additional equipment/personnel, and so forth). Capacity planning is used to assess the reasonableness of the production plan/master schedule.

Material Planning

Material planning uses the schedules defined by the production plan/master schedule and final assembly schedule to calculate material requirements based on the bills of material, lead times, and lot sizing parameters. With this information, buyers (responsible for obtaining raw material) and planners (responsible for scheduling each area of production) can take action on scheduling orders to meet the master schedule.

Procurement

Procurement involves periodic review of approved vendors and vendor agreements. It also requires daily coordination of vendor deliveries through a vendor schedule and purchase orders. For subcontracted items, the components may need to be picked and sent to the vendor. Receipts are matched to purchase orders and possibly placed in inspection for disposition by quality management. Receipt information is passed to accounts payable for matching with invoices and payment. Payment results in entries in the general ledger.

Production Activity Control

A manufacturing order defines the quantity and start/complete dates for producing an item. On a given order, the order-dependent bill/routing may be modified to reflect material substitutions or alternate operations. Material usage and labor/resource expenditures are reported against the manufacturing order. As an alternative to picking material components prior to starting production, the components may be backflushed or post-deducted after completion of an operation or receipt of the parent item. By reporting actual material and resource consumption, actual costs can be compared to planned costs for calculating variances. Production transactions (such as material/labor consumption and receipts) generate general ledger transactions.

Dispatch lists (reflecting the routings) coordinate various areas of production to meet the master schedule and final assembly schedule. In custom product manufacturing environments, the router/traveler (of detailed instructions) also acts as a coordination tool. In repetitive environments with standard routings, visible scheduling systems and replenishment goals can be used as coordination tools.

Accounting

Accounting uses shipment data for generating invoices, receipt data for validating vendor invoices, labor data for payroll, and costed manufacturing transactions for updating the general ledger and tracking actual costs versus budget.

Examples of Unique Requirements

While the major information flows and functions described above apply to most manufacturers and distributors, there are unique requirements in various segments of the manufacturing and distribution industries. Some examples illustrate the variety of specialized requirements that must be considered.

- *International business partners.* For firms with customers and suppliers in other countries, sales orders/invoices and purchase orders/payments may be expressed in foreign currencies. This requires currency conversion, different methods of taxation and payment, different date and currency formats, different character sets and descriptions for foreign languages, and so forth.
- *Foreign location of remote plants.* The users at foreign sites will probably require systems with documentation and screens in the local language. For standardized systems to be used, there must be language translations. Considerations of international usage and local customs may lead to changes in standardized systems to create an international system.
- *Data interchange requirements.* The standardization of Electronic Data Interchange (EDI) between customer and supplier has evolved over several years. Customers may require electronic data interchange communication of purchases, shipments, and payments. For example, the major automotive manufacturers (Chrysler, Ford and General Motors) communicate with their suppliers via EDI to provide close coordination of material shipments and receipts. This requires that supplier systems conform to the EDI standards.
- *Custom product manufacturing.* Complex job shop environments require configuration of multi-level bills/routings for unique jobs with project accounting for cost management. Labor or machine intensive job shop operations may require forward scheduling or finite loading logic for production scheduling.
- *Serial number product tracking.* Some products may require serial number tracking of individual items through production into end items or into assembly in other products. Examples are integrated circuits, PC boards, and personal computers.
- *Repetitive manufacturing.* Repetitive and process manufacturers typically use daily rate-based schedules to drive production rather than individual manufacturing orders. Production activity and cost accounting focus on periods rather than orders.

ALTERNATIVES FOR BUSINESS AND INFORMATION ARCHITECTURE

There are a number of alternative business and information system architectures. The chapter will present an overall taxonomy and focus on the major architectures rather than the variations that are possible. Two important issues that are reflected in architectures are integration and centralization/ decentralization.

Extent of Integration

Business integration refers to standardization, common business systems, agreement on interfaces, sharing of information, and other measures to reduce duplicate and inconsistent data. Integration can be with business functions and activities within a single business unit. It can also be among business units that are part of a larger company or that have established ad hoc or relatively permanent partnerships. Business integration can occur at various levels ranging from limited integration covering a few functions and interactions to extensive company-wide integration.

Information system integration refers to the extent to which there is a coherent businesswide information architecture with a common definition for data and a sharing of databases, applications that fit together and an information technology infrastructure that provides for shared use of hardware, software, and data. The integration can extend to interactions with suppliers and customers. Information system integration can also range from somewhat limited to very extensive. The integration schemes to be discussed in this chapter are the following:

- Business and information systems not integrated (using an example of one business unit)
- Integration of business and information systems within one business unit
- Integration of business and information systems among related business units or other business partners

Location and Control of Data and Facilities

In the design of an information system architecture, two characteristics of location and control are very influential:

• The location and control of computers and application software. This can be either centralized or distributed (decentralized). The choice has implications for hardware configuration, software design, and communications facilities.

• The location and control of databases. This can be centralized or distributed. Each alternative has implications for the design of databases, control of definitions and changes, control of data updates, and control of data access privileges.

Three variations on the location and control of hardware, software, and databases will be explored in this chapter: central control of hardware, software, and databases; mixed control with some central management and some distributed functions; and fully distributed hardware, software, and databases. Other activities such as application development can also be centralized or decentralized. These activities will be discussed later in the book.

Directions in Business and Information System Architecture

The trend in business organizations is to reduce the extent of centralized control and to distribute responsibility and control as much as possible. Centralization or decentralization can be mixed with some functions centralized and others decentralized. In the context of the trend, important business functions may remain centralized, but many functions that have been performed centrally will be decentralized.

The trend in information system architecture follows the changes in business architecture. The flexibility of information technology allows for a large number of variations in responsibility, control, location, and management of hardware, software, and databases. Distributing facilities and databases while maintaining the capability to share data and benefit from integration requires significant planning, configuration controls, and database management controls.

NON-INTEGRATED SYSTEMS IN A SINGLE BUSINESS UNIT

Information systems are important to an integrated business by aiding management to plan and control activities across functional areas and by reducing duplication and confusion as different functions and activities make use of data about the same objects of interest.

In many organizations, information systems have been developed to serve one functional area without regard for integration with other areas. For example, the accounting function has historically developed systems or implemented software packages with little consideration for manufacturing requirements. Even the functional areas involved in manufacturing (engineering, quality, production scheduling, procurement, and cost accounting) have often developed systems that provide overlapping functionality. The result is not only confusing but causes duplicate data maintenance efforts. Figure 3-3 illustrates non-integrated information systems in one organization, where each major box represents a standalone system maintaining duplicate data.

> *Example.* Prior to implementing an integrated information system, a manufacturer of scissor lift equipment used several non-integrated systems. The engineering department maintained a stand-alone system for documentation purposes with information about items/bills of material and workcenters/routings. Engineering also maintained item/bill information in their computer-aided design (CAD) system. Similar information was maintained by accounting on another system for product costing purposes and by materials management on still another system for the purpose of purchasing raw materials. Purchasing had to update a vendor master that was also being maintained on the separate accounting

FIGURE 3-3
An Example of a Non-Integrated System

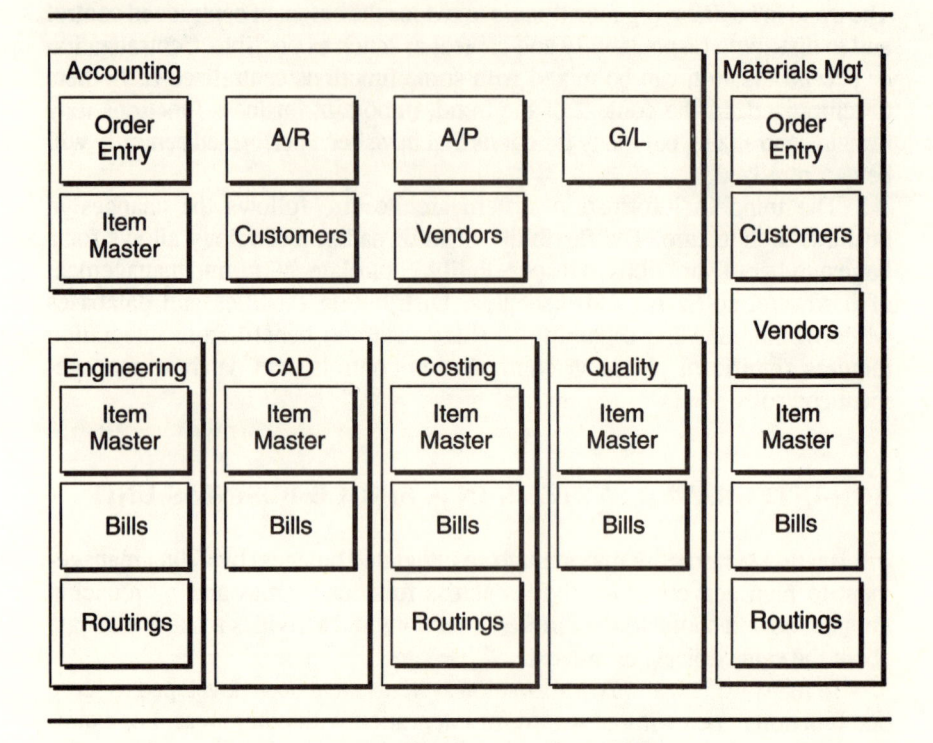

Accounting				Materials Mgt
Order Entry	A/R	A/P	G/L	Order Entry
Item Master	Customers	Vendors		Customers
				Vendors

Engineering	CAD	Costing	Quality	
Item Master	Item Master	Item Master	Item Master	Item Master
Bills	Bills	Bills	Bills	Bills
Routings		Routings		Routings

system. Quality control maintained yet another database about items/bills for the purposes of lot traceability and failure analysis. The sales order entry system, part of the accounting system, also required information about saleable items.

Materials management maintained a separate set of information about customer orders and customers, since the stand-alone sales order system used by customer service representatives was designed for accounting purposes. It did not capture information about customer-specified options and did not support materials management. Shipments had to be entered in both systems. Customer service also had to reenter overseas sales orders and invoices, since the system did not support multiple currencies and special value-added taxes.

Monthly management meetings involved lengthy arguments about the correct set of numbers, with hours of clerical effort spent on reconciling the numbers before and after the meetings.

INTEGRATED SYSTEMS WITHIN A SINGLE BUSINESS UNIT

The integration of business systems within the organization requires significant integration in the information systems, as exemplified in the earlier description of the major information flows for a manufacturing business. This integration can be handled in a number of ways with respect to the technical architecture of hardware, software, and databases. Two common approaches are a centralized, shared processor (computer) and a distributed approach using a client server system. In a client server system, each workstation does some processing and accesses data or programs located on a server computer. More technical details will be given in Chapter 6 on communication technologies.

Centralized Shared Computer

In the centralized approach, there is one (or more) computer under central management. The computer can be a large mainframe computer, midsize minicomputer, or microcomputer. The key issue is centralized processing; the size of the computer is not the issue. The central processor is shared by many users who access it through dumb terminals (with no processing capabilities) or personal computers being used as terminals. The terminals only serve as input devices (and output devices for screen images), while the centralized shared processor performs all other functions.

Any databases are maintained under the control of the central processor. A single set of data access and update controls is sufficient.

The advantages of this approach are its simplicity of design and high level of control over processing and data. The disadvantages are the amount (and possibly costs) of communication traffic and the difficulties inherent in handling the variety of processing needs centrally. Communication traffic is greater than on a distributed system because it is necessary to transmit all inputs and outputs between the terminals and the centralized processor to perform any processing.

Distributed Approach Using a Client Server System

The distributed approach is to allocate processing and data storage to computers that may be in different locations and under decentralized control. This does not exclude a computer under some centralized control to handle data and processing that is best done centrally. The difference between the distributed design and the centralized processor is the movement of processing and data to dispersed locations. Communication traffic is more limited because the decentralized processor performs local processing and manages local data. Technically, the use of decentralized processors can be implemented in several ways. A common distributed approach is to use a client server system.

A client server system, as explained more fully in Chapter 6, uses personal computer workstations to perform processing identified with the local user. The local user is connected by a local area network with a server computer that stores programs and data shared by many users. The local user obtains data and programs from the server and returns data to it. In other words, the processing power of each workstation is employed in using data and software that are maintained on a server computer that supports sharing. In its simplest form, a client server system may have only one network and one server; in a more complex configuration, there could be many interconnected networks, each with a server computer and workstations.

Shared databases are typically located at the central server. Each personal computer workstation may also store locally used data, such as an extract from the centralized database.

A client server system has several advantages in comparison to the centralized shared processor approach. Adding workstations to the network increases overall power, since each workstation performs some software functions. For example, user interface software can be run on the local workstation; this reduces the need for processing by the server computer. As a result, sophisticated user interface software requiring the extensive processing power of the local workstation (such as graphical user interface software like MicroSoft Windows) can be used to make applications more user-friendly (e.g., providing local edits, pop-up windows, and online documentation).

A second advantage is that communications traffic and often costs are reduced, since the network primarily transmits only the needed data records between workstations and the server computer. A third advantage is that failure at the server computer does not prevent users from performing work locally on their personal computer (such as a local decision support application with extracted data). In a client server system with multiple servers and interconnected networks, the user may still be able to access data and programs through other servers.

A distributed client server system does not eliminate the need for coordination, a data model to support data sharing, and the management of databases.

INTEGRATION ACROSS MULTIPLE BUSINESS UNITS

The movement toward decentralizing or "demassifying" operations into autonomous organizational units with profit/loss responsibilities leads to coordination requirements among these business units. This organizational structure directly affects the information system architecture. Some business functions may need to be coordinated or managed centrally, even though autonomous units have profit/loss responsibilities. Examples of these business functions requiring central coordination are described in this section. Coordinating of these functions also has implications for the information system architecture.

Consolidation of Financial Results

The general ledger information from each business unit must be consolidated into one set of corporate financial statements. When individual business units retain their own general ledgers, the financial information can be consolidated at an aggregate level on a periodic basis (such as monthly). This facilitates local profit/loss responsibility, since local management has immediate access to and control of detailed financial data. It also minimizes communication requirements to a corporate site. This approach involves the expense of maintaining accounting staff and systems at each business unit. Alternatively, the detailed financial transactions can be maintained and posted by a centralized accounting staff at the corporate site. This reduces the need for local accounting staff but increases communication requirements.

> *Example.* When a major consumer products manufacturer reorganized their manufacturing operations, they identified autonomous business units focusing on a particular facet of production. For example, one plastic molding plant supplies parts for several assembly facilities. Each business unit operates on a stand-alone basis, accepting sales orders from upstream customers and issuing purchase orders to downstream suppliers. In some instances, the individual business units operate under one roof, separated only by psychological boundaries. Each unit has its own manufacturing information system running on a client server system.
>
> A corporate accounting system processes the general ledger, payables, receivables, payroll, and fixed assets for all business units. In particular, the costed manufacturing transactions are passed to the corporate system for generating financial statements, with a complete audit trail to source transactions. The result has been a dramatic increase in local ownership of operations and systems and effective reporting of financial results.

Standardized Bills of Material

In organizations with strict standards for product formulations (such as paint, beverage, and perfume manufacturers), the item master and bills of material must be maintained by corporate engineering staff which generally implies a centralized system. Some duplicate information must also be maintained at each business unit (for applicable products). Other information will be unique to each business unit, such as the item planning parameters (lead times, lot sizing) and cost data and the specifications for bills and routings (e.g., phase-in of engineering changes and use of different equipment/processes). Ideally, the common information will be maintained once by the corporate engineering staff, and staff at the local business unit will maintain the unique attributes.

> *Example.* A producer of paint for a national chain of hardware stores has several plants that produce identical finished goods. Standard formulations are maintained by a corporate engineering staff to ensure a consistent high-quality product. Approved formulations are downloaded to each plant for subsequent use in production based on customer demand.

Product Costs

Some organizations insist upon corporate control and measurement of product costs in all business units. This generally requires a centralized system for maintaining information about items/bills and their associated costs, which may duplicate efforts to maintain item/bill data at individual plants. In one beverage manufacturer, this requirement was based upon the location of cost accounting personnel, since the remote plants did not have cost accounting expertise.

Centralized Master Scheduling

The scheduling of common products on common machines located in differing organizational units may require centralized master scheduling to optimize production based on customer service, transportation costs, raw material costs, machine utilization, or other criteria.

> *Example.* Kimberly-Clark, manufacturer of disposable diapers, has more than forty machines located in several plants to produce various diapers. The master schedule represents an optimization to minimize transportation costs to market and maximize utilization of machine capacity (they were running three shifts on a seven day week). The corporate master scheduler requires visibility of all customer demands, current finished goods inventories and machine capabilities at each plant in order to calculate the optimum daily schedules for each machine. This master schedule is downloaded to each plant on a periodic basis.

Centralized Purchasing

A corporate purchasing function is often used for sourcing critical raw materials, negotiating vendor agreements based on volume purchases, and even managing deliveries to specific organizational units. With a decentralized approach to information systems, purchasing requirements for each organizational unit can be periodically summarized for the purposes of sourcing/negotiations by corporate staff, with the subsequent vendor agreements/quotations accessed by local purchasing staff when releasing purchase orders.

> *Example.* A beer manufacturer produces items at several breweries to minimize transportation costs of getting product to market. The purchases of certain

packaging items (such as glass containers) and critical raw materials (such as hops) are coordinated by a central purchasing staff. In the case of glass containers, the corporate buyer negotiates volume discounts based on requirements for all business units and also manages deliveries to specific breweries. This requires visibility of bottle inventories and packaging schedules at each brewery, as well as the bottle inventory and schedule at the glass manufacturer. Deliveries of other raw materials, such as cardboard packaging and most ingredients, are managed by the local buyer.

Centralized Payables and Cash Management

Cash requirements for multiple business units may be planned and coordinated by a corporate staff, which frequently means accounts payable functions are performed centrally. This approach requires duplicate maintenance of the vendor information (for purchasing and payables) and communication of purchase receipt data to the central site. The matching of vendor invoices to purchase orders and receipts could also be performed at the local business unit (since they are closest to the information should questions arise) by accessing the centralized information system, or the accounts payable functions could be segmented for local matching and centralized cash planning and check writing.

> *Example*. Remote plants producing canned pet food for a New Zealand pet food manufacturer operate autonomously on stand-alone systems, with a corporate accounting staff performing accounts payable, receivables and general ledger. Information about receipts, shipments and costed manufacturing transactions are communicated to the Auckland headquarters via Wide Area Network (WAN) communication links for processing by a centralized system, and accounting reports are distributed to the plants by the same WAN.

Centralized Invoicing and/or Receivables

In some multi-plant operations, the local plants can operate completely autonomously in terms of entering/shipping sales orders for their own products. Further processing of the sales order, in terms of invoicing and then accounts receivable, can optionally be performed at the local plant or at the corporate headquarters. With decentralized order entry systems and centralized invoicing or receivables system, this requires communication of information about the sales order, customer, and shipment (or invoice) to a centralized system. With a centralized order entry system, the choice of how to perform invoicing and receivables is generally limited to a centralized approach.

Centralized Order Entry and Distribution Requirements Planning (DRP)

When sales order entry can promise and ship products from any plant/warehouse in a multi-site operation, the order entry system requires access to finished goods inventory and scheduled receipts in all sites to make valid delivery promises and to communicate shipping information to the appropriate site. The general ledger and invoicing functions must also be updated by the shipping transaction.

The complexity increases when the company requires interplant transfers of materials or when plants act as suppliers or customers for other sites. The coordination between the chain of plants/warehouses in the distribution network requires close coordination to effectively serve customer requirements. The coordinating systems are referred to as Distribution Requirements Planning (DRP).

DRP traditionally requires a centralized information system, with a centralized database maintained by various remote plants and order entry personnel. New advances in distributed database management and communications have made it possible for local information systems to access and update information at systems in other plants.

> *Example*. A consumer products manufacturer has a multi-tiered distribution network with two manufacturing plants (one supplying the other with some components) supplying regional distribution centers which in turn supply branch warehouses in different countries (Figure 3-4). Rather than using a centralized DRP system for calculating requirements across the entire distribution network, this firm uses distributed information systems located at each site. The DRP system at each branch warehouse site calculates net requirements and communicates demands to the regional distribution centers. With multiple levels in the supply chain, DRP calculations must be performed at each level and site to correctly communicate requirements to the two manufacturing plants.
>
> The distributed system uses a centralized database for all sales orders. To enter a sales order, the sales person at any location logs onto a centralized system containing the database of sales orders. The system automatically displays inventory availability at all sites, and the salesperson selects the best site to ship from. All MRP/DRP calculations are still done at the remote site. When the items are shipped from the remote site, the shipment is recorded back in the central sales order database. All invoicing and receivables functions are done centrally. General ledger transactions affect both the central and remote databases, so the system automatically posts the intercompany and cost variance accounts.

LESSONS FOR MANAGERS

The central concept of the chapter is a business architecture derived from business strategy and a matching information system architecture. The concept of architecture applied to these two systems is based on the fact that these systems have a structure that can be related to the functions to be performed,

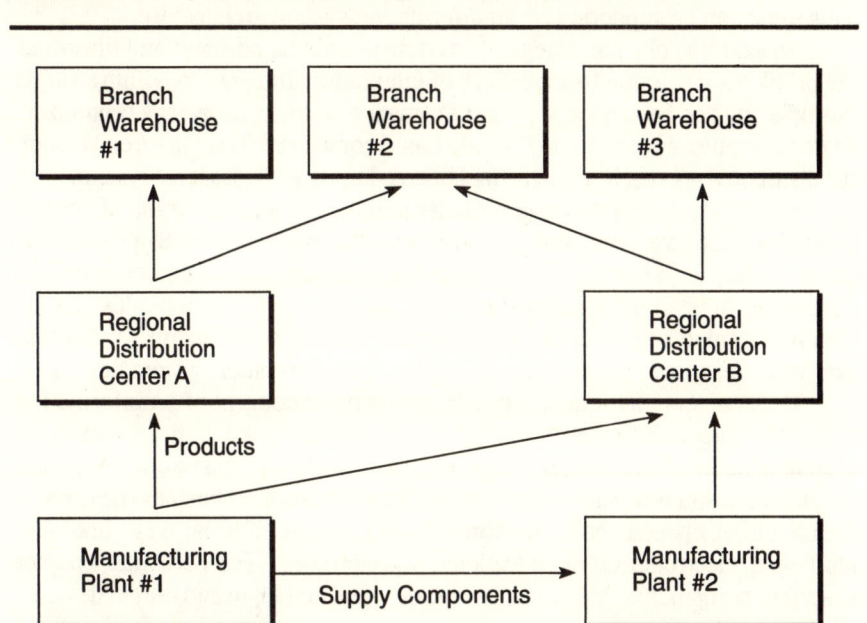

FIGURE 3-4
Distribution Requirements Planning for a Multi-Tiered Distributor

```
┌──────────┐      ┌──────────┐      ┌──────────┐
│ Branch   │      │ Branch   │      │ Branch   │
│ Warehouse│      │ Warehouse│      │ Warehouse│
│ #1       │      │ #2       │      │ #3       │
└──────────┘      └──────────┘      └──────────┘
     ▲            ▲       ▲               ▲
     │           /         \              │
     │          /           \             │
┌──────────┐                      ┌──────────┐
│ Regional │                      │ Regional │
│Distribution│                    │Distribution│
│ Center A │                      │ Center B │
└──────────┘                      └──────────┘
     ▲          Products                ▲
     │                                  │
┌──────────┐                      ┌──────────┐
│Manufacturing│                   │Manufacturing│
│ Plant #1 │──── Supply Components ──▶│ Plant #2 │
└──────────┘                      └──────────┘
```

communications and coordination requirements, objects of interest that the system deals with, and management and control processes.

Each of these factors helps define a model of the business. Decisions related to the four factors also affect the information system architecture. The activities of business functions are reflected in transaction processing systems. Transaction processing systems provide the basic framework for applications in support of management, such as management reporting, executive support systems, and decision support systems. Coordination and communications requirements are the basis for communication networks and applications. Objects of interest to the organization are directly related to the data model defining entities and attributes and to databases. Management and control considerations are reflected in decisions about the location of hardware, software, and databases plus the responsibility, control, and allocation of work.

The activities of business functions and information processing requirements must be analyzed in an organizational context, as illustrated by the discussion of a manufacturing business and MRP information systems. The alternatives for business and information system architecture must consider extent of integration and location of control. The business architecture trend appears to be away from complete centralization and toward autonomous business units that are coordinated by a few key, centrally managed activities. This trend can be supported by an information system architecture.

An example of a non-integrated system in a single business unit illustrates the problems stemming from the lack of integration. Integration within a single business unit can be supported by an information architecture using a centralized, shared computer system or distributed, shared computers. There is a trend toward the distributed approach which is implemented using a client server system.

Integration across multiple business units is generally desirable if coordination can achieve improved performance. The issue is how to provide the business unit with reasonable autonomy and yet have adequate coordination. Coordination is an information-intensive activity, so integration adds significant requirements to an information system. Several mechanisms for integration were described, each with implications for information system design.

The chapters that follow move from the basic concept of an information system architecture to the types of applications that make up the information system (Chapter 4). Having defined the way the information system models the organization and how various types of applications support business processes, the next three chapters cover the three major types of information technology: hardware, electronic communications, and software. The hardware chapter describes computer architecture, storage devices, and input and output devices. The communications technology chapter covers communications facilities and technology, networks, and applications affecting business systems. The software chapter describes the technology platform for application software and three approaches to application development: package, application generator, and programming language. The programming language approach to application development includes an overview of program structure and programming languages.

An understanding of these technologies is important in order to understand not only the power and opportunities available with information systems but also their limitations. The chapters provide the background for subsequent sections on building and implementing systems and managing information systems.

SELECTED REFERENCES FOR ADDITIONAL READING

McFarlan, F. W., and McKenney, J. E. A series of three articles in the *Harvard Business Review*: "The Information Archipelago Maps and Bridges," September-October 1982; "The Information Archipelago—Plotting a Course," January-February 1983 (with P. Pyburn); and "The Information Archipelago—Governing the New World," July-August, 1983.

Zachman, J. A., "A Framework for Information Systems Architecture," *IBM Systems Journal*, 26:3, 1987, pp. 276-292.

CHAPTER 4

TYPES OF APPLICATIONS IN AN INFORMATION SYSTEM

The information systems in an organization use the same information technology; however, they are not all of the same type, for the same organizational purposes, or for the same type of personnel. This chapter describes the types of information system applications that may be found within an organization.

As noted in Chapter 1, an application of information technology is often called an "information system." This is appropriate, since it is a system and a subsystem of the overall information system. This book will follow common terminology and refer to it as an application and as an information system (or application system). This means, for example, that an application of information technology to support decision making may be termed a decision support system (DSS) or a decision support application. Both are technically correct and both conform to common usage.

The types of applications can be broadly categorized into transaction processing applications, applications in support of management and control, and support for knowledge work by groups and by individuals. These are broad categories based on the type of problems addressed, organizational purposes, and personnel who are the primary users. They are useful in defining the primary orientation of applications of information technology. A knowledge-based system (or expert system) can be used as an application within one of the above types. However, because of the difference in design approach, knowledge-based systems will be described separately.

OVERVIEW OF TYPES OF APPLICATIONS IN AN INFORMATION SYSTEM

In the preceding chapter, the architecture of an information system was described in terms of the match with the business architecture. Relevant issues were the extent of integration, location of facilities, and the control of hardware, software, and databases. In this chapter, the information system is defined in terms of key characteristics. Two views of the information system are based on a classification of applications. The first view of applications is from the perspective of operations and management activities. Another view of applications is as a set of subsystems oriented to individual business functions (such as marketing or finance) and coordination of cross-functional activities.

Concepts of Data and Information

Is it data processing or information processing? The two terms "data" and "information" are not used precisely and are often used interchangeably. However, the two terms are different.[1]

Information is generally defined as data that is meaningful or useful, usually in the sense of letting the recipient know something that was not known or understood. Data items are the raw material for producing information. Another way to understand a distinction in usage is to regard attributes of transactions as data. In fact, attributes of an object of interest (attributes of a person, thing, transaction, etc.) tend to be called data. Therefore, the model that defines entities (related to objects of interest for the organization) and their attributes is termed a data model.

The outputs found in reports, results of inquiries, and results from management support applications are termed information because they represent processed data items that track performance, answer a question, relate to some issue, or provide insight into a problem. Information is sometimes defined in terms of surprise value, but in reporting systems, the reports may confirm rather than surprise. The reports are still considered as information.

The Definition of an Information System Based on Essential Characteristics

The comprehensive computer-based information system for an organization has been termed a *management information system* (MIS) to differentiate it from a simple data processing system. The MIS or information system for an organization is defined as

> an integrated, information technology-based, user-machine system for providing information to support operations, management, analysis, and decision-making functions in an organization. The system utilizes computer and communications hardware and software; manual procedures; models for analysis, planning, control, and decision making; and databases.

---

[1] In the field of information processing, it is common to use data with a singular verb as in "the data is processed." In other words, by common usage within the field, "data" is treated grammatically as if it were "a set of data items."

Some important elements of the definition are:

Information technology-based. One can conceptualize an information system without information technology, but it cannot be implemented fully as a manual system.

User-machine. The most effective system is designed to use the capabilities of both humans and computers. The division of labor uses computers and other information technology to enhance and expand the capabilities of human operators and users of the system. This aspect is often referred to as man-machine or human-machine systems.

Integrated system. Organizations share information internally and externally. This was explained in Chapter 3. Information captured or developed in one part of the organization is needed by other parts of the same organization. A well-designed information system reflects information interrelationships and supports sharing and joint use.

Database. The concept of databases follows from the concept of sharing and integration. The implementation of databases (instead of separate files belonging to applications) supports the shared use of data. It fits with the concept of data as an organizational resource to be managed like other organizational resources. An organization will generally employ several databases that fit together in an overall data architecture.

To support ... functions in an organization. The objective of an MIS is to support an organization. The functions being supported include operations, management, analysis, and decision making. The support may be structured in the form of models that support specific methods or approaches to these functions. The support may consist of access to data and software capabilities, where users develop their own models and analyses. The personnel being supported range from clerical personnel performing basic transactions to executives performing strategic planning. The information system support can include systems for routine data processing and reporting, systems for automation of operations, and systems to achieve competitive advantage and support organizational strategy.

Information Systems Based on Type of Application

The MIS or information system concept is comprehensive and envisions support to all levels of operations and management in an organization. As illustrated in Figure 4-1, the information system is congruent with the concept of a pyramid of organizational information activity and decision making.

- At the bottom are routine transaction processing applications and processing of inquiries seeking data from the databases. In terms of volume of activity, transaction processing and inquiries take up much of the time and capacity of the information processing facilities.
- The next level of activity consists of applications in support of operational planning, control, and decision making. Typical activities are scheduling production, controlling purchases, and tracking product costs.
- The management information at the next level is focused on management control through tactical planning and decision making. Budgets, management reports, and variance analyses are typical at this level.
- The highest level in the management information support pyramid is strategic planning and related decision making.

The pyramid is useful for explaining the relationship to information systems, decision support systems (DSS) and executive information systems (EIS). A DSS consists of computer software and related applications that support decision makers in decision processes, especially unstructured decision making. DSS have tended to focus on individual decision makers; another set of systems support group decision making (GDSS) and computer-supported cooperative work.

Executive information systems (EIS) are oriented to the needs of high-level executives. The executives performing strategic planning must deal with greater amounts of external information and data not normally available in the organization's internal information systems. Therefore, support for strategic planning and high-level executive decision making requires additional data and sets of analytical routines that are more or less unique to this level of management.

Information Systems as Subsystems for Organizational Functions

Although it is conceptually simple to think of the information system as being one large encompassing system, such a massive system would be cumbersome and difficult to build, implement, and maintain. Instead, there are natural groupings or subdivisions around which subsystems are built. The different business functions such as marketing, production, logistics, human resources, finance, and accounting have unique needs requiring information processing applications designed specifically for the functions and data bases used primarily for them. The concept of applications that support transactions, operations, control, and strategy are applicable for each function. Therefore, a subsystem for the marketing function will have applications for lead tracking and sales order transactions, sales history analysis and forecasting marketing management control, and strategic marketing planning. The subsystems for each function are not completely isolated. These system are designed to transfer data,

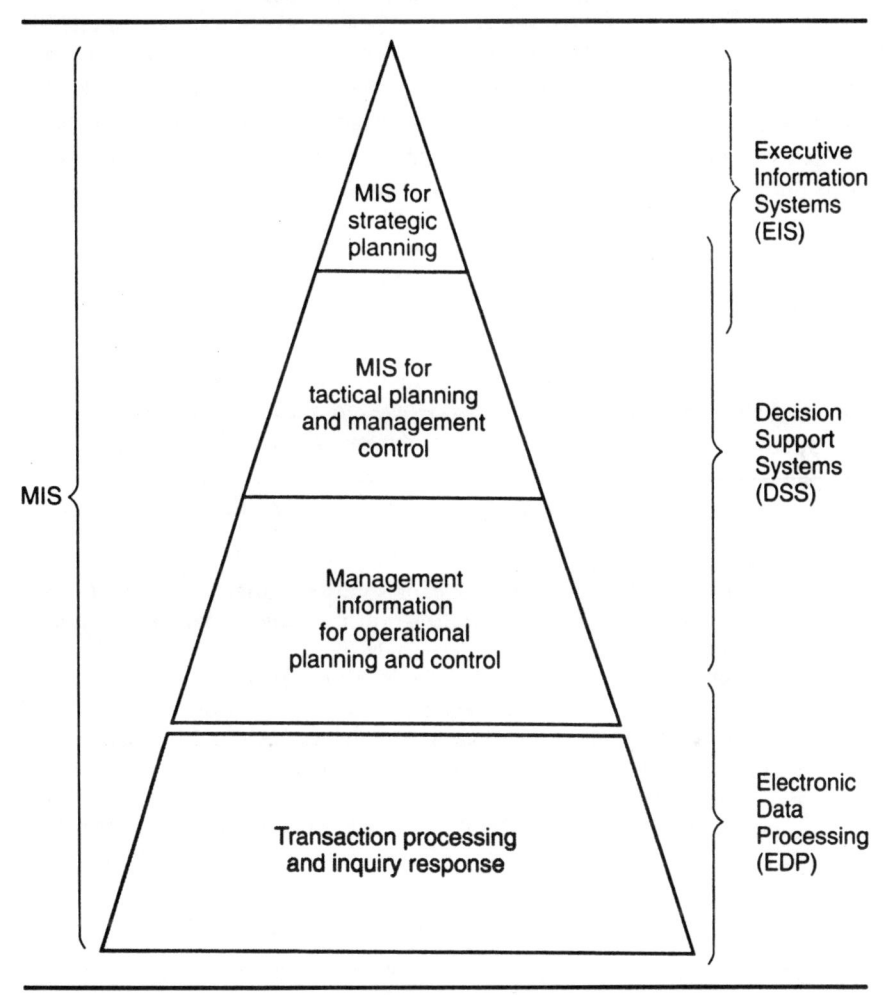

Types of Applications in an Information System   69

FIGURE 4-1
The Structure of a Management Information System

```
                    MIS for
                    strategic         }  Executive
                    planning             Information
                                         Systems
                                         (EIS)

                  MIS for
                  tactical planning
                  and management      }  Decision
                  control                Support
MIS                                      Systems
                                         (DSS)
                Management
                information
                for operational
                planning and control

                                      }  Electronic
              Transaction processing     Data
              and inquiry response       Processing
                                         (EDP)
```

share data, and operate as part of the larger information system within the enterprise.

TRANSACTION PROCESSING APPLICATIONS

Transactions are the basic activity of organizations. Examples include taking orders, billing, recording payments, ordering from suppliers, making payments, recording additions and subtractions from inventory, hiring employees, paying employees, and remitting taxes withheld. These transactions are necessary in order to record what happened and the economic effects.

In an accounting-oriented information system, every transaction directly affecting the income, expenses, liabilities, and equities of an organization will be recorded. The financial effects will be recorded, but this record will not necessarily include all data of interest. For example, it is necessary to record the sale of an item, but if the sale is for cash, it may not be necessary to record who purchased it. However, a business may have a number of reasons for wanting to know about cash customers. The business may wish to track the use of the product, offer upgrades or options after initial purchase, and use the initial purchase as a basis for advertising. In essence, it is often not sufficient to record the minimum data for processing a transaction; the transaction should yield more data if it will be useful to the business.

Some business transactions are not automatically recorded because they do not have direct financial effects. However, they may be important to management and control. For example, a customer complaint may be handled without recording it if no payment is made or received or product returned. For management purposes, it is very important to record the transactions and analyze and summarize them.

> *Example.* The maintenance facilities of Northwest Airlines represent "focused factories," where each hanger specializes in maintaining a certain type of airplane (such as Boeing 747s). Forecast demands for airplane maintenance can be predicted from information collected as part of the internal transaction processing systems that identify airplane usage (such as the number of flying hours and takeoffs/landings). Planned maintenance activities are also driven by external events, such as government mandated and customer requested upgrades, which must be translated into the impact on airplane maintenance (needed parts, personnel and schedule priorities). Forecasting the demand for maintenance activities and resources depends on constant monitoring of these external events in addition to the internal plane usage statistics.

There may be transactions that should be recorded which are not business transactions in the usual sense. These may be transactions that are reported in the community press or in general or specialized economic reports. For example, an organization may capture and store certain statistics about transactions of interest to the business even though they are not transactions with the business. A furniture manufacturer may wish to record key economic indicators describing housing starts, sales of houses, new family formations, and distribution of income in order to analyze and forecast future sales of furniture.

How can an organization decide what data should be recorded (or sought) when an internal or external transaction occurs? The key concept (described in Chapter 3) is that an organization has objects of interest. Generally, these objects will be defined in a data model for the organization and data will be collected and stored. The definition of these objects of interest (termed entities in data modeling) is one of the important tasks of information system planning.

> *Example.* A market research firm collects data about grocery store purchases. Using a microcomputer linked to each store's network of registers, the firm can selectively collect data about consumer purchases by utilizing the store's normal transaction processing system. On a periodic basis, the local microcomputer uploads a packet of data to the research firm's corporate mainframe system. The data packet represents consumer purchases over a given time period such as a week.
>
> Since a given product, such as a can of soda pop, can be sold in different ways (e.g., six versus twelve pack, standard packaging versus various promotional labels), data can be collected on more than a million variations of stockkeeping units. Coding the product correctly across all stores and over extended time periods is critical for subsequent data analysis.
>
> The firm's internal planning and control system for the grocery operations is very similar to that of a custom product manufacturing company, since it produces customized "finished reports" from the "raw material" of data. The transaction processing system tracks the packets of data collected from each store. Data packets go through quality control to ensure proper coding and computer processing to update master files of consumer purchase activity. The firm also collects other data about the store such as in-store displays and promotions and advertisements in local newspapers to correlate consumer purchases with marketing efforts. Before producing their finished reports, the firm must verify availability of the data. Customized reports, in printed or computer-readable format, are then prepared on a periodic basis according to customer-specified requirements.

MANAGEMENT REPORTING APPLICATIONS

Management reporting applications provide both traditional and non-traditional reports. The applications that produce traditional reports may be well defined by the functional discipline. For the accounting function, there are well specified standards for financial statements, cost and variance reports, and budget reports. This has the advantage that the figures shown in the managerial reports are computed in the same way as the figures in the reports to shareholders and creditors. The traditional accounting reports must follow a general reporting discipline that is useful for external comparability and for avoiding unknown bias. Recipients of the reports may deal with the bias from accounting standards, but they do not have to deal with unknown recording and valuation rules. The disadvantages are that the general accounting rules may obscure important trends and important relationships. The standard methods of recording and valuing transactions may not be appropriate for management decision making.

For manufacturing management, there are standards for many but not all reports. For example, the reports concerning supply/demand analysis, master schedule, cycle counting, and workcenter input/output have been delineated reasonably well. Many other reports have not been standardized, so there are wide variations among information systems.

Non-traditional (sometimes termed soft) reports contain data not normally collected by the financial or manufacturing transactions. They may include results of surveys and comments by dissatisfied customers. Applications to collect and report this data are not part of the traditional set of applications.

Regular management reports are basically of three types:

- *Report of results without comparisons.* The manager is responsible for providing a standard or benchmark for interpreting the results. Whether action is expected by the recipient of the reports can depend on the recipients and the benchmark used by them.
- *Report of results with comparisons or variances.* These are trend reports showing changes from prior periods and variance reports showing variations from standards or budgets. If there are variances of consequence, actions are implied.
- *Awareness reports.* The manager obtains information that is believed to be useful but no immediate actions are implied by the reports.

Since Chapter 3 explained transaction processing and management reports using manufacturing operations for illustrative purposes, the remainder of this chapter will examine other types of applications in support of executive management, decision making, group work, and knowledge work. The effect on applications of expert system methods will also be discussed.

EXECUTIVE INFORMATION SYSTEMS (EIS)

The two terms, EIS for executive information system and ESS for executive support system, refer to the same concept; the EIS term tends to be used most frequently. An EIS system is designed to provide a combination of regular executive-level reports plus on-demand executive-level access to large amounts of data. The on-demand access includes browsing through external and internal data at a high level of summarization with an option to examine breakdowns and detailed data. It also includes models of the organization that allow "what if" questions to be asked. The results are presented in a variety of formats ranging from lists and tables to graphs and charts (Figure 4-2).

FIGURE 4-2
Executive Information System

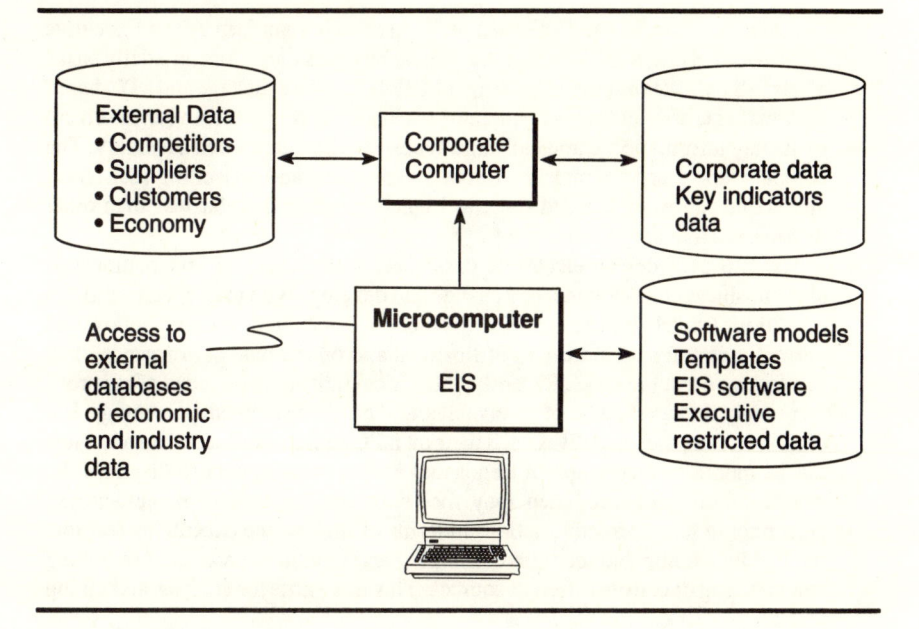

```
┌─────────────────┐                                  ┌─────────────────┐
│ External Data   │      ┌──────────┐                │ Corporate data  │
│ • Competitors   │◄────►│ Corporate│◄──────────────►│ Key indicators  │
│ • Suppliers     │      │ Computer │                │ data            │
│ • Customers     │      └──────────┘                │                 │
│ • Economy       │            ▲                     └─────────────────┘
└─────────────────┘            │
                               │
  Access to           ┌──────────────┐               ┌─────────────────┐
  external    ─────►  │ Microcomputer│               │ Software models │
  databases           │              │◄─────────────►│ Templates       │
  of economic         │    EIS       │               │ EIS software    │
  and industry        └──────────────┘               │ Executive       │
  data                       │                       │ restricted data │
                             ▼                       └─────────────────┘
                        [monitor]
```

The Need for an EIS

To understand the demand for an executive information system, it is useful to first think about how the information requirements of top executives may differ from others in the organization. It is not in the uniqueness of the information itself, because it is likely that any information needed by top executives may be needed by someone else in the organization. The problem is that no executive has the time and ability to read and process all of the information provided to the entire organization. The essence of an executive information system is to allow an executive to take a high level view of key variables, browse through information in order to develop an understanding of trends and issues, and to access detailed data when necessary. In other words, executives at the top level need to be able to monitor key variables, browse through organizational or external data when motivated by some external or internal event, and look at detailed data when focusing on a specific issue.

Since the information needed by high level executives is likely to be available to and used by others in the organization, why don't executives just get copies of all the reports and analyses used by others? This is not possible in a large organization. Also, it may turn out that information or critical analyses are not being used within the organization and would not be available if requested by executive management.

Example. The CEO and CFO at a division of a German firm use an Executive Information System (EIS) to monitor critical business indicators on a daily basis. Their EIS uses data extracted from their MRP II software package and a PC-based data management and report generator package (with graphical user interface) to display information graphically and access detailed data when necessary. The company spent approximately $10,000 on software and consulting assistance, and about one week elapsed time, to implement their EIS, far less than other alternatives that they investigated.

The EIS provides an electronic dashboard with "dials" of information that show business conditions as they change and develop. With user-specified alarm conditions (which indicate status with colors of critical red, warning yellow and normal green) for 96 indicators of financial and operational performance, they can focus on trouble spots. Recently, the critical indicators included gross profit by product line, cash, days of receivables, and on-time shipment percentage. For each indicator, the executives used their own PCs with downloaded data to view the 12 month history graph of trends and access detailed data to diagnose the source of the problem. Then they met with accounting and manufacturing personnel to take corrective action. In terms of impact, the executives feel that the EIS has minimized the time-consuming and repetitive process of searching and updating data from different sources. This frees time for analysis and taking action.

Now that they have a baseline EIS operational, the company executives want additional indicators (including some from external sources such as government and economic figures). The changing information requirements for EIS reflect an evolving sophistication among the executives about how they run the business. Rather than focus on easily obtained data such as financial measures and efficiency reports, the EIS implementation has prompted the management team to rethink what they should measure.

The Costs and Benefits of an EIS

Why would an organization fail to collect and evaluate critical information? It happens! The information may be difficult or costly to obtain. The analyses may be difficult to perform. No one may have been assigned to do the data collection and analysis. No organizational function may have perceived the importance of the data. For example, customer perceptions of product deficiencies may not be systematically collected and analyzed in such a way that the organization understands the nature of customer reactions and trends in customer perceptions. Competitor strategy with regard to pricing and service may be known to individual sales personnel but not collected and processed so that the strategic implications may be understood by executives.

The definition of requirements for an executive information system may overcome a tendency of executives to focus on available data rather than important data. In other words, the natural tendency of executives is to use whatever is available. If they receive reports that focus on internal efficiency variables, they will focus on these variables. The design of an EIS (by the executives who will use it) provides an opportunity to get the right combination of external and internal data and the right mix of effectiveness and efficiency variables. Ongoing comparisons with competitors and tracking of key government economic policies and economic indicators are critical components in an EIS. Without the EIS, these may have been done less systematically or less frequently.

The cost of an EIS consists of the costs of collection and processing of data and the facilities for presenting the information to executives as regular reports and on demand. The "on demand" portion of the system can be assisted by EIS software systems that manage presentation of data in executive formats and support browsing and access to detailed data.

The cost of data collection may not be excessive if the information should be or is already used by others in the organization. However, the behavior of an organization, in response to executive use, may be to spend more time and effort on collecting and analyzing the data. This may be worthwhile if prior efforts were inadequate; it may be an extra cost if the executive use does not justify extensive ongoing data collection and analysis. For example, competitor sales compensation policies may be of occasional interest and justify special ad hoc analyses; it may not be cost effective to track this data continuously.

An EIS can be established in a variety of ways and with different levels of sophistication and support. At the simplest level, the EIS may be some reports and analyses plus a comprehensive directory of information availability so that requests can be made for more detail. At the most sophisticated level, executives may use (or have an assistant use) a commercial software package or a system developed in house to browse through a range of databases. Some of the data may be specifically collected and stored for executive use; other data may be available in organizational files with the EIS making it accessible to the executives.

DECISION SUPPORT SYSTEMS

Decision support systems (DSS) are generally targeted at a class of problems described as complex and unstructured. Being unstructured means there are no well-defined algorithms or well-structured methods for solving the problems. The systems are not intended to replace human decision makers; rather, the intent is to support human judgment.

Example. A manufacturer producing environmental control systems uses a DSS to simulate the impact of changing MRP planning parameters. Leadtimes, lot sizes and lot size minimums/multiples are used by MRP calculations to plan material replenishment. Short leadtimes and small lot sizes have positive impacts on inventory turnover and negative impacts in terms of potential stockouts and increased transaction volume. For example, daily delivery of purchased materials may require many thousands of transactions to release and receive purchase orders. Disruptions in supply can create stockouts that prevent the smooth flow of production.

The material planner uses the DSS to simulate changes to planning parameters of individual items and groups of similar items. The impact on inventory turns is weighed against the impact on stockout exposures, setups (such as machine setups for each manufacturing order), and the number of transactions (to release and receive orders). When the material planner has finished the simulation, the DSS automatically updates the item master files with new values for the planning parameters. The DSS took several iterations to develop, since the task was initially unstructured. Feedback on the prototype developed after each iteration increased the DSS functionality and also resulted in more structured decision making.

Conceptually, a decision support system will contain programs or modules to perform three functions:

- *Manage data required for the analysis and decision making.* This involves management of a database and a data dictionary that defines the data used and a method for retrieving data requested during DSS use.
- *Manage models used in analysis and decision making.* A number of models are useful in analysis; others are useful in decision making. The model management facilities include storage, retrieval, and model tailoring to fit a specific problem.
- *Manage the dialogue and graphical user interface between the user and the system.* This module controls the interaction between the user and the data and model management modules. It specifies inputs to be provided and interprets inputs so the system can use them.

The requirements for a decision support system are usually developed iteratively. This is required because of the unstructured nature of the decision making process. Trial and error use of prototypes provides insight on how to modify the DSS for subsequent use.

A DSS can be built in a variety of ways. It may be built for use on a mainframe or on a microcomputer. When programming a DSS, two approaches are used. The first is a general purpose programming language; the second is the use of software packages. Software packages reduce the time and effort to program dialogue management, data management, and model management.

Example. A market research firm collects data about grocery store operations via on-site visits by field operations personnel. Periodic store visits involve identification of in-store displays/promotions, auditing product movement data (based on receipts, physical inventory and sales) and other activities. With several thousand store locations, tasks requiring specific skills, and several hundred field operations personnel (with differing skill levels and home locations), the firm developed a pilot DSS that managers could use to schedule store visits and specific tasks by field personnel.

The DSS combined the features of a transportation management system used by trucking companies (to minimize travel by each person to stores in his or her area) with a human resources management system (to optimize the match between the skill requirements of projects and skill sets of employees and to generate payroll based on labor reporting). The pilot DSS proved very successful in terms of acceptance by managers and field workers and in terms of effectively scheduling resources.

The fate of this DSS illustrates the vital relationship between a few executive supporters and the use of a DSS. The pilot program was not implemented in other geographic areas and ultimately canceled altogether. According to one participant, frequent changes in executive management of the organization led to changes in system development priorities. The DSS pilot was cancelled by the new executives who had not participated in the development and were not committed to this type of system.

COLLABORATIVE WORK SYSTEMS

Much of the work of organizations is collaborative and involves teams or groups. Activities often involve coordination or cooperative work among two or more individuals. This coordination or collaboration of groups or teams may involve activities such as idea generation, problem identification, ranking or rating or solutions, decision making, negotiation, conflict resolution, consensus building, report writing, and coordination of activities assigned to individuals. The coordination among individuals may involve such activities as inquiries, transfer of information, editing and review of reports, and evaluation of ideas and reports. In an organization spanning many time zones and many countries, collaborative work systems provide a new dimension for support of coordination across time barriers.

Since collaboration involves significant amounts of information exchange and communication, systems using information and communication technologies have been developed to aid and support collaborative work. They are sometimes referred to as *groupware*. Such systems are in use, but in many organizations they are in an early stage of use and diffusion. There is evidence of improvement in both effectiveness and efficiency by using groupware, but as with most technology innovations, achieving major impact requires rethinking the way work is performed, changing organizational norms, and redesigning work systems. If the introduction of collaborative work technology is accompanied by such organization changes, the technology may be a very significant use of computers and communications technologies. This suggests there is much innovation yet to be made with collaborative support technologies.

Proponents of groupware for collaborative work assert that it makes teams and groups more productive. Meetings using group technology capture more information, generate more ideas, elicit broader participation, and are more goal directed. Cycle time for activities involving coordination with individuals or groups, locally or remotely, is significantly reduced by using coordination technology. Many of the productivity benefits arise from the fact that electronic meeting systems support parallel processing in which many members at the meeting may be entering ideas or comments at the same time. The technology supports the formation of teams using the best individuals located in different places. The teams are formed for specific tasks and perform their work using group support technology. Because the teams are formed for a specific task and disbanded after the task is completed, they have been termed *adhocracies*. Some claim that groupware will lead to a leveling of authority because information will flow freely across the organization rather than through a hierarchy.

In terms of collaborative work, there are three variations with respect to meeting location and two variations for meeting time. The group size may also make a difference; group size can be categorized into large versus small (10 or fewer people). The meeting location may be with a group assembled at one meeting place, a group assembled at multiple sites, or a group located at individual locations (such as each individual in his or her office). The meeting time may be with all participants at the same time or it may be asynchronous with part of the group meeting at different times. This suggests five types of meetings to be supported:

- All participants in the same room at the same time.
- Participants divided among two or more rooms at different locations but at the same time.
- Participants meet in the same room but at different times.
- Participants are at individual offices but communicate at the same time.
- Participants are at individual offices but participate at different times.

A variety of systems can support the different types of collaborative meetings and communications. The two most important are electronic meeting systems (group decision support systems) and collaborative work electronic mail systems.

Electronic Meeting Systems

Electronic meeting systems are frequently termed *group decision support systems* (GDSS). They can support meetings in special meeting rooms or from offices. The meeting room support is for meetings at one location, meetings simultaneously at more than one location, or meetings at more than one location at different times.

In a typical electronic meeting room, a U-shaped room has tables with PCs for each participant (or pair of participants). A small room may support a meeting with up to 10 or 12 participants; a large room using a U-shaped gallery arrangement may have as many as 30 PCs. Each PC has a display for the person using it. There is a large public screen to display information to the group. The PCs are connected by a local area network and may also connect the system to a mainframe or minicomputer.

For meetings being held at the same time at different locations, each individual meeting room is connected to a computer that coordinates the exchange of information. In terms of the display of information, sharing of votes, and so forth, the different physical rooms can be viewed as one room. Special facilities may be provided to allow multiple screens to display the results from different locations. Television may be used to show the rooms to all locations.

For meetings held in electronic meeting rooms but at different times, there are additional facilities to allow the later meetings to access the results of earlier meetings, to add to existing files of ideas, and so forth.

The software on the PCs can include standard PC software such as spreadsheets. There is software specific to meetings and group decision making. These include software for agenda setting, brainstorming, rating and voting, and recording comments on ideas. The software not only makes a record of the meeting; it also allows the group to capture and use information from earlier efforts at a later point. All participants may enter data at the same time and entries may remain anonymous. The anonymity of input is said to be a significant benefit and improves participation.

> *Example.* Small groups of employees of a large oil company in three locations are each assembled in a group decision support room at their location. They are communicating about 12 proposals for a major new investment and will finally vote to rate each proposal on a scale from 1 to 10. At each site, the participants enter their comments or questions into personal computers connected first to a network in the room and through the network to a mainframe computer at a central location. On a six foot wide screen, the ideas they generate and ideas from other locations are displayed. After generating comments and ideas, the participants rank each proposal. The results of this very broad participation are summarized in an average rating plus other statistics about the ratings.

In addition to standard business meetings, GDSS rooms have been used for such innovative applications as crisis management, negotiation, interactive teaching, personnel selection, debates, eliciting of requirements for an information system, curriculum design, and deciding on a logo.

Collaborative Work Electronic Mail Systems

Electronic mail as a simple system supports communication in a mail format with messages being sent or received. For collaborative work, it is important for the participants to share access to files and databases and for the comments and ideas that are communicated to be available to all members of the group or team.

> *Example.* An auto manufacturer has installed a collaborative work electronic mail system at dealerships. It allows dealers to access manufacturer information on models and features. It also allows dealers to send the manufacturer comments about policies, plans, and features.
>
> *Example.* A software development firm had two software development groups, one in North America and one in Asia, collaborating on development of a new information system. Development activities were segmented between the two groups to minimize the need for communication and coordination. Subsystem design/programming and unit testing, for example, could proceed reasonably autonomously. At certain times, however, extensive coordination and communication were required (e.g., when requirements changed or when system testing was performed).
>
> The development groups used several methods to coordinate efforts. Meetings were arranged on middle ground (Western Europe); personnel were exchanged between groups; memos were faxed, data and memos were transmitted via electronic mail, and telephone calls were arranged to minimize the problems of a 12 hour time zone difference.

KNOWLEDGE WORK APPLICATIONS

There is a large investment in information technology to support knowledge workers (analysts, planners, managers, accountants, schedulers, etc.). The hardware investment is in personal computer workstations and communications equipment for networks, both local and wide area. The software investment is in system software and application packages.

Knowledge work applications are not identical with clerical applications because of the role perceptions of knowledge workers. They expect to bring personal knowledge to their work and to have significant freedom in structuring and managing their efforts.

Example. A software development firm specializing in planning and control systems implemented a project management system to coordinate efforts for software design, programming and testing, and development of related documentation and training materials. Each task was identified in various related projects and knowledge workers (e.g., programmers and analysts) were trained on how to plan and report their work using the project management system. In spite of management claims about improved coordination, control, and productivity that would be derived from the new system, the system failed and was removed after several months. The knowledge workers did not want to worry about detailed time reporting. Managers also resented the time-consuming efforts to collect and then reconcile the time reports. It appears that the experts in planning and control systems for others did not want a formal planning and control system for themselves.

In Chapter 2, a toolkit of generalized packages was described that virtually every knowledge worker should be prepared to employ. The chapter also explained how each function and each industry has packages that are commonly used by knowledge workers.

Knowledge work applications are of three types:

- *Software designed specifically for a knowledge work task based on approaches followed by most knowledge workers performing the work.* The knowledge worker provides input to the software and makes judgments relative to the inputs and processing choices that are required. The software applies the inputs to the problem and produces the outputs. Examples are software for tax return preparation, structural analysis (for engineers), geographic marketing analysis, project planning, and preparation of gantt charts and critical path analyses.

   Example. Tax return preparation software reduces the clerical effort to prepare tax returns. The package guides the process by requesting input data, asking for decisions that affect the computations, and offering alternatives that the user may select. When all inputs are complete, the package displays the return for review and, if accepted, prints it on a preprinted form or prints both the form and the data at the same time. Preparers who are part of the electronic submission system (for Federal tax returns) may transmit the return directly from the computer.

- *Software designed to support ways that knowledge workers perform important analytical and decision making tasks.* The spreadsheet processor is important as knowledge work software because it supports a fundamental way that knowledge workers perform analysis. Many problems are analyzed by placing data on a sheet in rows and columns and performing simple operations on them. The spreadsheet processor provides facilities to arrange the data items in rows and columns and perform operations on them. The DBMS package supports a fundamental knowledge work task of extracting data items from a database, performing operations on the data, and preparing a report of the results. The preparation of a financial model of a company is done by estimating current and projecting future relationships among measures of financial performance (such as sales and cost of sales). A financial modeling package supports a modeling approach to financial analysis by providing a modeling language for writing the model and routines to execute the model and output the results. Figure 4-3 is an example of a simple financial model and the output from it.

- *Software that can support innovation in the way tasks are performed or ways that knowledge workers perform analysis.* This requires software with programming facilities. As will be explained in Chapter 7, many software packages designed to support ways of doing analytical work processes also have program development facilities. This means that knowledge workers can innovate in the use of software.

KNOWLEDGE-BASED SYSTEMS

A knowledge-based system (often termed expert system) is presented as a different kind of application system, because it is designed for the solution of a problem requiring expertise. However, within the context of types of applications, knowledge-based systems are probably better understood as representing a different approach to the design of applications or an approach to the design of modules to be used within applications such as transaction processing, DSS, EIS, collaborative work, or knowledge work.

Most applications are based on flows of work or processing algorithms and operate on data in defined ways. There may be many processing paths and alternative algorithms, but the structures and logic of the application programs are well defined and change only in response to correction of errors or requests for enhancements. The methods of design and development focus on the flow of processing, the data needed or produced, and the behavior of the application in response to timing and order of events.

Knowledge-based or expert systems represent a different approach to application logic and design. Essentially, these systems seek to emulate the reasoning, analysis, and decision making of experts. In order to do this, it is necessary to discover the reasoning employed by experts in dealing with complex situations. This process is termed knowledge engineering. There are two major techniques or approaches to knowledge engineering: knowledge-based expert systems and data-based neural networks.

Knowledge-Based Expert Systems

There are several approaches to represent knowledge in order for a system to accept input and solve a problem. Two approaches in frequent use are rule-based systems and frame-based systems. In both approaches, the data and inference

FIGURE 4-3
Simple Financial Model Using a Financial Modeling Package (Encore! Plus 2.1 by Ferax Microcomputers, Inc.)

Output from financial model

```
                        Example Corp
                      Income Statement

                       1992        1993        1994
                      ------      ------      ------
Sales                  $750       $1,200      $1,500

Cost of Sales           300          480         600
                      ------      ------      ------

Gross Profit            450          720         900

Salaries                150          240         300
Advertising             105          168         210
Rent                    250          250         250
                      ------      ------      ------
Total Expenses          505          658         760

Operating Income      $(55)          $62        $140
                      ------      ------      ------

Taxes                    $0          $22         $49

Net Income            $(55)          $40         $91
                      ======      ======      ======
```

Logic for model

```
{Filename: Example}
{Income Statement for Example Corp.}
'Sales'
'Cost of Sales'= 'Sales'* 0.4
'Gross Profit' = 'Sales' - 'Cost of Sales'
'Salaries'= 'Cost of Sales' * 0.5
'Advertising'= 'Cost of Sales' * 0.35
'Rent'= 250.0
'Total Expenses' = 'Salaries' sum 'Rent'
'Operating Income' = 'Gross Profit' - 'Total Expenses'
ByColumn
If 'Operating Income' LE 0.0 Then
    Begin
    'Taxes' = 0.0
    End
Else
    Begin
    'Tax Rate' = 0.35
    'Taxes' = 'Tax Rate' * 'Operating Income'
    End
Endbycolumn
'Net Income' = 'Operating Income' - 'Taxes'
```

Description of input and format of output

Not shown

rules to be incorporated in the knowledge base come from having experts describe their reasoning as they do it (rather than based on after-the-fact reconstruction of reasoning). The method is time consuming and subject to errors arising from the small number of experts employed.

A rule-based expert system represents knowledge as a set of production rules expressed as IF . . . THEN statements. In other words, for each condition or a set of conditions, the actions are stated. Each set of conditions with set of actions represent a rule in the rule-based system. Special software is available to manage a large number of rules and simplify development. This type of expert system is quite close to a traditional procedural computer program but with a more complex set of rules and a structure that allows adding and deleting rules. This approach is used where there are many rules but each one can be stated with confidence in an IF . . . THEN statement. For example, the rules for configuring a computer hardware system, given many hardware specifications and site conditions, can be a large number. The expert system can be developed by starting with a small set of well-understood rules and adding additional rules based on experience and as experts recall added situations.

Example. A computer disk drive manufacturer required failure analysis on each of their customer replaceable units (such as a disk drive or PC board). Failure analysis is performed during the testing process on each serialized unit and also as part of the warranty work on returned units. The company's MRP software package provided limited functionality in recording and analyzing failures which forced them to develop a supplemental system.

As a first step, the quality management function developed a coding system to identify the type of tests, failures, and corrective actions. Second, they developed a system to record the failures and corrective actions associated with each serialized unit. As the engineers have identified correlations between tests, failures and corrective actions, the rules (expressed by IF . . . THEN statements) have evolved. The company started to embed this expert system approach in the training for new field service technicians even before the expert system application was completed. While the application is still in the early stages of development, feedback from the technicians indicates a large improvement in understanding, diagnosing, and fixing warranty work problems. This translates into faster and more professional customer service on any field problem and ultimately to higher quality product being delivered to customers.

A frame-based system employs an object approach in which frames represent relations and procedures in the knowledge base. An inference engine uses rules of inference for reasoning from information about the problem and problem domain. As new information and rules of inference are discovered, they may be added to the system.

One difficulty in the use of expert system modules stems from the principle that people will not rely upon reasoning or logic in a system if they do not understand it. In a simple program, the users are likely to understand the processing rules and logic. In a complex expert system, the reasoning or inference logic for a decision may become complex and not be understood. In many experts systems, this problem is being met by having the system produce an explanation of the rules or inferences that were applied. In other words, given a set of inputs, the expert system will apply a fairly small set of rules or inferences in arriving at a decision or conclusion. Providing this explanation to users helps solve the problem of not understanding the system.

Data-Based Neural Networks

Given data on a set of conditions presented to experts and data on their decisions, it is possible to infer the decision making rules that the experts follow. The inferences from the data are tentative since the set of conditions is limited in scope. Therefore, any new conditions and expert actions can cause the inferences to be revised.

A neural network approach is a data-driven, sophisticated method of dynamic correlation analysis to infer from the data how experts behave. As new information on conditions and outcomes is added to the model, the correlations are updated to yield revised rules. The advantage of the method is the dynamic, self modifying approach based on actual conditions and results. Applications generating large amounts of data are likely candidates for this approach. For example, a neural net approach might be used to develop a self-modifying expert system for recognizing causes of product defects by continuous analysis of many characteristics of the process and the product defects associated with them.

Although the knowledge-based expert system and the data-driven neural network approaches are quite different, they may be integrated in a system in which knowledge of rules and inference logic is obtained from experts and used to establish a framework for the data analysis by the neural network method. Rather than having the neural network analysis work entirely from the data in formulating rules, the knowledge-based rules are provided as a starting point and the analysis amends or improves them.

LESSONS FOR MANAGERS

Although other terms may be used, the term MIS or management information system is commonly applied to the organizational technology-based information system. The MIS concept is a comprehensive view of computer-based information systems as support for organizational operations, management, analysis, and decision making. The concept has been sharpened and expanded by executive information systems, individual and group decision support, and knowledge work applications.

Four types of applications are important in extending information systems support beyond traditional reporting. They are executive information systems, decision support systems, collaborative work systems, and knowledge work applications.

- *Executive information systems* (EIS) are a class of systems that support the needs of executives to a broad range of both traditional and non-traditional information plus methods for looking at data in detail and for doing ad hoc analyses.
- *Decision support systems* (DSS) are a type of application to support decision making, especially for difficult, unstructured problems. They support interactive analysis and decision making in which the models and data analysis of the DSS support human judgment and problem exploration.
- *Collaborative work systems* support a common organizational activity of group discussion, problem formulation, and decision recommendation. The systems operate in a variety of configurations involving time, place, and group size. The technology involves decision rooms and group decision support systems as well as electronic communications for group interaction.
- *Knowledge work systems* support analysis and related knowledge work.

Knowledge work systems or expert systems are a different approach to incorporating decision rules and decision making expertise in business systems. There are two major approaches to knowledge engineering: knowledge-based expert systems and data-based neural networks. Knowledge-based system techniques have significant potential for improving or enhancing information system applications.

SELECTED REFERENCES FOR ADDITIONAL READING

Davis, G. B., and Olson, M. H. *Management Information Systems: Conceptual Foundations, Structure, and Development.* Second Edition. New York: McGraw-Hill Book Company, 1985.

Gorry, G. A. and Scott Morton, M. S. "A Framework for Management Information Systems." *Sloan Management Review*, 13 (1):55-70, 1971. A classic framework article.

Nunamaker, J.; Dennis, A.; Valcich, J.; Vogel, D.; and George, J. "Electronic Meetings to Support Group Work: Theory and Practice at Arizona," *Communications of the ACM*, July 1991, pp. 40–61

Rockart, J. F., and Treacy, M. E. *Executive Support Systems.* Homewood, Illinois: Dow Jones-Irwin, 1988.

Sprague, R. H., and Carlson, E. D. *Building Effective Decision Support Systems.* Englewood Cliffs, New Jersey: Prentice Hall, 1982.

Turban, E., and Watkins, P. R. "Integrating Expert Systems and Decision Support Systems," *MIS Quarterly*, 10:2, 1989, pp. 121-136.

Watson, H. J.; Rainer, R. K.; and Houdeshel, G., Editors. *Executive Information Systems.* New York: John Wiley & Sons, Inc., 1992. A set of 26 articles describing various aspects of executive information systems. It includes experiences of several companies.

CHAPTER 5

COMPUTER HARDWARE SYSTEMS

In any computer system for information processing, there are four fundamental elements: hardware, software, databases and communications. This chapter will describe the hardware components including data storage devices. It will be a review for many readers and a short introduction for others. Chapters 6 and 7 will describe communications and software. Databases will be covered in Chapter 10, where data modeling and databases will be discussed.

MICROELECTRONICS

In the popular literature, there is a "computer" in your new automobile, multifunction telephone, multifont printer, video game, and so forth. Designing computers into such products is sometimes described as adding "intelligence." The term computer in these products is not describing a data processing system like the one in your company or even a personal computer system. They do, however, use a computer chip termed a microprocessor that is a "computer."

The basic building block for all computer hardware is the integrated circuit chip. This section will explain microprocessor and storage chips and how they are assembled onto boards with a bus that carries signals. It will also explain how general-purpose chips are made specific through microcode. The purpose of the section is to provide a broad survey rather than an explanation of all the technical options. The descriptions will often focus on microcomputers because these are most easily observed, and they are very similar in concept to the large mainframe computers.

Logic and Memory Chips

The process of producing integrated circuit chips starts with a crystal of silicon that is sliced into thin slices called wafers. Circuits are etched on the wafers by a process of masking and diffusion. The process forms and connects transistors, resisters, diodes, and other components that make up circuits. The wafer is sliced into several chips. In other words, a chip is a rectangular piece of silicon on which an integrated circuit has been etched. Each chip is mounted in a package with pins for plugging the chip into a board. The technology is termed VLSI for very large scale integration.

The circuits can be designed as microprocessor chips, memory chips, or input-output interface chips. A microprocessor is a chip that contains the traditional functions of the central processing unit of a computer. It contains an arithmetic/logic unit, a control unit (to direct and synchronize operations), and registers to use during operations. The microprocessor is essentially a computer on a chip. It can be programmed to perform arithmetic functions, execute logic, select among alternatives, and direct functions. High performance chips have extended features such as floating point arithmetic.

Chips are often referenced in the literature by numbers that indicate the progression of capabilities. For example, recent Intel chips have the designations 286, 386, and 486. Capabilities increase for the higher numbered chips. An SX following the designation of an Intel chip indicates a lower cost, reduced capability chip of that same series.

Memory chips are of two major types: read-only memory (ROM) and random access memory (RAM). The ROM chips are used for permanent programs (such as the microprograms described later). The programs are written as part of the manufacturing process and a user cannot alter them. The instructions are read from ROM as part of processing, but there is no writing to ROM chips. PROMs (programmable read-only memories) are like ROM chips but can be programmed after manufacture.

RAM chips are used for primary storage (main memory) containing user data and application programs being processed. Data may be read from this storage and stored in it. It is volatile in the sense that data stored there is lost if power is interrupted. As will be explained later, magnetic secondary storage is not volatile. The storage capacity is expressed in thousands (using the symbol K for thousands) of bytes of storage or millions of bytes (using the symbol MB for megabytes). A byte stores the coding for one character. The use of K for thousand is a rounding; because of the design of chips, the actual storage is in increments of 1024. This is the reason a computer with one MB of memory will display memory statistics with 1,024,000 bytes. Early personal computers had main memory as low as 64K; current personal computers have main memory in the range from 1MB to 16MB.

Boards and Buses

The microprocessor uses an internal bus for interconnecting its parts. In very early computers, wires were used to interconnect the various functional units in the central processing unit. As circuitry became smaller and large-scale integration was implemented, wiring everything together became unfeasible.

The alternative was to establish a common electrical "roadway" along which all signals are sent. All functional units connect to the roadway, called a bus. An electrical signal is sent down the bus and selects the connecting path that will take it to its destination. Different signals are kept from interfering by synchronizing signals and controls.

Internal architecture of the microprocessor varies depending on the number of internal buses. For example, a single bus architecture uses a single internal bus to move signals among registers in the arithmetic logic unit. A single bus architecture is simple but slow. Two or three internal buses may be used to increase speed.

Microprocessors accept input (from an entry device or sensors), execute a stored program of instructions, perform arithmetic and logic functions, and provide results to an output device or machine. To perform these activities requires not only microprocessor chips but also memory chips and input-output interface chips. They are interconnected by external buses. The different chips are packaged and connected to the external buses by the use of boards. A number of chips will be placed on a board and interconnections made by wiring circuits printed on the boards. The board has connections to the buses as well as a power supply. The board with the microprocessor chips is often termed a *motherboard* to distinguish it from boards with memory chips.

An important characteristic of chips and buses in personal computers is the size of the internal data path on the chip and on the buses, i.e., how many signals are sent and used simultaneously. By analogy, it is the number of lanes on which traffic can move in parallel. The early personal computer circuitry moved eight bits at a time; this increased to 16 bits in the next generation. As will be explained later, the 16-bit path is very constraining, so newer personal computers have changed to 32-bit chip architecture and some have been announced with a 64-bit design.

The explanation to this point is most appropriate to personal computers. Very large computers also use integrated circuits. However, the circuits are very dense and require special cooling and other design features. There are several technologies for microprocessor and memory chips, and some tend to be used mainly for microcomputers; others are used primarily with very large computers.

Microcode and Machine-Language Instructions

Computer instructions are usually written in a programming language (to be explained Chapter 7). The computer does not execute the programming language instructions directly; they must be translated into sets of machine-language instructions that are very specific and elementary. Examples of machine-language instructions are an instruction to read data from a memory location into a register, an instruction to add the contents of a second memory

FIGURE 5-1
Basic Functions in a Computer System

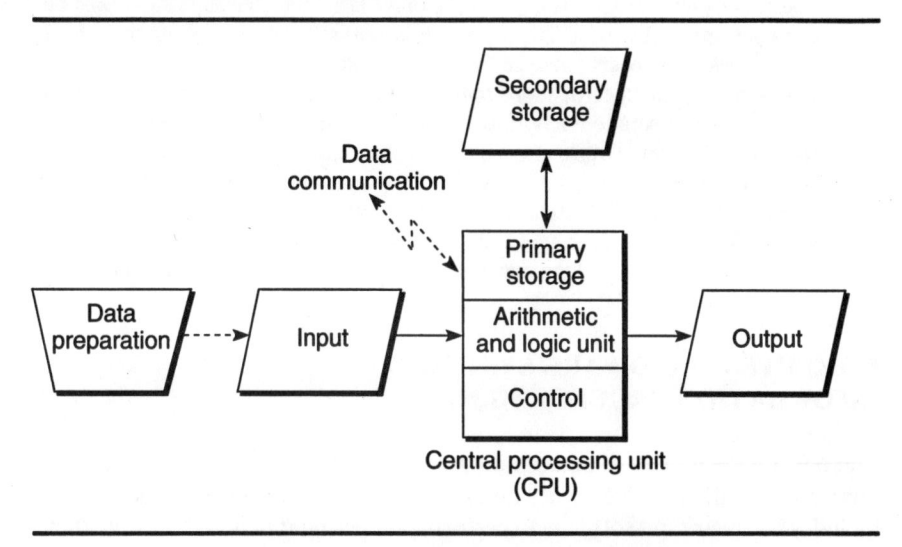

```
                          ┌──────────┐
                          │ Secondary│
                          │ storage  │
                          └────┬─────┘
          Data                 │
       communication           │
                               ▼
┌──────────┐      ┌──────┐   ┌──────────────┐    ┌──────┐
│   Data   │      │      │   │   Primary    │    │      │
│preparation│---->│ Input│──▶│   storage    │───▶│Output│
│          │      │      │   │──────────────│    │      │
└──────────┘      └──────┘   │  Arithmetic  │    └──────┘
                             │ and logic unit│
                             │──────────────│
                             │   Control    │
                             └──────────────┘
                            Central processing unit
                                    (CPU)
```

location to the data in the register, and an instruction to store the sum from the register in a memory location. The machine-language instructions are in turn each composed of a set of very elementary microinstructions. The machine-language instructions are interpreted and executed by a special computer program (a microprogram or microcode) permanently recorded in ROM.

Because of the basic power of the microprocessor design, one approach to design has been to create microprocessors with a large number of complex instructions. This design is termed CISC for complex instruction set computer. The advantage is the ability to create complex instructions that handle complex situations. The disadvantages are the decoding delays and the need for more than one instruction cycle. An alternative approach is RISC (reduced instruction set computers) in which instructions are limited to simple ones that can be executed in one cycle. As a result, for some applications, a RISC processor may require more instructions but may take less time to execute. For other applications, a CISC processor may be faster.

In the design of computers, both microcode and software can be used to present the user with a machine that has different characteristics from the physical hardware. The machine the programmer or user deals with is a conceptual or logical machine, often termed a virtual machine; the details of how the conceptual machine is implemented in the circuitry or software are not provided to the user.

Example. Some computer terminology may be confusing to the non-computer person. The term *virtual* is used to refer to something that appears to exist but doesn't physically exist. Thus, virtual storage is storage that appears to exist but does not physically exist. The term *transparent* refers to something that physically exists but appears not to be there. A program to translate user data retrieval requirements into specifications may physically exist but the user may not see evidence of its operation; it is transparent. The term *pseudo* is applied to a feature that looks like something else but is not the same. One use of the term is in pseudocode, which is a set of instructions that looks like a set of computer program language instructions but is not. Try applying the terms to a non-computer situation such as Santa Claus. He is a virtual person, the parent's role as Santa is transparent, and the man at the department store is a pseudo-Santa.

COMPUTER HARDWARE SYSTEM FOR INFORMATION PROCESSING

There is a wide variety of computer systems in terms of size, complexity, and power. Regardless of size, every computer system for information processing includes hardware and software to perform processing functions and store data. Not all computers have data communications capabilities. Although there are some hardware architecture differences, the basic concepts of hardware, software, data storage, and data communications are the same for all sizes of computers. Basic hardware equipment in a computer system for information processing supports the following functions (Figure 5-1):

1. Entry or input of data and instructions to the computer.
2. Computation, control, and primary storage in a central processing unit or CPU.
3. Secondary storage.
4. Output from the computer.
5. Data communications (not always present).

Equipment connected directly to the computer (through cables or communications lines) during use is termed *online*; equipment used separately and not connected is *offline*. In some cases, the same device may be used online for some applications and offline for others.

This section will provide an overview of the different types of hardware in a computer system. The next section will explain the operating system that is required in order for the hardware system to work. The chapter will then describe data representation for computer storage and processing. The last sections of the chapter will provide more detailed explanation of hardware for entry, input/output, secondary storage, and other system uses.

Hardware for Direct Data Entry or Data Input

Data for information processing comes from four sources: direct online entry from the keyboard of a terminal, microcomputer, or other input device; offline data preparation using terminals or microcomputers; reading of data from machine-readable documents or package coding; and data stored in files. Entry and input are often used interchangeably although recording data at a keyboard is usually termed *entry* while reading of stored data is usually termed *input*.

Data entry from documents or other inputs may be online or offline. In online data entry, the data items are sent directly from the entry device to the computer; in offline entry, data items are read or entered by using a device that stores the data for subsequent use. The trend is toward online entry but many applications are most efficient with offline entry. Some devices can be used for either online or offline entry depending on the design of the application. The most common data entry device is a terminal or microcomputer. Other input devices are small keyboards for limited data entry, card reading devices, and readers for optical reading of printed documents, optical reading of bar codes, or reading of magnetically encoded documents. A device to read and encode an image of a document is another approach to data entry.

Hardware for the Central Processing Unit (CPU)

The *central processing unit* (CPU) of a computer system contains the arithmetic logic unit, the control unit, registers, and primary storage or *memory*. A *clock* establishes the timing for operations.

- The *arithmetic logic unit* (ALU) contains circuitry that performs arithmetic operations (add, subtract, multiply, etc.) and logic operations (AND, OR, etc.).
- The *control unit* retrieves and interprets instructions, provides instructions to the other units, and sends timing signals.
- *Registers* are used to hold data during execution of arithmetic and logic operations. A computer will have a number of registers because of the need to hold several items at the same time.
- *Primary storage* is used for data and instructions to be processed. Access to primary or main storage is very fast compared to secondary storage access (to be explained later in the chapter) but still relatively slow compared to processing speeds. There are design methods to improve access; one of these is to use an additional, very fast access memory termed a *cache* memory to hold instructions and data that are actively being used. Data expected to be needed are transferred by the operating system from main memory to the cache memory. A chip may have a cache memory on it, and there may be separate cache memory chips on the board.

The clock for the CPU provides signals that are used in synchronizing operations. A crystal delivers these signals at a predetermined rate. This rate, stated in terms of megahertz (MHz), is the clock speed for a computer. For personal computers, rates may be in the range from 15 to 50 megahertz (for 1992 models). Clock speeds provide relevant comparisons only for the same type of computer.

To illustrate how the registers are used by the arithmetic/logic unit and control is exercised by the control unit, the following actions take place when two numbers are added together.

1. The control unit decodes the instruction and sends signals to access the first number contained in primary storage and transfer it to a register. The signals that make the transfer of data are synchronized by the control unit based on the clock signals.

2. The control unit decodes the location of the second number and sends signals to access it in primary storage and send it electronically to the arithmetic/logic unit that adds it to the first number in the register.

3. The control unit sends signals to copy the result from the register to a location in primary storage.

The above sequential flow of instruction processing is used by most computers. However, for many large-scale computational problems, a different hardware architecture may be used. Found primarily in supercomputers, the architecture uses either pipelining or vector processing. In pipelining, operations are divided into a number of independent steps to be performed in parallel by different parts of the computer. In vector processing, the same operation is performed simultaneously on all the elements of a vector or pair of vectors.

> *Example.* Hardware and software capacity has increased rapidly in response to business need for more powerful systems. The final assembly/testing process at a computer manufacturer in the early 1980s illustrates the need for increased computing power to coordinate a complex set of interrelated activities. Production of the various hardware subsystems (CPU, disk storage, front-end processor, terminals, and printers) and systems software (the operating system and communications software) came together in a final assembly and test area based on customer-specified configurations. The complex interaction of hardware and software made testing extremely difficult and time consuming and shipping deadlines added pressure.
>
> A smooth final assembly and testing process required tight coordination among sales order configurations, production schedules, and purchased material deliveries so that each subsystem (and tested software) would arrive on a timely basis. The coordination difficulties were increased by the number of component parts (more than 10,000), engineering changes (several hundred per month), customer configuration changes, and production disruptions, plus the similar difficulties in developing and testing the software to run the hardware.

Given the state of their manufacturing information system at the time, most of the planning and control for coordinating sales, materials, and production was performed on separate subsystems or manually. Without a common database and a means to translate overall plans into detailed plans, each functional area vigorously pursued its own agenda. The final assembly/test area had the difficult task of shipping complete computer systems.

Hardware for Secondary Storage

Secondary storage is supplementary to the primary storage contained in the CPU. It has larger capacity and is less expensive but slower relative to primary storage. It is therefore used to hold data files plus programs not currently in use. Also, unlike most primary storage, it is not volatile; stored data is not affected by shutting off power (or a power outage). The most common secondary storage media are magnetic disk, magnetic diskettes, and magnetic tape (reel and cassette). Storage technology is changing rapidly with the storage capacity of each storage medium increasing and the cost per character stored decreasing.

Most secondary storage utilizes magnetic media. A medium such as metal disk, plastic diskette, or plastic tape is coated with a metallic oxide. The coating can be magnetized. Tiny areas on the coating are treated as small magnets whose polarity is set in one of two ways in order to store one of two values. Data can be read without altering the polarity. Secondary storage is read or written by passing the magnetic media under a read-write head that either reads the polarity that is present in each tiny segment or changes the polarity to record new data.

Although much data can be stored by using a code for each character, other data can only be encoded by storing a pattern of tiny dots (pixels) that make up a picture or diagram. Since each dot can be identified with a location, storage and retrieval are conceptually easy, although storage requirements are much higher than for character coding.

To illustrate magnetic storage capacity characteristics, the rigid nonremovable disks (often called hard disks) on personal computers can store in the tens of millions of characters; sizes of 80MB to 200MB are common. In contrast, a diskette of the type used with small computers or word processors will store several hundred thousand characters or, at most, a few million characters. For comparison, a book of this size contains perhaps contains less than one million characters (perhaps 70K per chapter).

For large computer systems, disk packs hold hundreds of millions or billions of characters. Magnetic tape storage capacities vary depending on a number of factors, but a typical tape can store from a few million up to tens of millions of characters of data.

Another type of storage medium is compact disk read-only memory (CD ROM). The CD ROM medium stores huge amounts of data recorded in a read-only method. In other words, the disks are generally purchased with the data pre-recorded and the user accesses the data but does not change it. The recording method is patterns of tiny dots recorded on the medium. The dots are read by a laser beam. Applications are databases of text data such as an encyclopedia, reference volumes, or research literature. The technology is moving toward read and write optical storage; if so, this will open up new areas of application.

Hardware for Output

The most common output device is the printer, but output can be on a visual display terminal, a typewriter terminal, graph plotter, or other devices. There is a wide range of printer technology with high-speed printers using laser, electrostatic printing (the method used by most office copiers). Slow-speed printers use typewriter-like thimbles, daisy wheels, or dot matrix printing mechanisms.

One of the newer developments in hardware for output is multimedia output. Using the multimedia concept, a person using a computer may receive output from the display screen as text, graphics, or pictures. The picture can be still or moving; it can be a digitized picture from a photograph or film or an animation. At the same time, the person can receive sound in the form of music, tones, and spoken words. The combination allows new methods for output that may be powerful in getting and holding the attention of the person receiving the communication.

> *Example.* A computer-aided lesson in French can show the French words on the screen with English text explaining usage, there can be a picture, movie, or animation on part of the screen showing a scene in which the French words are employed and sound from the scene so the student hears the spoken French as well as sees the action.

CLASSES OF COMPUTER SYSTEMS

There is a wide variety of computer systems in terms of size and power. Four classes illustrate the differences:

1. Supercomputers.
2. Mainframe (large-scale) computers.
3. Minicomputers.
4. Microcomputers.

Supercomputers are designed for applications requiring very high speed computation and large primary storage. Large-scale or *mainframe computers* have very large secondary storage capacities, very powerful CPUs, and highly sophisticated operating systems. They can support multiple jobs executing concurrently and online processing from many remote locations at once.

Minicomputers are smaller than the large mainframes and relatively less expensive. Each minicomputer may support online processing from multiple remote locations. In many organizations, multiple minicomputers with communications capabilities are used instead of a single large-scale computer.

Microcomputers are small (will easily fit on a desktop) and typically have a simple operating system and (relative to larger mainframes or minicomputers) small primary and secondary storage, one keyboard input unit, one visual display unit (VDU) and one hardcopy output unit (a printer). Large capacity microcomputers are often termed workstations. Small, portable microcomputers are virtually equal to regular microcomputers except in size of monitor and availability of an online printer. The smallest portables, sized in width and length about the same as a standard 8.5 × 11 inch pad of paper and weighing about six pounds, are called *notebook computers*. The biggest constraint for notebook computers is the limited battery life before recharging is required, but this is increasing.

The classes of computers are approximate, and they overlap in various dimensions of speed, cost, and so forth. Multicomputer configurations (several CPUs linked together) of large computers can be as powerful as supercomputers. Super-minicomputers, especially multicomputer minisystems, are comparable in power to low-end large-scale computers. The low end of the minicomputer range and the high end of the microcomputer range are used for small business computers.

OPERATING SYSTEM SOFTWARE

The sets of computer program instructions that direct the operation of the hardware are called software. Software can be divided into two major categories: system software and application software. System software includes the operating system that directs and assists the execution of application programs, utility programs that do common tasks such as sorting, compilers that translate programs into machine-level instructions, and database management systems that manage storage and access to databases. System software is also required for data communications. System software is usually purchased or leased rather than developed by internal personnel.

One type of system software, the operating system, will be described in this hardware chapter because it is closely related to the hardware. It makes the hardware operational. Other types of system software and application software will be explained in the next two chapters.

The operating system manages the availability and use of computer resources. With multiple users or multiple applications operating concurrently, the operating system must allocate resources among the users and applications and manage switching of control among them. In a complex, large-scale system with multiple large processors, the operating system must not only allocate resources among many concurrent applications but must also manage a complex set of resources involving several processors. In a single user system, such as a personal computer, the problem of multiple, concurrent users is not present, so the operating system can be less complex.

The operating system performs several vital functions: memory management, process management, input/output device control, and user support. The instructions to an operating system are expressed in a command language. A few examples of instructions for the Microsoft operating system (MS-DOS) for the IBM personal computer, although simpler in scope than a more complex operating system, indicate the nature of operating system commands. There are two types of commands: *internal commands* that are associated with normal operations and *external commands* that perform diagnostic or process modification operations.

Examples of internal commands:
> chdir   change the directory being used
> copy   copy a file
> del   delete a file
> dir   list a directory
> mkdir   make a new directory
> time   display current system time (and allow changes)

Examples of external commands:
> backup   backup a disk by copying to another
> chkdsk   check a disk for errors
> format   format a diskette or disk
> mem   display the amount of used and free memory
> recover   recover a bad disk or file
> type   display the contents of a file

Since it is cumbersome to repeatedly enter sequences of operating system commands, MS-DOS provides for the creation of batch files that can be saved and run by typing the batch file name. As part of MS-DOS, a basic line editor, called Edlin, is available for creating batch files and other editing tasks.

The MS-DOS operating system provides instruction, warning, error, and diagnostic messages to the user. Three examples illustrates this feature:

- Invalid directory—the directory specified does not exist.
- Insert diskette for drive x—in connection with FORMAT command, it prompts for the disk to be formatted.
- Delete (Y/N)?—verify the action to be taken before the delete command is executed.

Memory management is required because memory is limited. For large-scale systems with multiple applications running concurrently, memory management is a major operating system activity. Several techniques can be used. The memory may be allocated as fixed partitions, as variable partitions, by using overlays, or using sections of fixed size called pages. The task of the operating system is to allocate the memory, keep track of what program or program segments are in each partition, and add or release partitions as needed.

Input/output device control is a major function of the operating system. Application programs issue standard commands; the operating system converts these to the specific commands for each device. *Device drivers* are the program routines used for this purpose. Through these routines, data can be transferred between memory and the input/output device. In the system, any errors, problems, or events to be handled send an interrupt to the computer. The interrupt is decoded by the operating system and action taken or messages sent to the operator.

As part of input/output control, the operating system provides users with commands for storage of programs and data. File access procedures are also supported.

The operating system manages processes. A process is either running (using the CPU), blocked (waiting for some event), or ready (waiting to be served). The scheduler, a part of the operating system, manages the execution of processes. Various algorithms are used depending on the type of job mix and other characteristics of the system.

DATA REPRESENTATION FOR COMPUTERS

Computers perform all calculation and storage with elements that have only two possible states. These elements include electronic switches that are open or closed, electrical pulses that are high or not high, or magnetized elements that have two directions of polarity. The two states are represented symbolically by *0* and *1*; they are called *binary digits* or *bits*. In essence, the computer moves strings of *0*s and *1*s through the circuitry to perform operations and stores strings of *0*s and *1*s in storage devices.

Since the computer needs to move and store a large number of characters but only represents the two values of *0* and *1*, there must be a method to represent and manipulate decimal numbers and alphanumeric characters (alphabetic, numeric, and special characters such as period and asterisk). Also, numeric data must be coded in a form which is suitable for computation.

The Binary Code for Alphanumeric Data

The way to represent many different characters using only binary digits is to take sets of *1*s and *0*s and establish a code such that a certain pattern of *0*s and *1*s represents *A*, another pattern *B*, etc. The set of *0*s and *1*s to represent the alphanumeric characters has to have enough different *1* and *0* combinations for each of the alphanumeric characters and any other characters needed. For example, a 3-bit set will have eight different combinations: 000 100 001 101 010 110 011 111.

The number of bits required to encode the most common alphanumerics is at least six, which permits 64 different combinations. Because of the need for more codes to distinguish between upper and lower case alphabetics and utilize many special characters, most computers use a set of eight bits to encode a character. Each set of eight bits is called a *byte*. For example, the three characters *1 - A* may be coded with three bytes as follows (an actual code being given only for illustrative purposes): 11110001 01100000 11000001. In other words, the computer moves and stores *1*s and *0*s (as represented by the two possible states), but 8-bit sets of the *1*s and *0*s represent (code) alphanumeric characters. The computer stores strings of these binary representations, moves them about, rearranges them, compares them, and so on.

In theory, each computer system could utilize a different set of 8-bit combinations to encode alphanumeric characters. In practice, two standard coding schemes are used. One is called ASCII (American Standard Code for Information Interchange); the code in use on most IBM mainframes is called EBCDIC (Extended Binary Coded Decimal Interchange Code).

When data items first enter the computer (say from keyboard input), the characters are coded into ASCII or EBCDIC, character by character. The codes also define the sequence by which data are sorted and ordered. This is termed the collating sequence. The numeric value of the 8-bit code representing *A* is less than for *B*, and so on.

Binary Coding of Numeric Data for Calculations

The coding of each character by an 8-bit byte works for numeric digits as well as for alphabetics and special characters. However, this is not an efficient scheme for arithmetic processing. For numbers on which calculations will be performed, some computers will split the eight bits into two 4-bit numeric coding sets. The coding concept is the same as with alphanumerics, with each 4-bit set representing a separate decimal digit. The computer can perform arithmetic on these sets much like arithmetic on decimal numbers. The approach is termed *binary-coded decimal* or *packed decimal*.

Another method of representing a decimal number for arithmetic processing is to encode numbers by using a string of binary digits, which holds the actual binary equivalent of the number. Depending on the computer, the string of bits can be 24, 32, 36, etc., bits in length. For example, the quantity 103 would be coded by a 32-bit binary string as:

00000000000000000000000001100111

Arithmetic performed on such strings is termed *binary arithmetic*. In general, it is faster and less complicated for computer hardware than binary-coded decimal arithmetic.

Representing Images in Storage

Unlike character coding using bytes, an image consists of a large number of very small dots. The dots may range from white to black with different shades in between. For color images, they may be different colors or shades of colors. Each dot is termed a *pixel*. By coding each pixel with a code that describes the shade or color, the image may be reasonably represented in storage and retrieved and restored.

Such a pixel representation consumes very large amounts of memory. There are various methods for compression of the coding. As a simple example, suppose that there is a large white space. It can be represented by codes that record that a large numbers of pixels in a certain space are white.

INPUT AND OUTPUT DEVICES

There are a number of input and output devices. This overview will describe some common devices that are important in business systems. These include individual data entry devices, readers for encoded data, individual output devices, and print and graphics output devices.

Individual Data Entry Devices

Individual data entry devices to be surveyed include keyboard, mouse, touch screen, pen, card, and voice.

- Keyboard entry is usually associated with a screen that displays instructions and messages. Data entry at the monitor typically follows a fill-in-the-form method with the form being displayed on the screen and movement about the screen by a cursor, tab key, or mouse.
- A mouse is a small box that is moved on a flat surface to direct the visual display cursor around the screen. Choices are made by pointing the mouse to a

location and clicking a button on the mouse. A trackball performs the same functions as a mouse.

- A touch sensitive screen is used for low volume input by touching designated points on the screen.
- Pen entry is by a stylus on a pad. The hand printing of characters is used to enter data.
- Card entry is data entry by a card that has a magnetic stripe that has access and user information. A small keypad is then used to enter more data. This approach is used for online entry of credit card transactions.
- Voice entry is used for limited entry of simple responses. However, the vocabulary that can be used is increasing rapidly.

Readers for Encoded Data

There are specialized input devices that read data documents or products coded with machine-readable data. Such devices are optical character readers (OCR), magnetic ink character readers (MICR), and bar code scanners (Figure 5-2).

- Optical scanners can read documents that are prepared on forms by typewriters or printers. An optical font may be used, but other typical type fonts can also be read.
- Magnetic character recognition is used almost exclusively with banking documents, especially checks and deposit slips. This allows the documents to be stamped, written on, get dirty, etc. without affecting the readability of the magnetic encoded bank number, routing, check number, and amount (the amount information is added by the bank where the check is deposited). Unfortunately, documents that are folded, spindled, or mutilated may not be readable.
- Bar code scanners are used to read bar codes such as the universal product codes (UPC). The most common use has been with grocery store products for automated pricing at checkout. However, they are also used for inventory control of books, tracking shipment of packages, and taking inventory of office equipment and furniture. A portable device scans the bar codes printed on or attached to the items.

> *Example.* Data collection systems have been employed in conjunction with manufacturing and distribution applications to reduce data entry efforts and errors. Typically, these systems collect data about material movement, labor activity, and/or quality statistics that are used by another application. A variety of devices can be used to record the data, such as bar code scanners or keyboards, and data can be transmitted to the application via immediate on-line transactions or delayed batch update (e.g., via hand held devices).

FIGURE 5-2
Three Encoding Methods for Automated Input

Font for Optical Character Reader (OCR-A)

```
Optical readers can read many fonts, but OCR-A was
designed to clearly differentiate letters and numbers.
Note zero (0) and letter O and o, one (1) and letter
L and l, two (2) and letter Z and z.  1 2 3 4 5 6 7 8 9
```

Font for Magnetic Character Reader (MICR)

⑆0910000481⑆ 023134018⑈

Bar code (example is Universal Product Code)

5 38000 55640 6   0 37449 13005 0

At a manufacturer of data collection devices, data collection via bar code scanners is used to collect data for their MRP system in terms of recording purchase order receipts, withdrawals from inventory, movements between operations, production completions and shipments to customers. The use of bar-coded documents and online edits/validations during the data entry process ensures timely, accurate data with minimal operator effort.

At a producer of computer components, the data collection system via bar code scanners is used in conjunction with a JIT approach to generate an electronic signal for replenishing floorstock inventories. When floor stock inventories run low for an item, the production person scans a bar-coded document on the floor stock bin. This generates a message (indicating item, quantity and delivery location) to the stockroom for replenishment action. Stockroom personnel use the same technology to indicate material issues to floor stock.

Individual Output Devices

Outputs to individuals can be a display screen, a voice response, or a printed output. The display screen and printed output have been explained and are well known. The voice response simulates a human response. The computer retrieves stored digital coding of words or phrases that are used in the response.

These are input into a voice synthesizer that produces the voice response. Common applications are customer call-in systems where a touchtone phone is used to enter codes and authorization information relative to an inquiry and the voice response system gives the reply. An example is a banking system that provides voice response to inquiries about last deposit, balances, and other transactions.

A relatively recent hardware innovation is the reading of documents that are stored as images. The images are retrievable by users with microcomputers attached to a network containing the stored images. The reader of the document image may attach comments and actions and store these with the image. Any subsequent retrieval of the document image will retrieve all notes and actions taken.

Print and Graphics Output Devices

Printed output is very common with various types of printers using a variety of technologies. Most laser printers can produce simple graphs and graphics outputs. Graphics output devices are less common. These range in size and sophistication from small devices producing page-size outputs to large devices that produce extensive drawings in blueprint size or larger. Color graphics devices are also available.

STORAGE DEVICES

The two types of secondary storage most widely used are magnetic disks and magnetic tapes. Both are used on both large-scale computers and microcomputers, although they differ in speed, capacity, and specific technology. Disk and tape technologies represent two different types of physical access mechanisms: direct access and serial access. Direct access devices, such as disks, support a variety of physical storage and access structures. Magnetic tape will efficiently support only serial access (called sequential access method).

Although both disks and tapes are widely used, the trend is toward disk for storage of active files and magnetic tape for backup and archival storage. This reflects a general tradeoff between the low cost and high capacity of tape and the faster direct access of disks. Optical disk storage is a storage technology for large read-only files.

Direct Access Devices

A *direct access storage device* (DASD, pronounced dazdee) can access any storage location without first accessing the location preceding it. The dominant direct access storage device is a disk. The storage medium is a round disk with a substratum of metal or plastic covered by a coating on which tiny dots can be polarized in two directions to store binary coded data. The recording areas are concentric circles called tracks on the surface of the disk. Depending on the design of the disk storage device, the tracks may be further divided into sectors. Each disk surface has an address; each track on a disk surface has an address; and each sector (if used) has an address. The address of a particular record in storage would thus be the surface, track, and sector addresses combined; these serve to locate the particular location at which the record is stored.

The small diskettes used on microcomputers (5¼ and 3½ inches) are based on similar concepts of addressing and access. A major difference between flexible disks and the fixed hard disks is that the hard disks are constantly rotating; the flexible disks are started before each access and stopped after it is complete. A second major difference is that the concentration of data on hard disks can be higher (because of its enclosure and close tolerances for head movement). This permits higher disk capacity. Thus, access is significantly faster with hard disks than with diskettes.

Reading or writing of data is accomplished by an "arm" with a read-write head that moves back and forth across the surface of the disk to the track desired. The disk revolves to position a sector or other location on the track under the read-write head of the arm.

Direct access storage devices have been called *random access devices*, implying that the time to access any record at random is the same regardless of its location. This term is not completely accurate because the time required to access a storage location is somewhat dependent upon the current location of the read-write head. If the record immediately preceding (physically) the one desired has just been read, the read-write head is already positioned over the record to be read. However, if the last record was on a different track, arm movement may be required to obtain the next record. This is in contrast to primary storage where there is no difference in read time among different storage locations.

Magnetic disk storage may be read and written in the same processing run. A record may be accessed and read into primary memory, changed based on a transaction, and written back to the same location in storage. This read-write capability is the basis for online, realtime processing, since the processing of a single transaction is instantly reflected in the data on the storage medium.

The time to read any location on a disk is composed of two major elements:

1. The seek time to position the read-write arm.
2. The time for the disk to revolve so that the location to be read moves under the read-write head (rotational delay).

The technical specifications for disk files are beyond the scope of this overview.

Serial Access Devices

Magnetic tape is termed a serial access device because a given stored record cannot be read until the records preceding it on the storage medium have been read. With a magnetic tape, the average time required to access a particular record at random is approximately one-half the time required to read the entire file, because on average half the records need to be read. Accessing of records in random order is therefore very inefficient and, because of this, files stored on magnetic tape are normally organized and processed in sequential order. Thus, magnetic tape is acceptable for applications for which sequential ordering of records for processing is natural, such as archival storage of transaction history.

There are no physical addresses on a magnetic tape to identify the location of stored data. The records are stored in blocks on the tape; a block is the amount of data transferred at one time from secondary to primary storage. Each block on the tape is separated from the next by an *interblock gap*. The block may contain more than one record. The gap allows the magnetic tape drive to accelerate to reading speed before sensing the data and to sense the end of the data and decelerate. The start and stop times are very slow relative to read time. This means that overall reading time is significantly reduced by having large blocks of data. The limit on the block size is the amount of storage space available for the block when it is read into primary storage.

Magnetic tape may only be read or written in a single processing run. In other words, it is not possible to read a few records, then stop and write a record on the tape. A tape is assigned as "read" or "write" by the operating instructions setting up the processing run. In order to protect against inadvertently writing over a tape, a *write ring* is used (no ring, no write).

The speed of access or data transfer rate for magnetic tape is based on three characteristics of the tape and the tape drive:

1. Tape density (characters per inch).
2. Tape speed (inches per second).
3. Size of interblock gap.

There are other tape unit designs. For example, tape units called streaming tape are designed for backup units that record continuously without blocking of records.

Optical Storage

Optical storage uses a metal disk with a coating. Data is recorded using binary coding and very tiny dots. The recorded data is read by a laser beam. The use of the laser means there is little danger of head crashes and the density of storage is much higher than with magnetic disks. The most common optical storage in use is write-once-read-many (often referred to as WORM) and CD-ROM (compact disk read-only memory). The high capacity and low cost per unit of storage makes optical storage very attractive for document images and large text databases. The disadvantages are fairly slow access time plus the write-once characteristic. In other words, data records or images are written permanently on the optical disks. There can be no updating. An area of development is rewriteable or erasable optical storage. This is not in common, operational use.

A USER VIEW OF INTERACTION WITH COMPUTER HARDWARE SYSTEMS

Most computer users do not have to deal with the technical details of the computer, but they do have to follow rather specific procedures. The procedures for use depend on the hardware and the design of the information system. Major differences in procedures can be observed for users of batch systems, users of terminals with online processing, and users of personal microcomputers.

Batch System Use

With a *batch system*, the user prepares data to be processed at a later time by the computer. The input data consists of a batch of transactions prepared over a period of time such as a day or week. A user responsible for processing data in a batch system must prepare input data in the exact format and with the exact codes required by the processing program, prepare control information used to ensure that no records are lost or remain unprocessed, and check output received for errors (including checking against the control information prepared with input data). The user is also responsible for reviewing error reports, preparing corrections, and submitting corrections for processing. A user manual describes how to prepare input data in the correct format, interpret error reports, prepare corrections, and interpret the output. Generally, the user submits prepared input data to, and receives output from, computer operations personnel rather than operating the computer directly.

Online System Use

In *online processing*, the user has a terminal for input of transactions and output of results. The terminal is connected by communication lines to a remote computer where processing actually takes place. Transactions are entered and processed one at a time as they occur (in real time). The user generally has to be identified to the system as an authorized user before transactions are accepted. System sign on and authorization usually uses a password protection scheme. Users may have different authorization levels that determine what types of transactions they may perform. For instance, a user may be authorized (via his or her password) to process certain update transactions (e.g., a sale) but not others (e.g., alteration of payroll data). The mode of operation is for the terminal to provide a dialogue with the user. The dialogue may be extensive and provide tutorial and help information for entry of data, or it may be very limited and require the user to understand what data to enter and how it should be entered.

A user responsible for processing data in an online system must sign on properly, enter transactions in the proper format based on a dialogue, a visual form, or instructions in a manual, respond to error messages (since the system should reject any invalid data) with corrected input, and review control information. At the end of a period of processing transactions, the user signs off, so that an unauthorized user may not subsequently enter data.

The computer application will normally provide some control information or control list of transactions entered during the period, so that the user may check the processing or be able to reference the work done during the session. During entry of transactions, the system provides both instructions and warning and error messages. Ideally, the messages should be so complete and clear that a user can respond with corrections or adjustments. This ideal is not always achieved, so a separate user manual may explain error codes and error messages and explain how to make corrections and adjustments.

Microcomputer Use

A microcomputer (or personal computer) is operated through an interactive dialogue; unlike online processing with a remote computer, all processing takes place locally. The significant factor is that the user of the microcomputer has direct control over processing. The microcomputer may be part of a client/server system in which several workstations share files and programs. This is described more fully in Chapter 6.

Microcomputer use places additional responsibilities on the user. The user must prepare for processing by "booting" the system (to load the operating system into primary storage) and loading the application program to be used. He or she must directly deal with setting up output and storage devices, inserting diskettes in the proper disk drive, and placing paper in the printer.

The user of a personal computer has some technical responsibility. Error messages may come from both the application itself and the operating system. The user is also responsible for backup of files and programs. Currently, security features for microcomputers are very limited, so the user must establish security controls if needed.

LESSONS FOR MANAGERS

The basic building block for all computer hardware is the chip. Microprocessor and storage chips are assembled onto boards used in computers. Basic hardware equipment in a computer system for information processing supports the functions of entry or input of data and instructions to the computer; computation, control, and primary storage; secondary storage; output; and perhaps data communications. The operating system is closely related to the hardware and makes it operational.

Since the computer needs to move and store a large number of characters and images but only represents the two values of 0 and 1, there is a method to represent and manipulate decimal numbers, alphanumeric characters, and images. Also, numeric data is coded in a form suitable for computation.

A number of input and output devices are important in business systems. There are individual data entry devices, devices to read encoded data, individual output devices, and print and graphics output devices. Disk and tape storage devices are important for data and the choice of device affects direct versus sequential access.

There are differences in the procedures for user interaction with hardware/application configurations. Three major types are batch systems, terminals with online processing, and personal microcomputers.

CHAPTER 6

COMMUNICATIONS TECHNOLOGY

Advances in communication technology are very significant for the use of information in organizations and in the design and redesign of business systems. The basic technology of communications employs much of the same electronics as computers, so changes in cost and speed for computers are reflected in communications as well. The cost of communications services has been dropping rapidly, and the capacity and speed of transmission channels has been rising. These trends have opened new possibilities for communication within organizations and with customers and suppliers. There are other effects. Stable, fast, low cost, high capacity electronic communications have aided communication between business units of multinational corporations, because the technology reduces the difficulties of coordination over long distances and different time zones. New applications of communications technology offer new capabilities and facilities for communication among individuals, within organizations, and among organizations. New communications services can be incorporated in business systems.

BASIC COMMUNICATIONS FACILITIES

In this section, the basic facilities for communication will be described. The additional requirements for data communication networks to support distributed systems will be discussed in the next section.

Model of a Communications System

A simple conceptual model of a communications system is shown in Figure 6-1. A transmitter provides coded symbols to be sent through a channel to a receiver. The message which comes from a source to the transmitter is encoded before being sent through the communications channel and decoded by a receiver. The channel is not usually a perfect conduit for the coded message because of noise and distortion.

FIGURE 6-1
Simple Conceptual Model of Communications System

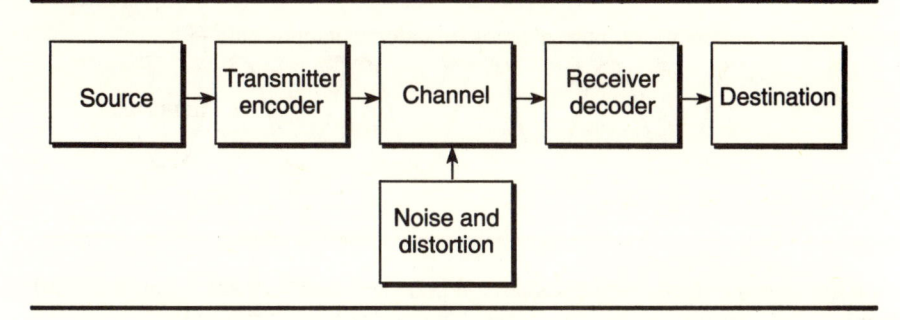

```
┌────────┐   ┌───────────┐   ┌─────────┐   ┌──────────┐   ┌─────────────┐
│ Source │ → │Transmitter│ → │ Channel │ → │ Receiver │ → │ Destination │
│        │   │ encoder   │   │         │   │ decoder  │   │             │
└────────┘   └───────────┘   └─────────┘   └──────────┘   └─────────────┘
                                  ↑
                             ┌──────────┐
                             │ Noise and│
                             │ distortion│
                             └──────────┘
```

The bits that encode data are carried through the channel by an electrical signal or waveform. The waveform has three characteristics that can be used in encoding data: strength of the signal (amplitude), direction of the "flow" of the signal in a cycle time (phase), and number of times the waveform is repeated during a specified interval (frequency). Frequency is described in units of hertz (Hz) or oscillation per second. These three characteristics are diagrammed in Figure 6-2. The standard unit of signalling speed is a *baud*, which is one pulse or code element.

Communication between a terminal or personal computer began in the 1970s with very low baud rates of 300 or 1200 per second. This increased in the 1980s to 2400 baud for most modems. Some modems offer 9600 baud and 19,200 baud. To put this in perspective, the coding means that 1200 baud is approximately equivalent to 120 characters per second, 2400 baud is 240 characters per second. For transmittal of text, this converts to about 1000 words per minute (for 1200 baud) and 2000 words per minute for 2400 baud.

> *Example.* The average reading speed for adults is about 300 to 400 words per minute, but many read at 600 or more words per minute. This means that text being transmitted at 2400 baud is coming faster than a person can read. Transmitting a 15-page single-spaced document (say 6500 words) to be printed by the recipient (rather than being read on screen) takes about four to five minutes at 2400 baud (with reset time) but only a little over a minute at 9600 baud.

In many applications, the transmission to or from a remote terminal or workstation is not just text but a screen with instructions, graphics, etc. The response time experienced by remote terminals/workstations accessing a computer (via telephone lines and a modem at each end of the line) is directly affected by the baud rate. Given a screen size of 25 lines by 80 characters, or 2000 characters, it can take between seven seconds (at 300 baud) and .2 seconds (at 9600 baud) to paint the screen. Graphics on the screen can take four

FIGURE 6-2
Diagram of Wave Form

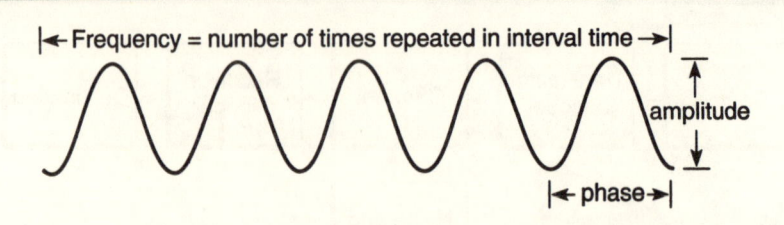

|← Frequency = number of times repeated in interval time →|

amplitude

|← phase →|

or five times longer than characters. When users need (or are accustomed to) sub-second response time, the faster communication is essential.

Communications between a host computer and a remote device such as a PC or terminal contain all the components of the conceptual model. When a message is sent from a terminal (source), the input codes are converted to signals (encoded) to be transmitted over a line (channel) such as a telephone line. When the message reaches the computer (destination), it is first converted back to the internal computer codes (decoded) for computer use. When the computer sends a message back to the remote device, the sequence is reversed, with the computer as the source and the remote device as the destination.

Older communications systems have used analog encoding in which the frequency of the signal changes continually to approximate the frequency changes of the voice signal; newer systems use digital signal encoding. When an analog transmission is used for the two values in binary coding, a modulator is used to encode the data before transmission and a demodulator reverses the process (Figure 6-3). The device, called a *modem* (abbreviation of modulator/demodulator), is not required if the communication carrier is designed for digital transmission.

Digitally encoded transmission of binary codes (*0*s and *1*s) is more efficient and has fewer errors. The reason for the increase in transmission quality is that a signal being transmitted becomes weaker after a certain distance. In analog transmission, at the propagation of the signals, they are amplified to strengthen them. The amplification also increases the noise, so that distortion may increase. In digital transmission, a repeater extracts the pattern of *1*s and *0*s and regenerates the signals without noise. It can also be used for voice transmission by encoding voice frequencies using digital codes and then reversing the process to reproduce the voice from the codes.

There are generally two types of data transmission: synchronous and asynchronous. With asynchronous transmission, each character is transmitted separately and therefore has a start signal transmitted in front of it and a stop signal at the end of it. In synchronous transmission, a number of characters are sent as a unit, and start and stop signals are required only for the whole unit. It

FIGURE 6-3
Use of Modems with Analog Transmission

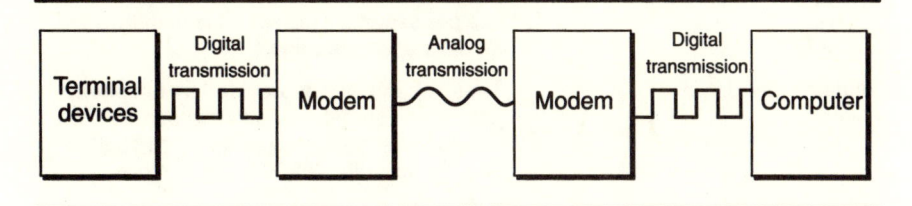

```
┌──────────┐  Digital    ┌───────┐  Analog      ┌───────┐  Digital    ┌──────────┐
│ Terminal │ transmission│       │ transmission │       │transmission │          │
│ devices  │─┘└┘└┘└─────│ Modem │─∿∿∿─────────│ Modem │─┘└┘└┘└─────│ Computer │
└──────────┘             └───────┘              └───────┘             └──────────┘
```

is used where faster transmission rates are required. The receiving device (e.g., computer or terminal) is synchronized bit for bit with the sending device; clocking mechanisms are required at both ends to achieve synchronization.

Transmission Media for Communications Channels

Communications channels, commonly known as lines, may use one or more of the following transmission media and technologies:

- Physical connection lines
    —twisted pair of copper wires
    —coaxial cables
    —fiber optics lines
- Microwave lines
    —line of sight earth microwave and infrared
    —satellite
    —radio

Example. A high-capacity disk manufacturer has a campus with several buildings connected via a local area network using twisted pair cables running through and between buildings. Personnel in each building require access to their manufacturing information systems running on the LAN. Running a cable to one building, located on the other side of a freeway, was impossible, so a laser beam was used to communicate across the freeway. The laser beam has been momentarily disrupted by flocks of birds, major blizzards, and showers, but error detection and retransmission have overcome these obstacles.

Example. A manufacturer of proximity sensors used radio frequency (RF) technology to provide wireless real-time data communication about material usage and shipments. It was not feasible to pick products and move them to a bar code scanner prior to shipping. They could not find a hand held data collection device with bar code reader that had sufficient memory and a large enough screen for processing/displaying transactions. They reasoned that if products could not

Speed and bandwidth	Explanation
Low speed (narrowband)	Data is transmitted in a range of up to 300 bits per second. This speed is usually used for slow speed terminals.
Medium speed (voice band)	These channels are provided by telephone and data communications companies. The typical transmission rates are from 1200 to 9600 baud, with 19,200 baud or more possible.
High speed (broadband)	Where it is necessary to transmit very high volumes of data at high speeds, a broadband service is appropriate.

be taken to a computer for scanning, they would take the computer to the products.

An automated inventory cart was used as the platform for data collection and materials handing. As stockroom personnel pick materials (based on consolidated picklists) from finished goods stock, they scan the bar code on the shelf and place material in a tray on the cart. Using a PC on the cart, picking transactions are communicated to their manufacturing information system using a radio frequency antenna mounted on top of the cart.

The full transmission capacity of a physical line is rarely required for transmitting data or voice. The physical line is divided into narrower channels (essentially sublines) based on the capacity required by users and technical considerations on keeping them separate. The bandwidth of a channel or line is the range of frequencies assigned to it. A wideband or large range of frequencies allows more data to be transmitted per unit of time than a narrowband, where the speed of the channel is in bits per second (bps). The speed is proportional to the bandwidth of the channel.

For medium-speed channels, the user has the option of leased (dedicated) or dial-up lines. With a leased or dedicated line, the channel is always connected and is only used for communication between the two points. In addition, a leased line can be "conditioned"; the line is treated to improve the transmission rate and decrease the number of errors in transmission. The cost of an unlimited-use leased line is usually a flat monthly charge based on the distance between the two points.

In dial-up lines, the channel is connected only during the duration of the particular communication. The source is linked into a carrier's switching network that assigns a channel. The charge for use of the switched network for data is roughly comparable to that of a long-distance telephone call over the same system. Because of the complex process of establishing a connection, delays in initial response times for dialing and connections may be unacceptable for some realtime response systems. Also, connecting through a telephone dial-up may be delayed when channels are busy. On the other hand, usage of dial-up lines has the advantage of portability (a terminal device at any location may be connected to the computer).

Data communication in general is performed in either half-duplex or full-duplex modes. *Half-duplex* is transmission in only one direction at a time; to provide a response back to the entry terminal, the line must switch directions. *Full-duplex* provides communication in both directions at once. Keystrokes entered at the terminal are sent to the computer and simultaneously echoed back to the terminal. Most personal computer communication is full-duplex.

A single slow-speed device, such as a terminal, will not use the capacity of a medium- or high-speed line. Therefore, a number of devices can share the same line by the use of a multiplexor. There are several approaches to multiplexing, but essentially the multiplexor divides the line into small segments and interleaves the slow transmissions of many devices to use the line capacity. A multiplexor at the receiving end reverses the process. A concentrator is a small computer that performs the same function as a multiplexor but also performs other functions related to validation of data, formatting of data, backup, etc.

> *Example.* A medical products manufacturer had two buildings located several miles apart which both need access to the same manufacturing information system running on a LAN. A standard phone line linking the two network servers together could not provide adequate service. A faster dedicated data line would have worked but was too costly for the number of users needing access. After several trial-and-error efforts, the MIS department successfully used two communications software packages to provide access for multiple PCs across a single inexpensive standard leased phone line. Performance for the remote users is comparable to any station on the host network, since only keystrokes and screen images travel across the line.

Front-End Processors

The management of data communications requires a complex set of computer programs. Terminals may need to be checked for transmission and messages assembled and checked prior to any processing. Error checking and error recovery procedures are required. Many computer systems use a special front-end processor to handle all data communications. A software program or a small computer performs all functions required to assemble and check a message that is then sent to the main computer for processing (Figure 6-4).

COMMUNICATION NETWORKS

In many instances, a computer within an information system is "stand alone" and self-contained with no data communications; however, the more typical

FIGURE 6-4
Use of Front-End Communications Computer and Multiplexor

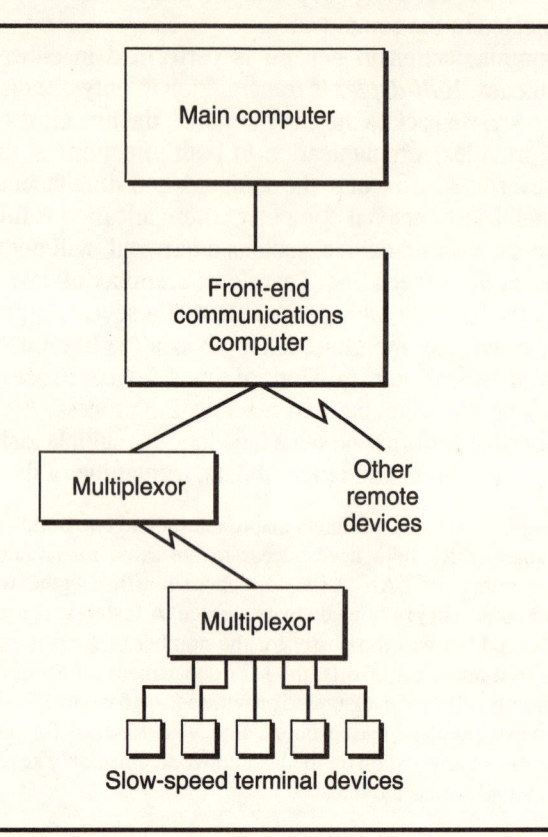

```
                    ┌──────────────┐
                    │ Main computer│
                    └──────┬───────┘
                           │
                    ┌──────┴───────┐
                    │   Front-end  │
                    │communications│
                    │   computer   │
                    └──┬────────┬──┘
                       │         \
              ┌────────┴───┐    Other
              │ Multiplexor│    remote
              └─────┬──────┘    devices
                    │
             ┌──────┴─────┐
             │ Multiplexor│
             └┬─┬─┬─┬─┬─┬─┘
              □ □ □ □ □ □
          Slow-speed terminal devices
```

situation is that the information system is a network of devices interconnected by a communications network.

Need for Communication Networks

Communication networks are needed to connect:

- Remote devices (PC or terminal) to a central computer.
- A computer in one location to computers in other locations; the locations can be within the same organization or among business partners.
- PCs within a workgroup or department to each other and to a computer serving the group or department.

These communications capabilities are significant because they allow the following functions to be accomplished:

- Communication among users of computer systems.
- Communication among applications being executed on different systems.
- Sharing of computer resources, including databases, package software, and applications.
- Distribution of computer applications among computers in different locations.

There are two broad classes of communications networks: local area and wide area networks. A *local area network* (LAN) can be used to support interconnections within a building or set of buildings close together; a *wide area network* (also termed a long haul network) can be used for communications among remote devices, including those close by if there is no local area network.

Concept of a Communication Network

Communication networks are formed from the interconnection of a number of different locations through communications facilities. There are multiple devices on the network with multiple users able to choose among them.

One way of describing the concept of a network is in terms of "layers" of function or interconnection. The end user is the source or destination of a message. In network terminology, an end user is not necessarily a person; it may be an application program inquiring into a file, an application program interacting with another application, a terminal or PC user talking to another terminal or PC user, etc. The access path is the connection between the two end users that allows them to communicate.

A path is established by pairwise linking of nodes in the network. A node is a physical box that can accept and redirect a message along an access path: it may be a computer, a multiplexor, or a terminal controller. It also buffers messages (holding characters and waiting until it receives the entire message before transmitting it to the next node) and performs error control.

A network can be configured in many different ways, depending primarily on the applications and geographic locations to be supported. The placement of the nodes and the number of alternate communications paths between them determine the configuration. The common network configurations (star, ring, and irregular) are shown in Figure 6-5. In a star network, all messages are received by the central computer and switched to the proper location; this process is called message switching. In the ring network, messages are passed from one node to another in a given direction. A multiple-connected irregular network may be structured to have multiple access paths between any two nodes. The control and management of an irregular network is usually more complicated than a star or ring.

FIGURE 6-5
Star, Ring, and Irregular Networks for Data Communications

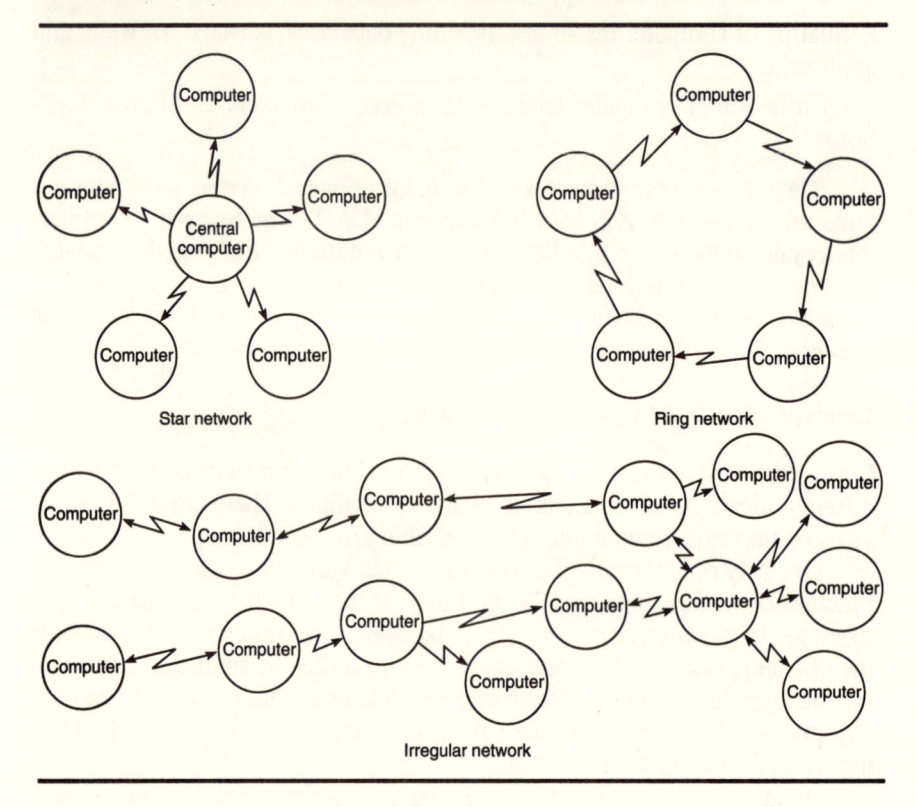

Star network

Ring network

Irregular network

Local Area Network (LAN)

If the professionals in an organization each have a microcomputer and every clerical person doing typing, filing, and retrieval has a microcomputer, it is probably useful to communicate among the devices. Stringing wires between a few devices is feasible but does not deal with the management of the communications. The alternative is to connect the devices to a local area network (LAN).

> *Example.* In a manufacturing application of one Computer-Aided Design (CAD) package, each engineer's workstation performs all data access/updates, calculations, and screen management functions. The workstation is connected to a LAN so that a file server manages the physical disk storage device of centralized files for all drawings. The file server processes individual requests from each workstation for drawing files.

A local area network is constructed of high-capacity lines. Early local area networks required coaxial cable, but improvements in communications technology allow the use of twisted pairs, which means cabling can be less expensive and even utilize telephone wiring. If the cable is long, electronic devices are attached to keep signals strong and clear as they move along the line. A device to be attached to the network cable has an interface (connection) containing a microprocessor that manages the logic of the attachment and transmission. If the local area network is small, the attachment logic may be handled by a computer that controls the entire network. There are a number of proprietary designs for building a local area network and a number of software packages for managing a LAN.

Messages to be sent over the local area network are assembled by the sending device into short packets of data with a code that indicates the destination. The communications interface decides if the line is available; if it is, the message is sent. The communication protocol of a local area network determines how a receiving device is addressed and how contention for the line is handled. The most important local area network contention-handling designs are *token ring* and *carrier-sense multiple-access collision detection* (CSMA/CD).

In token ring design, the line has a token consisting of a code (set of bits) that is continuously circulated around the ring on the line connecting the devices. A device ready to send "takes the token" by changing the set of bits in the token code. Transmission from that device has full use of the line. When transmission is complete, the token code indicating network availability is put back on the line. In carrier-sense multiple-access collision detection design, the transmitting device checks to see if there is a signal on the line; if not, it puts the message to be sent on the network. Only if it detects a collision (another device started at the same time) does it retransmit, waiting a random interval before attempting to do so.

Another alternative for local communications is to have all devices connected to a PABX (Private Automatic Branch Exchange) which acts as a central switchboard to connect devices needing to communicate. This is a logical method of integrating voice and data communications.

Local area networks designed only for data communications (and perhaps telephones) are termed *baseband* networks. A *broadband* network is a larger capacity cable than baseband. It can be divided into separate channels, each channel acting as a separate line. The extra capacity means the broadband network can carry data communications, television, telephone, and other communication on the same cable. It is more expensive than a baseband network and is therefore cost-justified only where there is a consistently high volume of communications.

Wide Area Network

In contrast to local area networks in the same building or small area, the wide area network provides communication over long distances. For almost all organizations, long-distance communications make use of facilities and services of public communications companies. In most countries, this is a monopoly of the government postal, telephone, and telegraph company (PTT); in the United States, it can be one of the regional Bell System companies, AT&T, or other private communications companies. There is however a worldwide trend to more competition and away from the PTT monopolies.

> *Example.* A clothing manufacturer and distributor must coordinate activities between multiple warehouses and manufacturing plants. Using a software package that supports Distribution Requirements Planning (DRP) with a distributed database approach, each site runs their own system on a local area network. Sales order information, however, is maintained on a centralized database. When one site enters sales orders, the order entry person may check availability at other sites using a wide area network (WAN) to access information on the centralized database.

Wide area network communications can use the regular telephone network, but this is expensive and relatively poor for large volumes of data transmission. The alternative is a packet switching network. The packet switching network is accessed via a local connection. The data file to be transmitted is received by a node in the network (a special purpose computer operated by the packet switching vendor) and divided into packets (strings of data characters) with each packet having a sequence number and address of destination. The packets are sent over high speed communications facilities with error detection on each packet. At the destination, the packets are assembled in the proper order to form the original message.

Protocols

When two devices are communicating, there must be agreement as to the meaning of control information being sent with the data and agreement as to how the control information and data will be packaged. This agreement is the *protocol*. There are a number of standard communication protocols. A common standard protocol is the international RS-232 physical connection standard for connecting two devices with a cable. It specifies, for example, what each pin on the cable is used for. Most microcomputers use RS-232 cables.

A broader standard approach to communications protocols is the international standard X.25 open systems interconnect model. The X.25 model consists of seven layers in a hierarchy of communication protocols. The first three layers are physical, link, and network:

Physical layer	Physical interface between data terminal equipment
Data link layer	Flow of data control between adjacent nodes
Network layer	Public packet-switching interface for public data networks

There are standard protocols for these three levels, and standards are being developed for the remaining layers of transport, session, presentation, and application. Thus, using X.25, networks can have a common protocol for communicating with packets. IBM has SNA (System Network Architecture) for interconnecting devices in data communications. SNA uses SDLC (Synchronous Data Link Control), which is a subset of the X.25 data link layer standard.

DISTRIBUTED SYSTEMS

Each CPU (mainframe or PC) represents processing power, each terminal device represents capability to enter and retrieve data, and each output device represents the capability to receive output. All these devices can be grouped in one location (centralized); they can also be dispersed, so that the power is distributed to different locations.

There are a number of variations of distributed systems depending on the distribution of hardware and data. A central computer can distribute data entry and data access hardware to other locations. Separate computers in each location can have their own data for some functions. For other purposes, they may share data maintained on different computers or share data managed by a computer designated for it.

Distributed Computing

When physically separated computers are interconnected through communications facilities, the configuration is called distributed computing. Distributed computers may be organized as a hierarchy or a ring. A hierarchy of processors is shown in Figure 6-6. The lowest level of processors consists of microcomputers or minicomputers that have some local data storage and perform local processing. Tasks too large to be processed at this level or requiring data not available in the local database are transmitted to a higher-level regional or centralized computer. The highest level in the hierarchy of processors has the capacity to handle large-scale problems.

Alternatively, there may be a ring structure of minicomputers of equal power and no large central processor. Each minicomputer does local processing and accesses data from the other locations as required. The way a distrib-

FIGURE 6-6
Distributed Processing Using Hierarchy of Processors

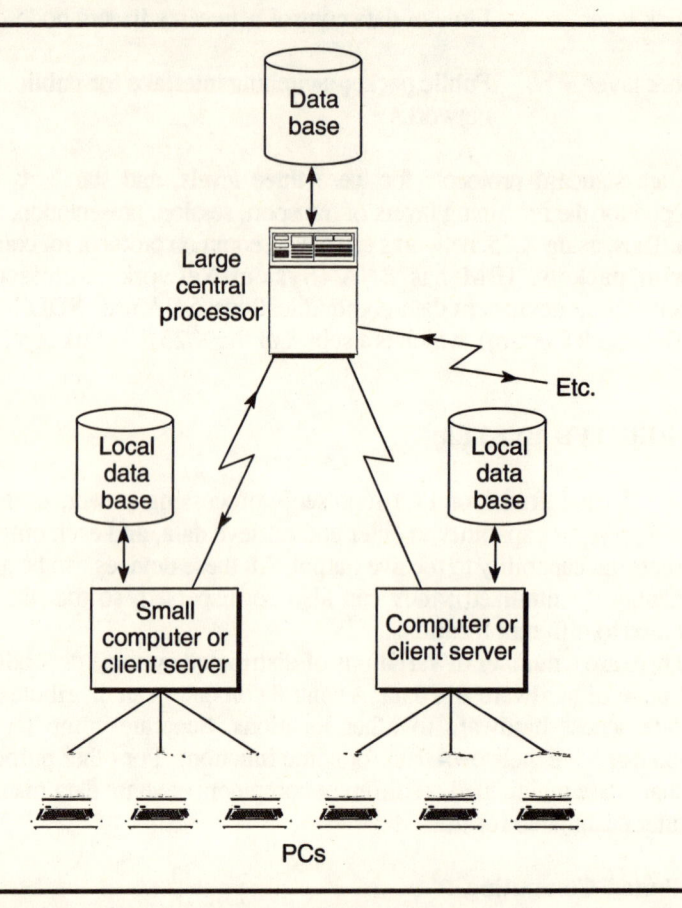

uted processing system is configured usually depends on the needs of the application.

There are several advantages of distributed computing over a centralized computer. Since the bulk of computing is perormed at the local site, communications costs can be significantly reduced. Furthermore, if one processor is "down" (cannot function), its processing can be shifted to other processors, and there is minimal disturbance to the entire system; if, on the other hand, a central computer goes down, all processing stops. In the case of the hierarchical configuration in particular, users at an organizational unit or department may benefit from control over a relatively inexpensive system and still have access to more powerful computers as needed.

Client Server Systems

A client server system represents a step in the evolution of LAN and PC-based file and print servers. Applications are divided into separate processes operating on separate computers connected over a network thus forming a loosely coupled system. Tasks are divided between client workstations and servers. A server is a computer that "serves" other computers by managing a shared resource such as a database or a printer.

In terms of task division, each client workstation manages the user interface software, security and access control checks, and queries to local databases (including integrity checks of queries), and forms queries for processing by the server. The client workstation also performs analysis with both its own local data and data sent from the server.

The use of one or more server computers to provide services to the client workstations that are connected via a LAN requires system management and interface software. The workstation interface with applications is through a system called by one vendor a network basic input/output system (NetBIOS). This communication method is a de facto standard in PC LANs. Several vendors provide local area network management products, although there has been dominance and a de facto standard by one vendor.

Servers provide service in response to queries from the client workstations and hide the composite client server system from the end users. For example, a database server provides intensive processing power for managing the database for tasks such as searching for data records, providing record level locking and concurrent access control during database updates, and logging and recovery. A file server manages the network and network communications, security and administration, the library of applications software, and the physical storage devices.

Example. A leading MRP software package employing a client server architecture divides the computer processing into front-end and back-end processes. The back-end is an intelligent database server that controls all data access and updates through a database management system. The front-end is the user's intelligent workstation that performs calculations and creates screen displays. The back-end uses the file server as a physical disk storage device for centralized data files.

Network traffic is minimized by the transmission of data records only between the front-end and back-end processes. The back-end reads database indexes to find requested records for transmission to workstations, minimizing the number of actual reads performed by the file server and the amount of data transmitted on the network. This maximizes the price/performance of powerful servers and relatively less powerful workstations. Database location is transparent to users and applications.

The client server architecture is in sharp contrast to a host computer and dumb terminals, and also to LAN systems employing only a file server (a file server system).

> *Example.* A useful analogy to understand the effects of distributed computing is a mail carrier. Client server systems are like efficient mail carriers taking the right piece of mail to the right recipient. The recipient then takes the necessary actions on the mail received. File server systems are like inefficient mail carriers. They must take the entire mailbag to the door and ask the recipients to sift through the bag and find the letter addressed to them. Host computer dumb terminal systems take the right piece of mail to the right recipient. However, the recipients on the mail route cannot do anything; they must ask the mail carrier to read the mail and act upon it for them.

COMMUNICATION APPLICATIONS

Electronic communication technology has provided a number of new services. These can be incorporated into work procedures and business systems. Examples of these are voice mail, electronic mail, fax, electronic data interchange, and integrated services digital networks. The first three provide new ways for communications to add to traditional written document, face-to-face, and telephone. The voice mail, electronic mail, and fax are similar in some respects but also have unique features. A person communicating in the information age therefore has more choices for communication media. Electronic data interchange is a replacement for traditional mailing of documents. Integrated services digital networks provide multiple communications at the same time; they offer interesting capabilities that will start to appear in redesigned business systems. There are other telephone services that can be used in business system design; these are surveyed.

Voice Mail

Also termed voice messaging, voice mail is a sophisticated extension of the recorder that some users have attached to their telephones. The difference is that the voice mail system performs a digital storage of the message. This allows a number of features to be included. Examples are broadcasting messages to a number of users, sending messages at a specified time, and forwarding messages. The user of a telephone can record a message telling the person to leave a message or how to contact a receptionist or other person. Messages can be stored or discarded. If desired, they can be read more than once.

The major advantages of voice mail are the avoidance of telephone tag when the objective is to leave a message. There is a record of a call being made and a message requesting a callback may be left. The ability to send a message to multiple recipients or to have a message sent at a designated time are useful features.

Voice mail can be part of business systems. The features allow customers or others to leave messages that can be handled when the person being called is available. It has some of the same characteristics as e-mail in terms of providing asynchronous communication but also allows more media richness because the sound of a voice message also communicates content. The disadvantage is that it is not suitable for sending longer messages or messages that need to be read or that have data within them.

Electronic Mail (E-Mail)

Electronic mail (or e-mail) is used for the electronic transmission of messages. The most common use is for text, but many systems can handle graphics as well. Essentially, each user has an electronic mailbox maintained by a computer and accessed by the user's personal computer or terminal. In a large network, there are many clusters of users around a computer (a node in the mail network).

> *Example*. In the large-scale worldwide educational network, each node has a code for the computer and the country (or in the United States for the institution and network. Thus, a user at the Technical University of Delft in the Netherlands might have an address that consist of a personal identifier plus TUDELFT.NL with TUDELFT being the institution computer node and NL being the Netherlands. A faculty member at the University of Minnesota using the St. Paul campus computer center might be addressed by a personal identifier plus SPCS.UMN.EDU which specifies the St Paul Computer Services at the University of Minnesota and Edunet as the network. No country code is used. Messages can be sent across networks in different countries and within the United States. A faculty member on Bitnet or Edunet can send or receive a message to someone on the other network or someone on a commercial network such as COMSERVE.

A message is sent from a personal computer by data communications to the computer at the user's node. From this computer, the message is routed through one or more computer nodes until it reaches the destination. If it is misaddressed to a nonexistent node or a nonexistent personal identifier, it is returned to the sender. The sender may send short messages or prepare long messages separately and send them as files.

It is possible to address the message to multiple recipients or to one recipient with copies to others. There are bulletin boards that are accessible by many users, and procedures to send notices to a large list of interested parties.

When a person receives a message, it is retained by the system with a log of time received, sender, sender node, and subject of the message. When the message is read, the recipient may do one or more of the following: leave it in the mailbox for later disposition, store it in a file (notebook), forward it to someone else, reply, or delete it from the mailbox. Thus, it is possible to retain messages related to persons or subjects in separate files (notebooks). These may be retrieved electronically and viewed by personal computer or printed.

> *Example.* The computer that manages e-mail for a user will keep a log of messages for backup and recovery purposes. In some systems, the log may be kept for some time as an archive in order to provide access to past messages. In other systems, the log is maintained for a short time only. In both cases, the backup and recovery log is a system feature; e-mail users are expected to delete messages they do not wish to save and save messages in their files or notebooks that they wish to use later or to archive. The user deletion does not affect the system log. This distinction was important in the evidence against the conspirators in the Irangate affair in which members of the White House staff engaged in illegal activities to sell arms to Iran. One person used the electronic mail system of the White House but deleted all incriminating messages. What he did not realize was that the system was maintaining a log that was not affected by his deletions. The log provided the evidence of the illegal activities.

Electronic mail is widely used. An average of 30 to 50 million messages are exchanged each day. It has been found to facilitate communication, especially under certain conditions: where face-to-face or telephone communications are difficult to arrange, where messages need to be read by the recipient (contain data or there is a need to make sure the recipient can read and reread the contents), and where the issue can be resolved by short inquiries or messages. Electronic mail messages have lower formality than letters or memoranda but do not deal with ambiguous situations as well as telephone or face-to-face communication. Therefore, e-mail is a very useful addition to the set of communication media but is not suitable for all communications.

> *Example.* The vice-president for production of a food products company used electronic mail to keep in touch with the managers at each plant. When he first used e-mail, he became very involved with plant decision making. Soon he observed that his e-mail messages prompted local managers to spend too much time dealing with him and too little time dealing with critical operating problems. He adjusted his use of e-mail to keep information flowing but to avoid getting involved with details.

Facsimile Transmission (Fax or Telefax)

Fax (also termed telefax in some countries) is the transmission of an image (facsimile) of text or graphics (or combination) by a communications channel. It is an old technology but was further developed and diffused in the Orient during the 1960s and 1970s. The reason for the rapid diffusion in that part of the world was the comparative advantage in transmitting documents written in Oriental language symbols (that are cumbersome to convert to standard data transmission coding). Diffusion in other parts of the world began in the early 1980s. By the early 1990s, fax machines are found in virtually all businesses and in many homes. Copy services, drugstores, hotels, airports, and other consumer service locations offer fax services. Fax is now an integral part of communications services.

A fax machine works by scanning the document and converting it into codes that describe very small dots on the page as either white or black. Advanced fax machines may code various shades of darkness. The codes are transmitted to a receiving machine that uses the coded dot locations to reproduce the document. Transmission is normally over the voice network. Some fax machines use special paper; others use plain paper. There are international standards for fax transmission. The standards are expressed in terms of Group 1, 2, 3, or 4 machines. The Group 3 machines are most common; they send pages at about 15 to 20 per page. Group 4 machines are for use with ISDN (explained later in the chapter). Fax boards for PCs are available for taking images directly from a computer generated text (with or without graphics) and transmitting to a fax receiver. The fax board also receives fax transmissions and converts to pixels that reproduce the transmitted document on the computer screen.

Electronic Data Interchange (EDI)

Electronic data interchange (usually referred to as EDI) is an application of communications technology in which companies exchange standard business documents electronically. Common business documents such as purchase orders, bills of lading, and invoices are converted to a standard format and transmitted electronically on a telecommunications network. This replaces the preparation and mailing of paper documents.

> *Example.* General Motors, Ford, and Chrysler require their parts suppliers to use EDI during the procurement cycle from purchase order and release notice to shipment and payment.

> *Example.* A small company may not want to invest in the hardware and software for EDI to establish connections with its customers or suppliers that require its use. The company can use an EDI network vendor that accepts batches of EDI documents from a company, separates them, and transmits them to the recipient. The EDI vendor will also accept EDI documents for the company.

The main problem with EDI is to agree on the format of records to be exchanged. Although individual companies might make such agreements, it is more common to have industry standards or to use national or international standards. Two important standards are the American National Standards Institute (ANSI) standard X.12 and EDIFACT which was developed internationally. When a company's internal document format is different than the EDI format, it is necessary to use translation software.

EDI has some obvious benefits. It improves the speed and accuracy of document transmission (thereby reducing business transaction cycle time) and may do it at lower cost. The use of EDI encourages a company to have a smaller number of suppliers or trading partners. It will tend to develop a closer relationship with them. There are also some costs. There are costs associated with the conversion to EDI, the costs of conversion from internal formats, and the costs of EDI transmission. It also introduces security issues not present with paper documents. EDI may make it more difficult for new suppliers to obtain orders because of the need to keep the number of suppliers smaller when using EDI.

Integrated Services Digital Networks (ISDN)

The change of the telephone system from analog transmission to digital transmission opened up new possibilities since digital transmission is more versatile, not only for voice but also for data, graphics, pictures, video, etc. A digital voice transmission channel is quite small; to transmit combinations of voice and nonvoice (data, graphics, pictures, video) requires a larger channel. With a larger channel, it is possible to have two-way communication with combinations of voice and nonvoice traffic. ISDN opens up new possibilities in the design of business systems. It promises to be one of the important technologies for business in the 1990s.

> *Example*. A business use of the larger capacity of ISDN is a customer order entry system that allows the customer to use voice communication at the same time graphic images are being sent to describe the product or its specifications. For example, a software user on a help line might send a printout of diagnostics or other evidence of errors while at the same time talking with the vendor help line person.
>
> *Example*. With ISDN, two or more authors in different locations might not only talk but at the same time share access to the same display screen showing pages of the manuscript and instantly reflecting changes by any author.

Other Telephone Services Useful in Business Systems

When designing business systems using information and communications technology in the system, there are a number of telephone services that may be incorporated in the designs. Examples are 800 and 900 numbers, identification of caller number, dialing software, touchtone direct inquiry systems, and public database access.

The 800 and 900 numbers are examples of customer services that are useful in business systems. The 800 numbers allow customers to call in without charge to place an order, inquire about services, reach a help line, etc. This allows one number to be used in advertising in all parts of the USA. The 900 number is a more recent innovation. It allows the caller to be charged for the call. This is appropriate in cases where the caller is receiving technical advice or diagnosis that has not been included in the price of goods or services already purchased.

> *Example.* A vendor of a software package to psychotherapists sells the package with video tape training and support manuals. If users want more technical advice or help, they call a 900 number and are charged $2.50 per minute. The company promises prompt no-waiting service. Since the purchasers of the package will vary significantly in their knowledge of software, they will vary in their need for help services. The 900 number allows the vendor to price the package for the user with computer knowledge and obtain compensation from those who want more assistance.

Caller identification is a controversial feature. It is technically possible to provide the person being called with the telephone number of the person calling. This is useful in business systems where customers call in. The business computer can use the caller number to retrieve the customer file. By the time the call is answered by a customer service representative, the file for the customer is available. This reduces service cycle time and allows more personalized service. There is opposition to the feature because callers may not want to be identified automatically.

Dialing software dials numbers for service or sales personnel. This reduces the time spent waiting for an answer. With a group of telephone sales personnel, telephone numbers will be dialed automatically. When there is an answer, the call is switched to a sales person who is also provided with the name of the person being called and other information.

> *Example.* Bill collection personnel make contact by phone, but it often takes several calls to reach the person who is delinquent. Calls must be repeated to home or job before making contact. Dialing software can double the productivity of such collection personnel by taking over the task of dialing and waiting for a response.

Touchtone telephones allow direct customer inquiry or routing of customer calls. This feature of the telephone system allows customers to obtain information from computer files at any time of day or night. It also allows them to select from a menu of options. Responses from computer files are converted to voice responses by a voice response system that assembles digital recordings to make up the response.

> *Example.* A bank offers a 24-hour service to customers to make inquiries about their checking or saving account balance, last deposit, and available credit. The customer dials a telephone number and responds via touchtone keys to indicate the service desired, the account number, and a security code to prevent access by unauthorized persons. The information is retrieved from a computer file and a voice response is assembled from a file of digital recordings. This provides

excellent service, eliminates the need to return receipts for deposits made by mail, and virtually eliminates inquiries to bookkeeping.

Touchtone services are limited to fairly short responses, although pre-recorded messages of some length may be provided. If customers are to be provided access to significant amounts of data, they may be given access to a database through the use of a PC and a modem. Access can be free, charged by a 900 number, or billed separately.

> *Example.* The Federal Reserve Bank of Minneapolis offers a free information service called Kimberely. Accessed by modem and PC, the service is a database with economic and financial information. Examples of information are daily interest and exchange rates, financial markets data, economic indicators, texts of speeches and articles, and catalogs of materials.

LESSONS FOR MANAGERS

Communications technology employs much of the same technology as computers, so the speed and power advances in computing have parallel developments in communications. Useful information and concepts for managers to understand are basic communication facilities, wide area and local networks, and protocols and standards.

Each CPU (mainframe or PC) represents processing power, each terminal device represents power to enter and retrieve data, and each output device represents the capability to receive output. All of these devices can be grouped in one location (centralized); they can also be dispersed, so that the power is distributed to different locations. Distributed processing is an important alternative to centralized computing. The client/server architecture is often used in newer distributed systems.

Electronic communication technology has provided a number of new services that can be incorporated in business systems. Examples are voice mail, electronic mail, fax, electronic data interchange, and integrated services digital networks. The first three provide new ways for communications that add to traditional written documents, face-to-face, and telephone. Electronic data interchange is a replacement for traditional mailing of documents. Integrated services digital networks provide multiple communications at the same time; they suggest new features in redesigned business systems. Services of telephone companies that are being incorporated in business systems include 800 and 900 numbers, caller identification, dialing software, touchtone inquiry systems, and database access.

CHAPTER 7

COMPUTER SOFTWARE

The chapter will survey the hardware/software platform for applications and their development. It will describe three approaches to acquisition and development of application software: package, application generator, and programming language. The programming language approach will be described in some detail because the approach is used for developing not only in-house applications but is also used by software vendors to develop packages. It will describe the different types of instructions and languages for programming a computer. The approach to software development, termed software engineering, will be explained and the structure of programs described. The chapter concludes with a short description of some of the more common programming languages used for business applications.

THE ROLE OF SOFTWARE

Software consists of sets of instructions that are not permanently stored in the computer. A set of instructions called a *program* is input in the computer when needed for a specific purpose. A question is why have instructions that are not permanently stored in the computer. Why not "hardwire" the instructions in microprocessors? The answer is that the software provides a more flexible approach. It allows the use of many more sets of instructions than could be permanently stored.

Computer software defines procedures to be followed, but it can be written to respond to a huge variety of conditions. The set of instructions that comprise a computer program can be written so that it modifies itself as the instructions are executed. There are usually numerous program paths that may be selected; the actual path of instructions executed depends on the data being processed, instructions provided by the user at execution, and the way the solution process was programmed. A program can, in essence, build the execution path as the program is run. The potential number of unique combinations of instructions that can be executed by a program can easily number in the millions. This is why software is so useful in processing complex procedures required for human systems. It is also a reason why it is difficult to make sure software is correct.

An application program is part of a larger business process that includes manual procedures and connections to other processes. All business systems that use computers are designed as *human-machine systems* in which software is used in connection with human input, human review, and human decision making. The advantage of computers is that they are very fast and do not make errors (if the program and the data are correct). The consistency of processing is very valuable in performing procedures required by organizations. If the computer is such a perfect organizational robot, why have humans in the systems? The reason for human-machine systems is that software, even though flexible and having millions of program paths to deal with different situations and contingencies, cannot innovate and deal with new situations that arise. The program can be programmed to change in response to new data (as explained with neural nets), but the program cannot innovate and respond to unanticipated inputs in the same way as humans.

THE TECHNOLOGY PLATFORM FOR APPLICATION SOFTWARE

The technology platform for information systems is often described as the hardware and software platform. Software in the information system is of two general types: *application software* and *systems software*. The application software performs the information processing required by the organization; system software supports the development and execution of application software. The implication is that the dominant uses for application software (and availability of application software packages) should determine the choice of system software and hardware.

The Hardware/Software Platform for Applications

An application program is not the only software in the computer when it is loaded and ready for execution. The *operating system* is always present, because this software is fundamental to the operation of hardware. In the typical computer system, the application software also makes use of user interface software, database management software, and communications software. These may be thought of as extending the services offered by the operating system to application software. The application software cannot run without the operating system; when application software is written to use facilities of these other software, it cannot operate without them as well.

FIGURE 7-1
Hardware/Software Platform for Application Software

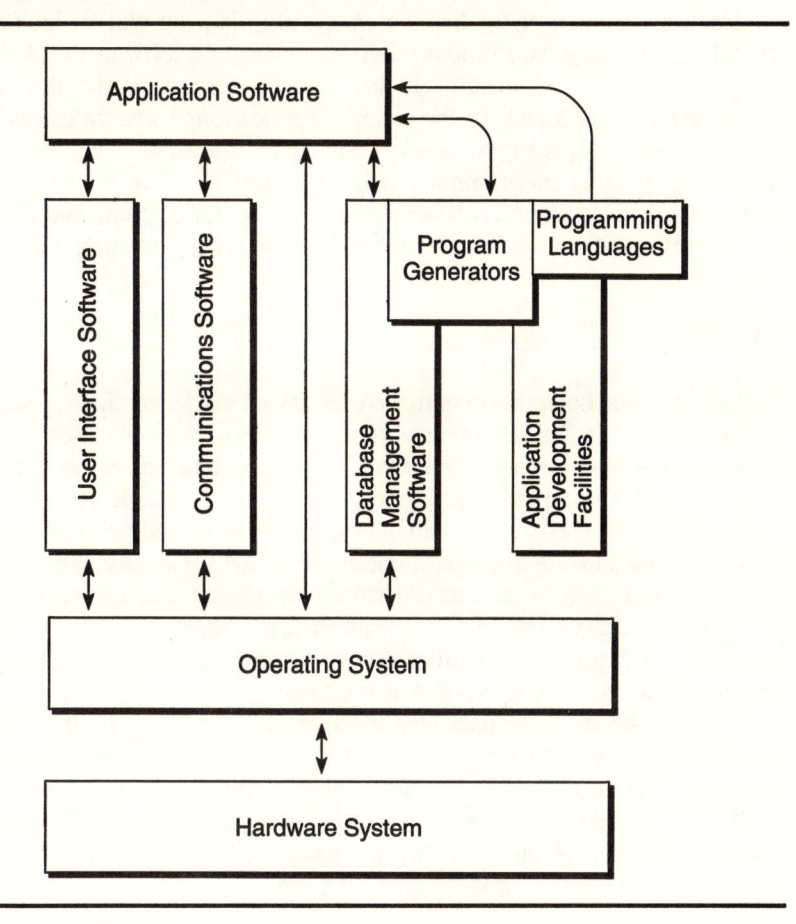

[Diagram: Application Software connects to User Interface Software, Communications Software, Program Generators, Programming Languages, Database Management Software, and Application Development Facilities, which all connect to the Operating System, which connects to the Hardware System.]

The development of applications requires software development tools, such as high-level software to generate programs from specifications, computer language software for writing processing procedures, and software to assist in various parts of the program development process. The database management software package that supports application programs also contains program development facilities.

The hardware/software supporting the execution of application software can be explained separately from the hardware/software that supports the development of the applications. However, the hardware/software platforms for execution and development are so interrelated that it is useful to describe them as a single technology platform supporting both purposes. The structure of hardware and software for this purpose is diagrammed in Figure 7-1.

Each component of the hardware/software platform will be briefly described, along with considerations related to application software development and execution. Application software differs in how it is acquired or developed. As will be explained later in the chapter, applications software can be purchased as complete packages, developed using high-level program generators, or developed using programming language facilities. The way they were acquired or developed affects how they use the operating system and software for the user interface, communications, database management, and development tools.

The Hardware and Operating System

The hardware and operating system were explained in Chapter 5. The operating system provides facilities for hardware utilization by the application program and it monitors the program execution for various types of errors related to hardware use. The basic operating system functions include job execution control, allocation and management of system resources, and standard methods for use of input and output devices. For example, the application program may specify reading data from a record stored on a disk; the operating system provides the instructions to manage the physical reading of the record from disk storage. It also provides facilities for common activities such as sorting, although these are often referred to as utilities.

Application software packages are typically written to be used with a certain operating system. For example, an application package for a microcomputer may require a specific operating system and version number; a large mainframe package may require a specific mainframe operating system. In other words, an application software package often dictates the operating system and permissible hardware configuration.

User Interface Software

The operating system may provide only minimal features for the user interface. User interface software is added to improve user friendliness. It provides facilities that improve the user interaction with the operating system and allows switching among programs, transferring data between them, copying files, and other user support facilities. Application software may make use of the user interface software packages such as Microsoft Windows. User interface software can also be embedded in other software, such as the operating system, database management system, and local area network software.

Example. A consistent user interface is one of many critical factors that makes software user friendly. By using the same user interface in all applications, developers can enforce consistent standards and users can learn/use systems more easily. Graphical user interfaces offer many advantages over traditional character-based command-driven interfaces. Users tend to find the graphical presentation intuitively appealing. Reducing reliance on keyboard skills is also important to many users.

Communications Software

Communications software provides facilities for applications that rely on data communications, as explained in Chapter 6. Managing data communications is a specialized task. Rather than having each application contain its own data communication programs, a single data communications package is installed to manage the transfer of data, deal with transmission errors, handle protocols, and so forth.

In a local area network, each workstation has communications software and a LAN communication board. The network is managed by a local area network operating system. In a wide area network, the communications software installed in the personal computer (or on the mainframe) manages the communications over telephone lines or other facilities. Numbers to dial for different uses can be specified directly or through command files. Once the number is specified, the communications software dials the number, handles busy signals and redials, handles the communication and retransmits if errors are detected.

Database Management Software

The database management software extends the data and file management facilities of the operating system. The database management system (DBMS) may be used by application software to manage access and storage of data. Some application software packages are written for use with a specific DBMS, so the selection of an application may govern the choice of a DBMS.

The database management software typically has facilities for program development and may constrain options for user interface software. The development facilities include programming a database query, commands for selecting data and producing a report, and programming language commands for developing an application that uses the database management software in its execution.

Application Development Tools

Two broad classes of application development tools are program generators and programming languages. Program generators are software packages that support the development and, in some cases, execution of application software. The application is programmed by writing specifications, for example, about inputs, outputs, and transformations. The specifications are interpreted and an application program produced by the program generator. A common example is a report generator that may be a separate development package or be provided as part of the DBMS application development facilities. General-purpose application development packages for a certain type of problem may be considered program generators.

The programming language development approach utilizes software called compilers and assemblers to translate source program instructions written by programmers into the machine-level object program instructions that are executed. There are also a number of programs to assist in linking programs, editing programs, testing programs, and maintaining programs in libraries.

Choices for Application Software Acquisition or Development

In the early days of computing, every application was programmed using a low-level procedural language. Higher level languages were soon developed to support programmers. The computer translated the high level instructions to machine-level instructions. The process of reducing the time and cost for applications has proceeded to the point that there are several options to be considered in the acquisition or development of software. Three major choices for applications software will be described in the chapter: package, application generator, and programming language.

THE APPLICATION SOFTWARE PACKAGE APPROACH

Commercial application packages are written to be used by a large number of organizations for a common business processing application. They are identical in general purpose to application software written by an individual company. They are, however, written and maintained by a software company that sells or leases the software. The software vendor takes responsibility for all aspects of development and maintenance including documentation, user instruction manuals, error corrections, and enhancements. The vendor usually provides training for users and maintains help lines to answer questions about the software. There is a growing trend toward acquisition of application packages.

Advantages and Disadvantages of Application Packages

There are a number of advantages to commercial application software. It has typically been written by specialists who have considered industry practices and standards. They have created a package that satisfies all important requirements associated with the business processes. The application is typically very well tested. The exact cost is known in advance. The software is available for

FIGURE 7-2
Three Approaches to Use of Application Packages

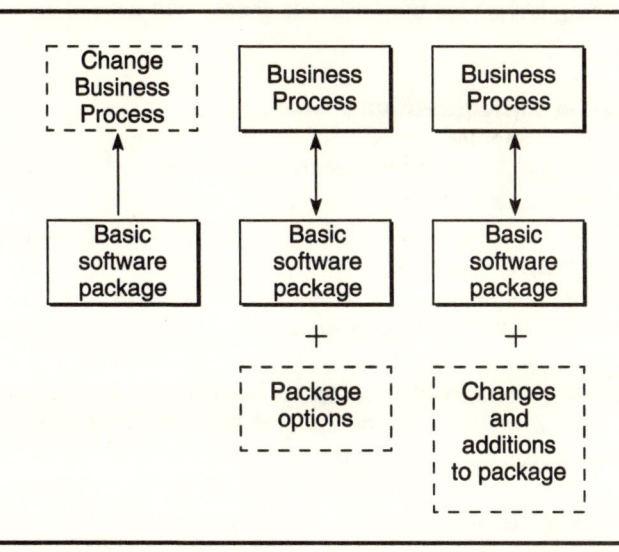

immediate use; there is no development delay. The vendor has economic incentives to keep the package up-to-date and running on industry-standard hardware/software platforms. For fairly standard applications, packages tend to be very cost effective.

One disadvantage of a package is generality, so the package cannot meet unique requirements as well as applications software developed in-house. Another disadvantage is that the organization cannot be innovative in the same way as with in-house-developed software. If the company has very innovative, competitively valuable ideas, they are not likely to be available in package software.

The analysis of buy versus build follows traditional cost analysis methods. Various risks are included in the quantitative and non-quantitative analysis. Examples of risks to consider are completion risk, cost overrun risk, requirements determination risk, software maintenance risk, obsolescence risk, and innovation (too little or too much) risk. The risk analysis is very important because inhouse and package development are different with respect to these risks.

> *Example.* A completely integrated MRP system typically involves 15 to 25 modules (such as inventory control, purchasing, and accounts payable) and a significant development effort. Approximately 200 man-years and more than one million lines of code are needed to develop a commercial MRP system. Hence, most companies opt for a commercial software package rather than trying to develop one as an in-house application package.

There are three major approaches to using application packages (Figure 7-2): use without change, customizing with input/output changes, and customizing by adding unique features. The one chosen will depend on a number of factors.

Use Application Package without Change

In this approach to application package use, the company changes its processes and procedures to adapt to the package. This is often a useful approach to process redesign, especially if the package is based on leading-edge practices. The inputs, outputs, reports, and procedures are all defined by the package. The configuration options provide a limited number of alternatives for modeling company operations; these permit users to select the alternative that provides the best fit with company procedures. For example, the handling of accounts receivable can be designated as open item or balance forward. Material requirements planning calculations can be directed to ignore availability of certain locations. Reports can be displayed based on selected, predefined parameters.

Customizing Application Package with Input/Output Changes

Many commercial packages have a number of options for making input/output or cosmetic changes to the package. Examples of input/output changes include the design of inputs, reports, external documents (such as purchase orders and invoices), and the meaning of user definable codes. The input/output changes do not change the basic logic and functions of the package. One major advantage of input/output changes is fitting the package to the company in the design of forms and reports. A second advantage is that the company will maintain the ability to upgrade and enhance the package. In implementing a new version, the input/output changes will typically not impair compatibility with the vendor's standard package.

Supplemental applications can be developed that interface with the software package using data import and export features. These supplemental applications do not change the software package. Using standard methods of data input and output provided with the software package, a user can transfer data to/from a routine in another package such as a spreadsheet processor.

Customizing Application Package with Unique Features

The application software package defines the basic requirements and forms the starting point for adding unique features. The changes can be done inhouse or by the package vendor. The advantage is that the basic features are well tested and meet general requirements, while the additions or changes provide unique capabilities for the company.

The disadvantages are that the company may be constrained by the package's basic functionality and must take responsibility for updating the application when the basic package is altered. There is a risk that modifications may interfere with a well-designed package. Every time the package is updated with new features, the modifications will again need to be examined for interference. The issue of modification by inhouse personnel versus vendor personnel is whether control over the innovations is worth the risk associated with inhouse personnel modifying a package and perhaps interfering with its functions. Also, it may depend on whether or not the package is designed to be modified.

The ability to customize or modify a package depends on the availability of source code. Packages can be modified when programmers have access to the source code. Source code consists of instructions in a programming language (such as COBOL). Source code is not executed directly. It is translated by a compiler to object code that runs on a specific computer. Source code can be modified by any programmer who can program in the source language. Object code is in a format that is not easily modified. Because of this, almost all software is distributed as object code. However, a company that pays a vendor to develop a program will generally insist on ownership of a copy of the source code.

THE APPLICATION GENERATOR PACKAGE APPROACH

In traditional programming languages, most of the processing procedures have to be specified. In general-purpose application generator packages, much of the application is generated from simple user-defined specifications. Such packages have facilities for common tasks such as spreadsheet computation, statistical analysis, and data management. When a person uses a software package for a task such as preparing a spreadsheet, the package does the processing based on the specification that the user has given. It is a very cost effective way to generate a program for a simple application. It fits the concept of end-user computing, although such application generator packages are also used by professional developers for certain types of applications.

Software packages such as spreadsheet processors and database managers are a type of general-purpose application generator software. The packages perform common tasks based on user specifications. They can also be programmed to do more processing. Simple commands create an application complete with input/output screens, editing of input data, storage and retrieval of data, computations, and other processes. Examples of application development facilities in software packages are a macro language, user-defined menus, and user-defined error handling.

Because of the widespread use of general-purpose generator packages, many applications are available. For example, templates for applications using spreadsheet processors are available from software vendors. These templates, in connection with the general-purpose package, constitute a complete application.

ISSUES IN SOFTWARE PACKAGE ACQUISITION AND USE

There are several key policy issues in dealing with the acquisition of software packages. There are so many application packages and general packages that a company needs to consider issues relative to portability; company package decisions versus individual package decisions; and use of freeware, shareware, or pirate software.

Portability

There are two aspects to package portability. One is to be able to use the same software package on different computers; the other is portability between versions of the software package.

Portability of software packages across computers is achieved by using well-known standard (or virtually standard) languages. For example, a program written in a language such as COBOL, FORTRAN, C, or SQL (to be described later) is highly portable because these languages have compilers for almost all computer hardware and operating systems.

Portability of packages across versions is the responsibility of the package vendor. Version 3.1 should be easily installed and use all files and commands of version 3.0. Portability across versions is jeopardized by user customized changes (but not by input/output customization).

Portability of application software packages is especially critical to businesses requiring different types of hardware/software platforms. The processing requirements of different business units, for example, may require that an application software package run on both small and large computers.

The software vendor typically provides guidelines for using the application package with certain hardware and systems software and may even specify versions of systems software. The interdependence between packages in the hardware/software platform can limit portability across versions and computers.

> *Example.* An application software package was written in a standard language. It utilized a database management system, user interface software, local area network, and operating system. In each case, the software package followed (or had established) de facto industry standards. The interdependence among packages in the hardware/software platform meant that the application software was not immediately portable across new versions. After the release of a new version of the operating system, for example, the vendors for the database management

system, language facilities, local area network software, and user interface software needed to release new versions. Only after these updates had been made could an update of the application software package be released. The database management system was not portable across all machines using the operating system. These factors limited the portability of the application package.

Individual versus Company Package Decisions

When a central computer has a number of users sharing a software package, there is only one software selection decision. In the case of microcomputers, there are a number of competing packages for the knowledge work toolkit (described in Chapter 2). Although the basic functionality is the same, individual preferences may result in a number of different packages being selected. This situation supports individual initiative and preferences, but it has significant organizational costs. The three most significant are training, coordination, and loss of purchasing discounts.

Although many software packages in the toolkit claim to be easy to learn and use (with manuals, help screens, and tutorials), it is likely that most users will benefit from formal training. Although the basic features of packages such as word processors or spreadsheet processors are easily learned, productivity and performance are enhanced significantly through the advanced features. These are often best introduced by formal training on the advantages and use of the features. A spreadsheet processor may have 20 or 30 basic commands or features that permit simple models and printing. However, there may be a hundred additional features and options. These features and options are often not used because the users have never understood the advantages from their use.

Coordination costs are increased if more than one software package is used. Packages can communicate via conversion features that either convert to the format and codes used by another package or convert to a standard interchange format. However, conversions are time consuming and often do not convert all features.

Obtaining purchase discounts may become an issue, either through volume discounts or individual versus site licenses. If a company purchases multiple copies of a software package, there is usually a volume discount. If five or six different packages are used, the volume discount may be reduced or lost. Package vendors often provide a site license that provides the use of the software to anyone at an organizational site. For example, all personnel using a software package in an office would be covered by a site license.

When a client server system is employed, it introduces additional software purchase considerations. One of the advantages of a client server architecture is that one copy of the software can be stored on the server and loaded by any user on the network when needed. This raises the question of whether a site license is needed when only one copy of the software is used. An alternative approach used by some vendors is to price the software in terms of maximum number of users who may concurrently employ the software.

Freeware, Shareware, and Pirate Software

There are large numbers of packages that are free (freeware) or shared with an honor system payment (shareware). Some are available without cost because they were produced under a government grant that made them available in the public domain; however, most free software is available because someone developed a package and is willing to share it. In many cases, shareware is available without initial cost, but a modest payment to the author is to be made if the software is used.

Sometimes freeware or shareware can be very good, and some innovative and unique software solutions may be available only with free or shared software. There are two problems with freeware or shareware. First, the support, updating, and quality assurance provided by a regular commercial vendor are not available. The second problem is that some freeware or shareware diskettes may have been infected with computer software viruses. A company can protect against this by having the diskette examined by a virus protection software package; virus concerns are not usually present with commercially available software packages.

It is relatively simple to pirate software and use it without making payment to a vendor holding the copyright. Most vendor protection schemes are easily circumvented by a computer expert. The use of pirated software is, by definition, a violation of normal trade practices and a violation of societal laws and norms. A recent court case by a software vendor against a company with a record of widespread use of pirated copies of the vendor software resulted in a significant financial judgment against the company.

To guard against abuse, most companies have a strict policy against use of pirated software. Software vendors recognize the value of trial use of their products before purchase. Therefore, they often provide a demonstration copy of the software for evaluation. The question of loading a regular copy of software for trial use is an ambiguous practice. Given the desirability of trial, vendors might not object to a trial use of limited duration; keeping an unpaid copy of software on one's disk after a limited duration trial suggests pirating.

THE PROGRAMMING LANGUAGE APPROACH TO APPLICATION DEVELOPMENT

The programming language approach is used for many applications developed by professional information system staff within a company; it is also the approach used in programming the packages described earlier. Even though a typical end user will not program using a programming language, some knowledge of the process is useful for understanding software.

As explained in Chapter 5, the computer hardware is instructed by a program of machine-language instructions in primary storage. For all practical purposes, programmers never write computer instructions in machine language. The programmer writes instructions in a language more suited to human use and the instructions are translated to machine language. The translation process uses a program called an assembler (for low level languages) or a compiler (for higher level languages).

It is useful to think of three levels of programming languages: the lowest level is a language close to the machine level, the middle level is a language oriented to the procedures and computer processing steps, and the third level is problem-oriented programming facilities which focus on describing the output to be achieved or the problem to be solved (rather than detailed processing or solution procedures).

High-level languages obtain human productivity at the expense of extra storage and inefficiencies in execution. The gains in human productivity come through reduced time to code instructions and less time to debug and document the programs; the languages are less error-prone and at least partly self-documenting. High-level languages are also easier to learn and are not dependent on a particular type of computer, so the programmer's skills are more transferable. Machine costs have decreased to the extent that high-level languages are almost always preferred.

The section will explain the programming process (very simplified), symbolic assembly languages, and three types of high level languages: procedure-oriented languages, problem-oriented programming facilities, and very high level languages. A new approach to programming is object-oriented programming. This requires new languages or substantial modifications in existing languages. This development will also be surveyed.

The Programming Process

The process of programming using a language consists of the following steps after program specifications have been prepared. The process is simplified by considering a short program and ignoring the common need to subdivide a large program and manage a programming group working on the different parts.

1. Decide on the structure of the program.
2. Code individual statements for describing data, input and output formats, and processing procedures. These are coded in the source language understandable to programmers. The program is a *source program* or *source code*. A programmer will usually walk through the logic of the program as a first test.

3. Translate the source program into an *object program* using a compiler (or assembler for low-level languages). The compiler checks for syntax errors. Correct these until the program has no errors in terms of program statements. It may still have logic and processing errors.

4. Execute the object program (object code) using test data. Correct errors on the source code, recompile, and retest. Repeat until the program executes correctly.

5. During the programming, various documents were prepared to record the program specifications, source code, test conditions applied, operator and user instructions. This documentation is assembled and completed. Operator and user instructions are tested.

This very simplified view demonstrated the flow of program coding, translation, testing, and documentation. It does not deal with requirements and how to do good design, coding, testing, and documentation.

Assembly Language

Coding a program in machine language is very complex, tedious, and prone to error. Assembly languages are close to machine language but allow the programmer to use symbolic operation codes and symbolic addresses. For example, a symbolic instruction to add two quantities stored in memory might be

AP WKGRDTOT,MPLYANS

where AP is the symbolic code for adding the contents of a storage location given the symbolic name MPLYANS to the contents of a storage location given the symbolic name WKGRDTOT. In this case, the names are programmer shorthand: WKGRDTOT for a storage location for a grand total and MPLYANS for a storage location containing the result of a multiplication.

The symbolic operation codes and symbolic addresses must be translated to actual machine operation codes and machine storage addresses. This translation is performed by an assembly program or assembler. Each class (or brand) of computers has a somewhat unique assembler language appropriate to the machine architecture.

Procedure-Oriented Languages

The languages most commonly used for development of information processing applications are procedure-oriented languages. There are two general types: *data processing languages* for programming the processing of large volumes of data records and *algorithmic languages* for programming of algorithms and mathematical computations. An additional programming consideration is handling time-dependent transactions, such as in realtime systems with many transactions arriving concurrently.

The common element of procedure-oriented languages is that the programmer specifies the step-by-step procedures to be followed. There are many commonalities of form and logic among procedure-oriented programming languages. Once a person has learned programming in one procedure-oriented language, it is generally simpler to learn another. The most common business-oriented procedural language is COBOL; the most common algorithmic languages are BASIC and FORTRAN. An important language incorporating data processing, algorithmic, and realtime programming capabilities is ADA. It is specified for many government contracts.

Procedure-oriented languages are able to use a database system for data management by coding data access instructions in a DBMS host language specified by the database management system.

Problem-Oriented Programming Facilities

This category is characterized by an emphasis on describing the problem to be solved or the output to be achieved rather than describing all of the procedures. Procedural descriptions are not eliminated, but they are not the focus of the programming facilities. Examples that illustrate this type of programming are a DBMS language, application development facilities, and a report generator.

Database languages are similar but specific to the database management system with which they are used. There are three reasons for employing the programming facilities of a DBMS. The first is to use the DBMS to access data and produce regular reports. The second is to use the DBMS for ad hoc queries. The third is to use the DBMS as the vehicle for developing a complete application with input, processing, and output. Some DBMS language facilities are oriented to programmers; others are sufficiently simple that they can be used by a nonprogrammer (i.e., a manager) for ad hoc queries.

Procedures can be quite complex for formatting a report and performing subtotals and breaks for each group of items, page breaks, page headings on first and subsequent pages, page numbering, grand totals, and so forth. However the procedures and rules are quite regular. This is the basis for report generators. Using a report generator, the programmer describes the format of the report and characteristics of the data. The detailed procedures are generated by the software.

Very High Level Languages (4GLs)

Very high level languages or fourth generation languages (4GL) are a general class of languages designed to improve the efficiency of the applications development process. Some of these languages are designed to improve the

FIGURE 7-3
Simple Program in FOCUS, a Very High Level Language

```
PROGRAM IN FOCUS

        PROJECT: TS3017        MEMBER: GORDON4        DATE: 84/02/24
        LIBRARY: SPFSRC        LEVEL:  01.02          TIME: 18:27
        TYPE:    CONTROL       USERID: TS3017         PAGE: 01 OF 01
  START
  COL   ----+----1----+----2----+----3----+----4----+----5----+----6----+----7----+----8
      1 REPORT EMPLOYEE
      1 HEADING CENTER
      1 "SALARY ANALYSIS BY JOB CODE"
      1 " "
      1 SUM CSAL AS 'CURRENT,SALARY'
      5     MAX.CSAL AS 'MAXIMUM,SALARY'
      5     MIN.CSAL AS 'MINIMUM,SALARY'
      5     AVE.CSAL AS 'AVERAGE,SALARY'
      1 BY CJC AS 'JOB,CODE'
      1 END
```

```
OUTPUT
                       SALARY ANALYSIS BY JOB CODE

        JOB       CURRENT        MAXIMUM        MINIMUM        AVERAGE
        CODE      SALARY         SALARY         SALARY         SALARY
        ----      -------        -------        -------        -------
        A01       $9,500.00      $9,500.00      $9,500.00      $9,500.00
        A07       $20,000.00     $11,000.00     $9,000.00      $10,000.00
        A15       $26,862.00     $26,862.00     $26,862.00     $26,862.00
        A17       $56,762.00     $29,700.00     $27,062.00     $28,381.00
        B02       $34,580.00     $18,480.00     $16,100.00     $17,290.00
        B03       $18,480.00     $18,480.00     $18,480.00     $18,480.00
        B04       $42,900.00     $21,780.00     $21,120.00     $21,450.00
        B14       $13,200.00     $13,200.00     $13,200.00     $13,200.00
```

productivity of programming professionals, while others are designed to be used directly by the end user. In very general terms, these languages are designed for specification of what needs to be accomplished, as opposed to the procedure-oriented languages which specify how. They represent a generalization of the problem-oriented programming facilities. Many fourth-generation languages use SQL (Structured Query Language) as the basic model for the language. An example of a simple program in a very high level language called FOCUS and the resulting output are shown in Figure 7-3.

Object-Oriented Languages

A programming language should aid the programmer in thinking about the information processing solution to a problem. Languages that emphasized numbers, algorithmic processes, and processing procedures are useful, but do they provide a good match with the way programmers think about the application? An object-oriented approach provides a different way to program. There are some object-oriented programming languages (such as C++) that support the approach, but the ideas can be implemented in some conventional languages.

The basic unit is an object, either concrete or abstract. The programmer describes the objects that are important to the program and specifies the actions each object can perform and the data associated with the object. In other words, an object has data and possible actions. In fact, the object stores the program that controls its behavior. Unlike some other programming approaches, there is no separation of data and actions.

In object programming, questions and requests (called messages) are given to an object. The object uses a set of procedures in its program (method) to act on a message. After defining objects and the data and methods associated with them, a program consists of messages to the objects (that act upon the messages). To illustrate the concept, assume a program object is a display screen used for input and editing of data. The input/edit screen object contains all of the procedures for responding to any message received by the screen. A programmer writes the messages to the screen object in the order that actions should be taken by it.

The reason object programming is of interest is that the notion of objects allows the definition and testing of objects with associated methods and data. Once an object has been well tested, it can be used in other programs. In maintenance, it is not difficult to isolate a fault, because the object contains both data and methods that caused a certain type of response. In other words, it is not necessary to look through the entire program to find out what happened when an object operated on a message; it is all in the message and the object.

THE STRUCTURE OF COMPUTER PROGRAMS

Software development is a complex human problem-solving activity. It is termed software engineering to highlight the systematic, engineering-like approach to development of complex products.

> Software entities are more complex for their size than perhaps any other human construct because no two parts are alike (at least above the statement level) . . . In this respect, software systems differ profoundly from computers, buildings, or automobiles, where repeated elements abound. (F. Brooks, "No Silver Bullet: Essence and Accident of Software Engineering," *Computer*, April, 1987, pp. 10-19.)

Dealing with Program Complexity

In a system approach to the problem of building an information system application, the complexity is handled by decomposing the problem so that

1. The system is organized into a hierarchy of subsystems,
2. The system is loosely coupled, and
3. The internal components of an individual system are tightly coupled.

The hierarchy of systems and relationships of subsystems are the basis for a design approach termed top-down or structured design. The concept is widely used; perhaps half of all development personnel use structured design. Based on the structured design, the software engineering approach applies structured methods to computer programs. During the process, there is emphasis on methods to reduce errors and ensure quality.

Some Program Definitions

Software consists of instructions or code organized into groups or modules. Programs of even small size can be too complex to be developed and maintained without some simplification of design. The simplification follows a basic engineering principle of division into modules based on tasks, functions, and actions to be performed.

Some major terms that describe software are explained below.

Program. A program is a set of instructions that performs the processing for a task. Examples of programs are Update the Payroll File, Depreciation Analysis, Apply Customer Payments to Accounts Receivable, and so forth.

Routine. A routine is a set of instructions within a program that performs a specific function. Routines are a way of subdividing the program into parts for purposes of development and maintenance. A routine is a program within a program.

Module. A module is a program building block consisting of a set of instructions. A module is often smaller than a routine, so that a routine may contain several modules.

Subprogram. A routine that is part of a library of routines. They are available for use in a program.

Subroutine. A routine that is designed to exist separately as a small program and is used (called) by another program when the function it performs is required. For example, a program doing simulation may need a sequence of random numbers. The program could be written with a routine to do random number generation or the program could have an instruction which calls upon a random number subroutine (available in a library of mathematical and statistical routines). The subroutine is made available to the main program by special instructions.

Macro instruction (macro). In writing a program, there are sequences of instructions that occur frequently with only some key parameters being changed. A macro instruction is a code word that creates the set of instructions and inserts them in the program. The term "macro" is used in microcomputer software to refer to a code word, defined by a user, that executes a set of instructions.

Reusability. This refers to the design of modules so that they can be used in any program requiring the processing performed by the modules. The reusable code modules support standardization. Since they are carefully checked for errors, they reduce potential program errors. They are stored in a code module library accessible by programmers.

Structured Program Design

Structured programming of software is based on the principle of decomposition and modular design. Key issues are the way modules are defined and the structure of the program itself. A structured program is a linear line-by-line representation of a hierarchical structure in which modules are part of routines that are part of programs (Figure 7-4). The program also represents (in linear fashion) program loops in which the program repeats actions until some condition is satisfied, then a different program path is chosen. The hierarchy of the program code is represented by comments, routine names, etc. Loops and selection of program paths are shown by indentations and other formatting. For example, Figure 7-5 shows a short section of a COBOL program that uses indentations and key words to represent a loop and a selection. A program flowchart segment is shown alongside to visually display the logic of the program code.

There are a number of conventions that are followed in structured coding of programs. The rules are too detailed for this text; the concept is simple. The idea is that programs should be modular with functions grouped, so that there are no unknown effects when a change is made. In other words, if a programmer makes a change in a module, there should be no instruction in some other module that affects the module being changed. If such a change occurs, it should be programmed so that it is very clear and apparent. Structured code is often called GOTOLESS programming because the flow of logic should move clearly from module to module rather than jumping around.

The effect of following structured coding conventions is a program that is clear and documented within the code itself. A programmer can use the code with minimal other documentation when making changes. This requires a significant number of comments as documentation lines within the program. Each module or logical set of code will have comment lines that explain its purpose. This may extend to comments before small groups of instructions.

FIGURE 7-4
Hierarchical Structure of a Computer Program

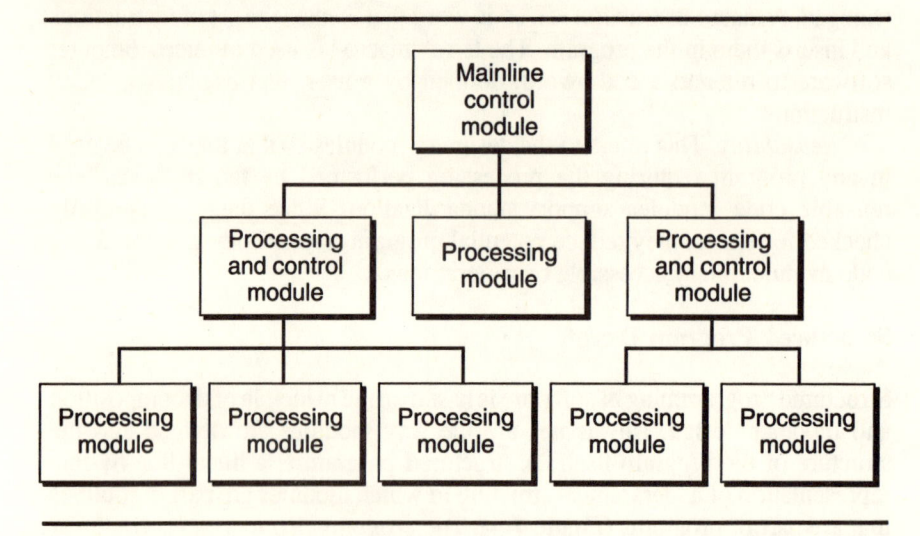

```
                    Mainline
                    control
                    module
         ┌─────────────┼─────────────┐
    Processing     Processing     Processing
    and control    module         and control
    module                        module
   ┌────┼────┐                   ┌────┼────┐
Processing Processing Processing Processing Processing
module     module     module     module     module
```

For example, a selection instruction may be preceded by a comment explaining the condition for selection and the alternative processing paths. The reason for the emphasis on self-documenting code by formatting and comment lines is the fact that the lines of code and related in-program comment lines are usually kept up to date, but outside documentation such as program flowcharts and narratives are often not updated and cannot be trusted.

Routines and Subroutines

When a program uses routines and subroutines, it further simplifies the design by reducing the interactions among parts of the program. The idea of a routine or subroutine is that control will be transferred from a mainline part of the program to a routine and when the routine has completed its processing, control will be returned to the mainline.

Routines and subroutines are conceptually very similar. The major difference is that a subroutine is usually more independent and constrains the interaction (in terms of data provided and results produced).

Object-oriented program design, explained earlier, is a variation on the concept of subroutines. A program object is somewhat similar to a subroutine in the sense of containing all data and procedures associated with the object when it is called by receiving a message.

FIGURE 7-5
Code Indentation and Key Words to Show Program Structure

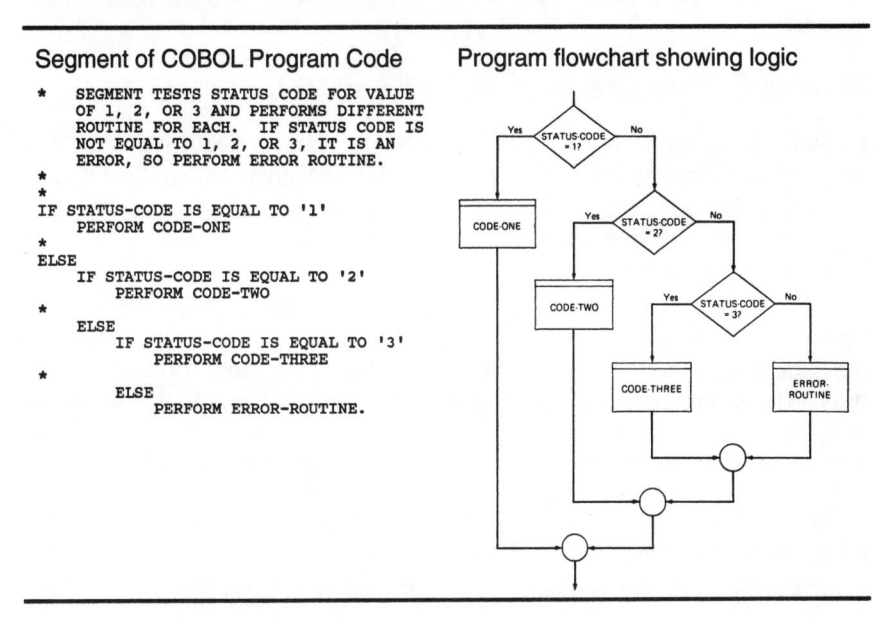

Segment of COBOL Program Code

```
*    SEGMENT TESTS STATUS CODE FOR VALUE
     OF 1, 2, OR 3 AND PERFORMS DIFFERENT
     ROUTINE FOR EACH.  IF STATUS CODE IS
     NOT EQUAL TO 1, 2, OR 3, IT IS AN
     ERROR, SO PERFORM ERROR ROUTINE.
*
*
IF STATUS-CODE IS EQUAL TO '1'
    PERFORM CODE-ONE
*
ELSE
    IF STATUS-CODE IS EQUAL TO '2'
        PERFORM CODE-TWO
*
    ELSE
        IF STATUS-CODE IS EQUAL TO '3'
            PERFORM CODE-THREE
*
        ELSE
            PERFORM ERROR-ROUTINE.
```

Program flowchart showing logic

INTRODUCTION TO SOME COMMONLY USED PROGRAMMING LANGUAGES

This section will provide an overview familiarity with a few of the commonly used languages. It is not a survey of the structure of the languages and the instruction sets. Rather, it describes the major characteristics of the languages and the types of problems for which they were designed.

C and C++

The C language is probably the most important programming language for microcomputer applications that need attention to machine characteristics to achieve high performance. It can be thought of as a high-level symbolic assembly language. Instructions can take into account machine level considerations, but there are a number of somewhat high level instructions to simplify programming. Programs written for one brand of microcomputer can be quite easily executed on another. In other words, the programs are portable.

The C++ language is a variation of the C language that incorporates principles of object-oriented programming. It has the advantage of being similar to the C language; it has the disadvantage of not meeting all of the conditions of object-oriented programming in order to keep its connection with C.

Common Business Oriented Language (COBOL)

COBOL is designed for typical business applications requiring repetitive processing of large numbers of data records. It is the most commonly used data processing language with perhaps 60 to 70 percent of all installed business applications written in this language. A simple but complete COBOL program is shown in Figure 7-6.

The structure of a COBOL program is based on the idea that the description of data to be used should be separate from the procedures that operate on the data. Also, general information about the program and information about the hardware environment on which the program will run are also separated from the data descriptions and the procedures. In the simple COBOL program in Figure 7-6, the four divisions of a COBOL program are shown.

- *Identification Division* is for documentation purposes and identifies the program and the date it was written and compiled.
- *Environment Division* contains two sections that specify the hardware environment for the program and associates file names in the program with program names defined by the operating system.
- *Data Division* describes files and individual data items. It separates the description of data from the procedures that operate on it. Input and outputs are defined with descriptive headings where they are to appear. The length of data items, the type of item, and initial value (if needed) are also specified by picture symbols.
- *Procedure Division* contains program sections and program procedures. The individual instruction lines are somewhat English-like. The data names are those defined in the Data Division. For example, a line such as ADD STORE-SALES TO STORE-SALES-TOTALS is intuitively obvious. The sales for an individual store are being added to a total for all stores.

Algorithmic Programming Languages

There are a number of languages designed for programming algorithms. They are used in applications where many computations are to be performed on a relatively small amount of numeric data. Examples of such languages are FORTRAN, PASCAL, BASIC, and APL.

FORTRAN (FORmula TRANslator) has been extensively used in mathematical and scientific programming. It is the language of choice for supercomputers and is frequently used in engineering applications. A sample computational statement in FORTRAN is:

FIGURE 7-6
Simple but Complete COBOL Program

```
IDENTIFICATION DIVISION.
PROGRAM-ID. PAYROLL-REPORT.
AUTHOR. GORDON B DAVIS.
    REMARKS.  SIMPLE COBOL PROGRAM TO READ HOURS-WORKED AND
        RATE-OF-PAY AND TO COMPUTE REGULAR-PAY, OVERTIME-PAY,
        AND GROSS-PAY.  OVERTIME-PAY IS ONE-AND-ONE-HALF THE
        REGULAR RATE FOR HOURS OVER 40.
ENVIRONMENT DIVISION.
CONFIGURATION SECTION.
SOURCE-COMPUTER. CYBER.
OBJECT-COMPUTER. CYBER.
INPUT-OUTPUT SECTION.
FILE-CONTROL.
    SELECT PAYROLL-FILE ASSIGN TO FILE1.
    SELECT PAYROLL-REPORT-FILE ASSIGN TO OUTFILE.
DATA DIVISION.
FILE SECTION.
FD  PAYROLL-FILE LABEL RECORD IS OMITTED
    DATA RECORD IS PAYROLL-RECORD.
01  PAYROLL-RECORD.
    05  PAYROLL-ID              PICTURE X(5).
    05  HOURS-WORKED            PICTURE 99.
    05  RATE-OF-PAY             PICTURE 9V999.
    05  FILLER                  PICTURE X(69).
FD  PAYROLL-REPORT-FILE LABEL RECORD IS OMITTED
    DATA RECORD IS PRINT-PAY-LINE.
01  PRINT-PAY-LINE.
    05  FILLER                  PICTURE X(10).
    05  PAYROLL-ID              PICTURE X(5).
    05  HOURS-WORKED            PICTURE ZZ99.
    05  RATE-OF-PAY             PICTURE ZZ9.999.
    05  REGULAR-PAY-PRINT       PICTURE $$$$$$9.99.
    05  OVERTIME-PAY-PRINT      PICTURE $$$$$$9.99.
    05  GROSS-PAY-PRINT         PICTURE $$$$$$9.99.
    05  FILLER                  PICTURE X(89).
WORKING-STORAGE SECTION.
    77  REGULAR-PAY             PICTURE S999V99.
    77  OVERTIME-PAY            PICTURE S999V99.
    77  GROSS-PAY               PICTURE S999V99.
    77  MORE-RECORDS            PICTURE X(3) VALUE "YES".
PROCEDURE DIVISION.
MAINLINE-ROUTINE.
    PERFORM INITIALIZATION.
    PERFORM PAY-PROCESSING UNTIL MORE-RECORDS EQUAL "NO".
    PERFORM CLOSING.
    STOP RUN.
INITIALIZATION.
    OPEN INPUT PAYROLL-FILE OUTPUT PAYROLL-REPORT-FILE.
    READ PAYROLL-FILE AT END MOVE "NO" TO MORE-RECORDS.
PAY-PROCESSING.
    IF HOURS-WORKED OF PAYROLL-RECORD IS GREATER THAN 40
        PERFORM PAY-CALCULATION-WITH-OVERTIME
    ELSE
        PERFORM PAY-CALCULATION-NO-OVERTIME.
    COMPUTE GROSS-PAY = REGULAR-PAY + OVERTIME-PAY.
    PERFORM WRITE-REPORT-LINE.
    READ PAYROLL-FILE AT END MOVE "NO" TO MORE-RECORDS.
PAY-CALCULATION-NO-OVERTIME.
    MULTIPLY HOURS-WORKED OF PAYROLL-RECORD BY RATE-OF-PAY OF
        PAYROLL-RECORD GIVING REGULAR-PAY ROUNDED.
    COMPUTE OVERTIME-PAY = 0.
PAY-CALCULATION-WITH-OVERTIME.
    MULTIPLY RATE-OF-PAY OF PAYROLL-RECORD BY 40 GIVING
        REGULAR-PAY ROUNDED.
    COMPUTE OVERTIME-PAY ROUNDED = ((HOURS-WORKED OF
        PAYROLL-RECORD - 40) * 1.5 * RATE-OF-PAY OF
        PAYROLL-RECORD).
WRITE-REPORT-LINE.
    MOVE SPACES TO PRINT-PAY-LINE.
    MOVE CORRESPONDING PAYROLL-RECORD TO PRINT-PAY-LINE.
    MOVE REGULAR-PAY TO REGULAR-PAY-PRINT.
    MOVE OVERTIME-PAY TO OVERTIME-PAY-PRINT.
    MOVE GROSS-PAY TO GROSS-PAY-PRINT.
    WRITE PRINT-PAY-LINE.
CLOSING.
    CLOSE PAYROLL-FILE, PAYROLL-REPORT-FILE.
```

$$X = SQRT\ (Y+Z-(ALPHA**2))$$

This means that the variable ALPHA is squared and subtracted from the sum of Y plus Z. The square root of the result is stored as the value of the variable X.

PASCAL (named after the mathematician) is widely used in instruction because it enforces elements of good programming style. It is not as widely used in practice.

BASIC is a very simple language to learn and use. It contains only eleven fundamental statements. It is the most widely used procedure-oriented language for personal computers.

APL (A Programming Language) is an interactive language for algorithmic processing. It is especially powerful in programming computational procedures involving vectors and matrices.

Structured Query Language (SQL)

SQL is a language for programming in connection with a relational database. It is important because of the extent of use, the fact that it can be used across a large number of computer types and sizes, and that it has been standardized.

Using relational concepts, SQL can be used to program retrievals from a relational database. Data can be combined in various ways and data selected using various criteria. SQL also provides facilities for data entry, report formatting, and other procedures to produce an application.

LESSONS FOR MANAGERS

Software consists of sets of instructions that are not permanently stored in the computer. Application software refers to software programs written for an individual application such as payroll processing or personnel skill analysis. A platform of hardware and software supports the use of application software. The hardware has an operating system that supports hardware use by the application programs; three other software systems in the platform supporting application use are user interface software, communications software, and database software. Development software is provided by general purpose software packages and programming language facilities.

Three approaches to acquisition or development of application software are commercial application packages, general-purpose application generator packages, and programming languages. The first has classic make or buy implications and questions of tailoring and customization. The second approach is more likely to be used with smaller applications or end-user applications. The use of packages has management issues related to portability, company package decisions versus individual package decisions, and policy questions relative to use of freeware, shareware, or pirate software.

The third approach of programming languages is used in large-scale inhouse applications development and is the way packages are developed. There are different levels of programming languages. The lowest level is a symbolic assembly language close to the machine level, the middle level is a language oriented to the procedures and steps in processing or problem solving (such as COBOL), and the third level consists of problem-oriented programming facilities and very high level language (often called fourth generation languages or 4GLs) designed to focus on describing the output to be achieved or the problem to be solved (rather than detailed processing or solution procedures). Object-oriented programming is a fairly new approach that centers program design around program objects each of which encapsulates all the data and procedures associated with it.

Software engineering is a systematic approach to the development of quality software. The hierarchy of systems and relationships of subsystems in applications are the basis for a design approach termed top-down or structured design. The software engineering approach also applies structured methods to computer programs. The process follows a basic engineering principle for dealing with complexity by division into modules, routines, and subroutines based on tasks, functions, and actions to be performed.

For business purposes, the most common programming languages are COBOL (for data processing) and FORTRAN and BASIC for algorithmic processes. Structured Query Language (SQL) is a language for databases.

CHAPTER 8

APPLICATION DEVELOPMENT AND IMPLEMENTATION

There are different strategies for developing an information system application; the best approach depends on the situation. For each development strategy, there are methodologies for performing and managing the process. One difficulty with development strategies and methodologies is that they tend to ignore resistance associated with organizational change; they assume a well-designed, well-engineered system will be accepted and used.

The chapter explains four approaches to the development of an application: traditional, prototyping, package, and end-user. Each approach is described in terms of a system development life cycle (SDLC) that delineates the flow of work, decisions, and deliverables starting with project initiation and extending to the maintenance of the system after installation.

Automated methods, called CASE tools, are explained. Implementation of systems for application development and the issues of overcoming resistance are explored. A simple model of quality for the results from application development is introduced.

APPLICATION DEVELOPMENT METHODOLOGIES AND STRATEGIES

Methodologies are based on the concept of an application development cycle of activities. The way that the steps in the cycle are defined and the methods included will depend on the development perspective employed. The organization of the steps in development, the emphasis on each step, and omission of certain steps will depend on the development strategy or development approach. There are four major development strategies. They are introduced in this section and explained more fully in the sections that follow.

Development Methodology and Development Strategy

The development of an application can be conceptualized as a cycle starting with initiation of a project through design and building to implementation and finally to evolution through corrections and changes. This logical cycle of processes and events is termed a *system development life cycle* (SDLC). The concept of an SDLC is achieved through a *development methodology*.

A development methodology provides a well-defined process by which an application is conceived, developed, and implemented. The methodology gives structure to a creative process. In order to manage and control the development effort, it is necessary to know what should have been done, what has been done, and what has yet to be accomplished. The phases in the system development methodology provide a basis for management and control because they segment the flow of work into phases for managerial purposes and specify the documents or other deliverables to be produced in each phase.

There is a difference between a development methodology and a development strategy. A development strategy defines how much trial and error should be incorporated into development efforts, how much of the development effort will be original work versus building from existing work, and whether parts of the methodology can be eliminated or simplified. In other words, the strategy addresses the issue of how the development methodology should be modified to fit the situation. For users and developers, the first issue to be decided is the strategy or approach to development, because it determines what activities are needed. Having selected a strategy, the methodology helps to plan and manage the conduct of the activities.

Methodology Perspectives

All methodologies are similar, but there are differences in perspective. Three major perspectives are process-oriented, data-oriented, and behavior-oriented.[1]

The process-oriented perspective is the traditional one. The emphasis is on defining the functions to be performed and the flow of work. The data-oriented perspective is based on the idea that data requirements should be the primary basis for design. It is associated with the availability of database technology. The behavior-oriented perspective is a response to applications that require careful attention to the order and timing of events. This could also be termed a time-dependent or temporal perspective.

Since all methodologies must accomplish the same objective, what is the effect of the perspective taken? One perspective is dominant in the design of

---

[1] W. T. Olle, J. Hagelstein, I. G. Macdonald, C. Rolland, H. G. Sol, F. J. M. Van Assche, and A. A. Verrijn-Stuart, *Information Systems Methodologies: A Framework for Understanding*, second edition, Assison-Wesley Publishing Company, Workingham, England, 1991.

the methodology, but all perspectives must be used in development. A methodology may have process as the dominant perspective, but data requirements must still be described and temporal behavior of the systems defined. In other words, the effect of the methodology perspective is primarily on the way tasks are defined and the order in which they are accomplished and the emphasis on some issues. It may also affect the ease with which the methodology can be used for certain types of problems.

Four Development Strategies

There are four main strategies that determine how methodologies will be applied.

Traditional approach. This strategy incorporates a linear flow of activities starting with the initiation of the project and requirements determination. Underlying the traditional approach are two assumptions: there is a stable set of requirements that can be obtained and documented, and users can verify that the development project is on track from abstract specifications and representations of progress.

Prototyping approach. This strategy emphasizes explicit iterations (rather than a linear flow of activities) in development based on prototypes that can be examined and tried out by users. The prototyping approach overcomes the difficulties of the traditional approach when requirements are not stable (or being formulated) or cannot easily be determined because users find it difficult to specify them. It also works well when users must see and try out concrete prototypes in order to verify the development project is on track in meeting needs.

Package approach. This strategy emphasizes the use of application software packages as the starting point for design and development. It is similar to the prototyping approach because of the existence of concrete representations and opportunities to try out the system. The difference is that most of the development has been done.

End user development approach. This strategy emphasizes a simplified approach to end-user application development. The end-user development approach is most applicable for small applications for a microcomputer and may also be applied with either the prototyping or package approach. Small end-user developed applications do not require the extensive controls of the traditional approach.

TRADITIONAL APPROACH TO APPLICATION DEVELOPMENT

A significant amount of new development work involves major operational applications of broad scope. The application systems are large and highly structured. User task comprehension and developer task proficiency are usually

Application Development and Implementation   159

FIGURE 8-1
The Application System Development Strategies

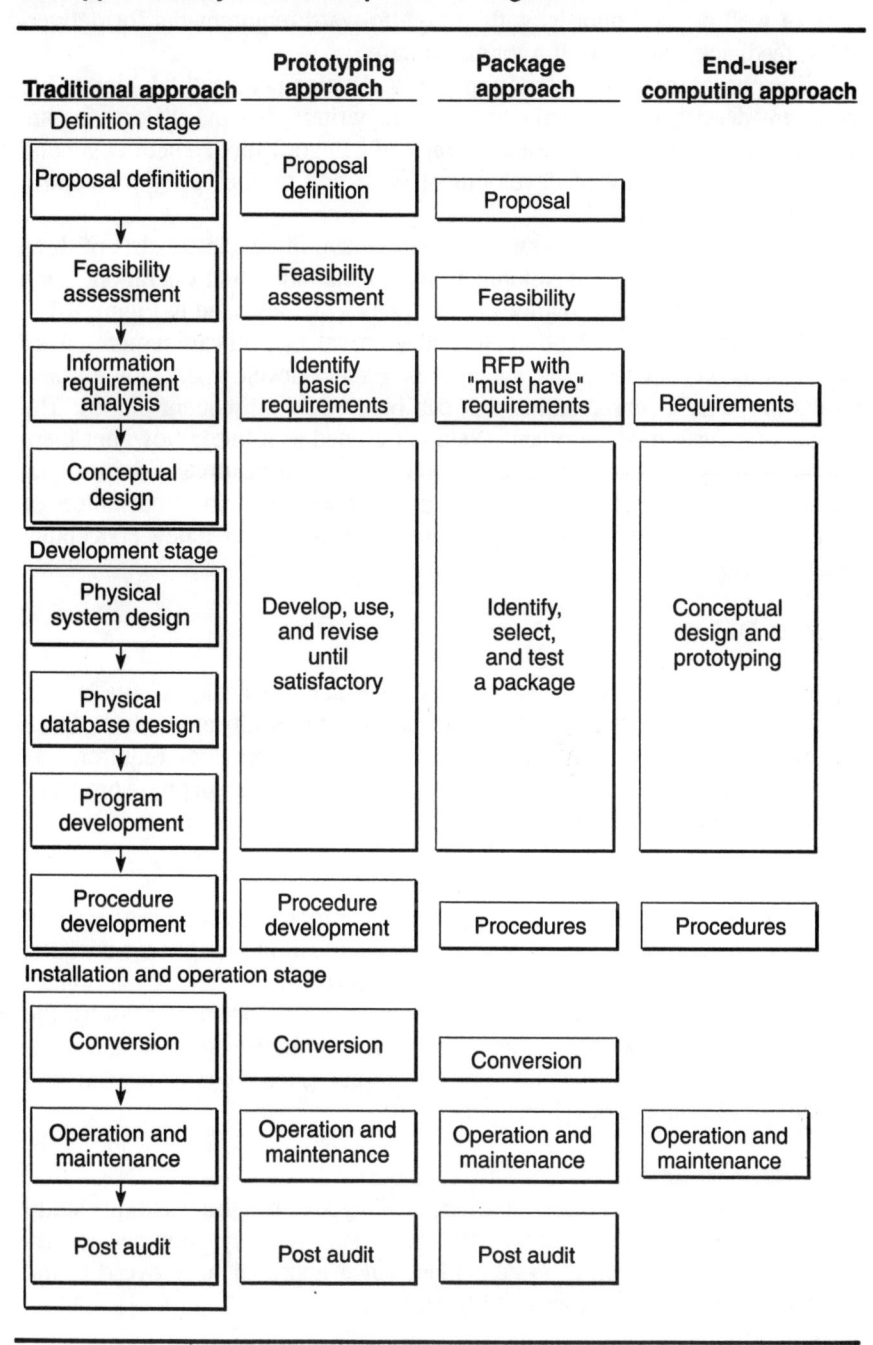

Traditional approach	Prototyping approach	Package approach	End-user computing approach
Definition stage			
Proposal definition	Proposal definition	Proposal	
Feasibility assessment	Feasibility assessment	Feasibility	
Information requirement analysis	Identify basic requirements	RFP with "must have" requirements	Requirements
Conceptual design			
Development stage			
Physical system design	Develop, use, and revise until satisfactory	Identify, select, and test a package	Conceptual design and prototyping
Physical database design			
Program development			
Procedure development	Procedure development	Procedures	Procedures
Installation and operation stage			
Conversion	Conversion	Conversion	
Operation and maintenance	Operation and maintenance	Operation and maintenance	Operation and maintenance
Post audit	Post audit	Post audit	

high. These factors suggest a traditional approach as a development strategy. In this approach, a comprehensive development methodology follows a linear flow of well-defined phrases with straightforward requirements for deliverables, feedback, and sign-off after each phase.

The phases in the traditional application development methodology or life cycle are described differently by different writers, but the differences are primarily in amount of detail and manner of categorization. There is general agreement on the flow of development steps and the necessity for control procedures at each stage.

A traditional application system development life cycle consists of three major stages: definition, development, and installation and operation. Each stage can be divided into smaller steps or phases as illustrated in Figure 8-1.

At completion of each phase, formal approval sign-offs are required from the users as well as from the manager of project development. Each phase results in formal documentation that can be used in subsequent phases. The information system development cycle is outlined as a linear flow, but there can be an iteration to go back to a prior phase for modifications. For example, the review after the physical design phase may result in cancellation or continuation, but it may also result in going back to prepare a new conceptual design.

Stage 1: Definition

A proposal represents the first step in a development life cycle. After a project is proposed, the next step in the definition stage is feasibility assessment. Once a proposed alternative is approved, the next phase is information requirements analysis. Following requirements analysis, a conceptual design phase produces a high-level design emphasizing the application as seen by its users.

Proposal Definition
Proposals may be for entirely new applications or for enhancements to existing applications. A proposal provides sufficient justification to support a decision to proceed with a feasibility analysis. The proposal might include the organizational need for or benefit from the application (the business reason), the requirements for organizational support (such as a budget, sponsor, and management support), and schedule considerations (such as date needed and availability of user and developer personnel).

Feasibility Assessment
When a new application is proposed, it normally goes through a feasibility study before it is approved for development. The feasibility study examines consistency with the information system plan, since approval may override the priorities of other applications already planned.

Five types of feasibility should be addressed in the feasibility study. Both risks and benefits should be recognized in each factor.

Technical feasibility. Can the proposed application be implemented with existing technology? The analysis of project risk relative to technical feasibility includes not only whether the technology is available on the market but also the degree to which it is "state of the art," both in absolute terms and relative to the company's current technical sophistication.

Economic feasibility. Will the system provide benefits greater than the costs? The feasibility study presents intangible as well as tangible benefits in a formal way. A relatively detailed analysis of the costs of both development and operations of the various alternatives should be presented.

Motivational feasibility. This identifies the probability that the organization is sufficiently motivated to support the development and implementation of the application with necessary user participation, resources, training time, and so forth. This motivation is usually demonstrated by an owner or champion for the application who has sufficient organizational power to marshall the resources and motivate others to assist and cooperate.

Schedule feasibility. This identifies the probability that the organization can complete the development process in the time allowed for development.

Operational feasibility. Will it work when installed? This analysis may involve a subjective assessment of the political and managerial environment in which the system will be implemented. In general, the greater the requirements for change in the user environment in which the system will be installed, the greater the risk of implementation failure.

Once the feasibility study has been accepted, information requirements analysis can begin.

Information Requirements Analysis

The information requirements analysis phase defines the reports (including the data items on the reports), queries (both regular and ad hoc), conceptual schema for database (from data modeling or other analysis), functional requirements (including operational characteristics), and user interface requirements. This information is used in subsequent phases to develop the application. It is one of the most critical steps in the development life cycle (for any strategy). The process of information requirements analysis is described in more detail in Chapter 9.

Conceptual Design

The conceptual design emphasizes the application as seen by those who will operate or use the outputs of the system. It is different than physical design (the next phase) that translates requirements into specifications for implementing the system. In general terms, conceptual design treats the actual processing functions as "black boxes"; physical design specifies the actual processing functions.

Typical contents of a conceptual design are the following:

- A user-oriented application description that documents the flow of the application activities through the organizational units providing inputs and using outputs and that distinguishes manual operations from automated operations performed by the application system. Figure 8-2 shows a simplified process-oriented description (dataflow diagram) for a diet drink manufacturer.
- Inputs for the application with a general description of each input (such as visual display screens, source documents, forms, and queries).
- Outputs produced by the application with a general description of each output (such as visual display screens, query responses, printed outputs, and reports).
- Functions to be performed by the application system.
- A general flow of processing with relationships of major programs, files, inputs, and outputs.
- Outlines of operating manuals, user manuals, and training materials needed for the application.
- Audit and control procedures for ensuring appropriate quality in the use and operation of the application.

Stage 2: Development

The development stage of the application system development life cycle consists of four classes of activity that may occur somewhat concurrently: physical system design, physical database design, program development, and procedure development.

Physical System Design

The physical system design phase, also called internal or detailed design, consists of activities to prepare the detailed technical design of the application system. The physical system design is based on the information requirements and the conceptual design. In turn, it provides the basis for physical database design, program development, and procedure development. Testing should be defined as a separate phase. However, testing is really part of each phase. Some life cycles include physical database design in the physical system design phase. However, the trend is toward more independence between programs and data and specialized skills are often required for physical database design, so physical database design is considered a separate design phase in this explanation. The results of the physical system design phase are specifications and designs for the following:

- System design showing flow of work, programs, and user functions.

Application Development and Implementation **163**

FIGURE 8-2
Dataflow Diagram for Process-oriented Description

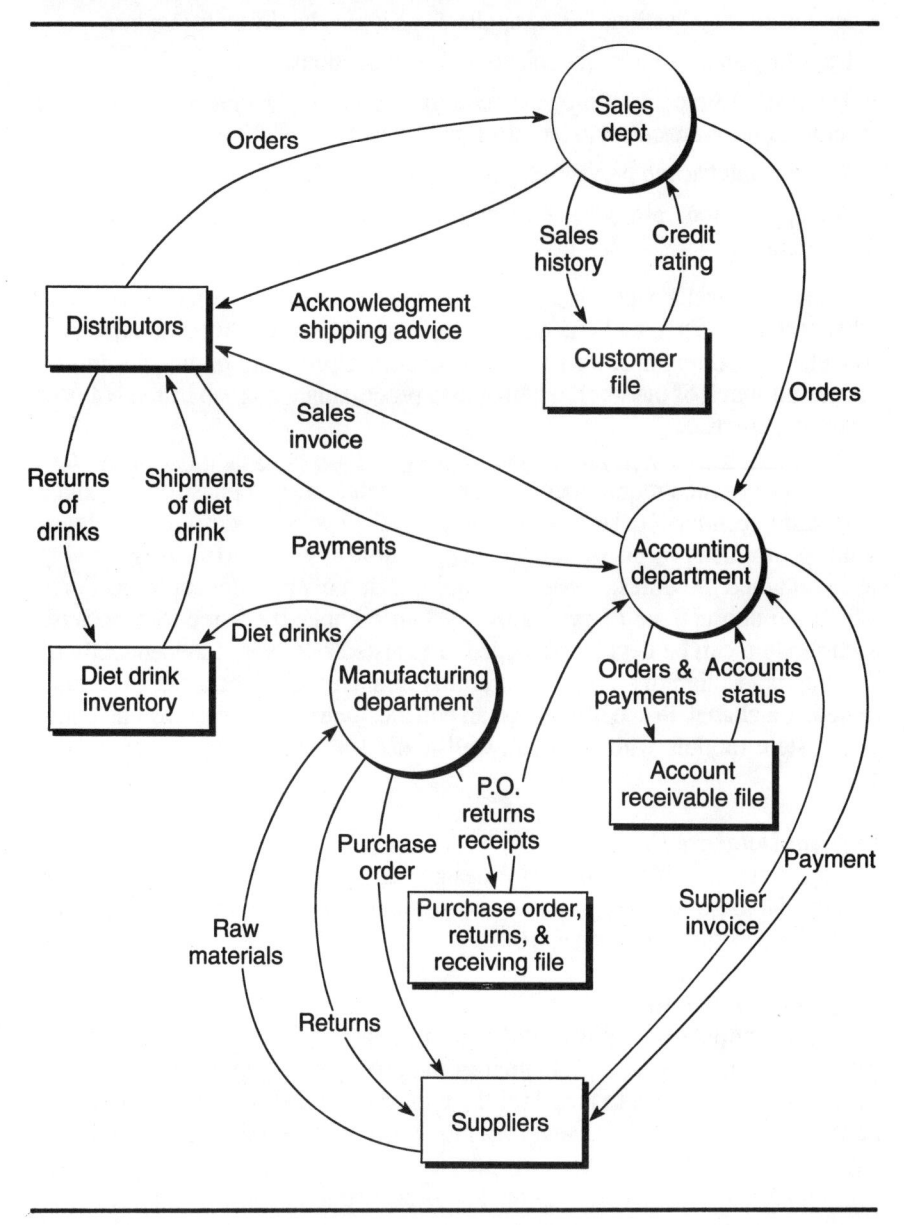

- Control design showing controls to be implemented at various points in the flow of processing.
- Hardware specifications for the applications if new hardware is required.
- Data communications requirements and specifications.
- The overall structure of programs required by the application with procedural specifications on functions to be performed by each.
- Security and backup provisions.
- An application test or quality assurance plan for the remainder of the development.

The physical system design work is performed by systems analysts and other technical personnel (such as controls specialists, quality assurance personnel, data communications specialists, etc.). Users may participate in this phase, but much of the work requires data processing expertise instead of user function expertise.

The work of the physical system design phase is to take the fairly high level, user-oriented requirements of the conceptual design phase and produce a specific technical design. Generally, physical system design techniques achieve simplicity by subdividing the application system into small, relatively self-contained modules. System modules can be programs or procedures which are subsections of programs. System complexity is reduced because each module can be developed, coded, and tested relatively independently of the others. Reliability and modifiability are enhanced because a change (whether a change in specifications, an enhancement, or a repair) can be made to a system module with minimal, well-understood effects on the rest of the system.

Physical Database Design
The approach to physical database design for an application depends on the existing database and the approach followed for database requirements determination, as described in Chapter 10.

Program Development
A primary output of the physical design process is a set of specifications that define programming tasks. The goal of the program development phase is to code and test programs required for the application. Testing of each module is performed on test data representing a fairly complete set of variations in input data in the user environment.

Problems encountered during the programming phase are typically a result of incomplete specifications provided during conceptual or physical design. This often results in extensive reprogramming efforts. The techniques for formalizing the conceptual and physical design process are aimed at alleviating this problem. Another problem in this phase is inadequate program testing prior to system test and conversion. A number of program development techniques reduce program complexity and aid in achieving program correctness. Important examples are structured design and structural coding.

Testing represents a critical factor in application development. It can take from 15 to 50 percent of the total development effort depending on the size and complexity of the application. Formal approaches to system testing involve a discipline which begins early in the program development phase. Program designs and program coding are usually reviewed by peers in a "walk through" process. A senior or chief programmer in charge of a team may also review the work of members of the team. There are three distinct phases of program testing as the parts of an application are developed separately and assembled:

1. *Module testing.* Each individual program module is tested.

2. *Integration testing.* Groups of program modules are tested together to determine if they interface properly. This may be done incrementally as they are developed until the entire program is tested.

3. *System testing.* This involves testing of the complete set of programs for an application.

It is useful to distinguish between reliability and correctness for programs. A *correct* program meets specifications; a *reliable* program operates in an acceptable manner under both intended and unintended input data and operating conditions. In other words, a reliable program will perform satisfactorily (even to the extent of rejecting further processing) under a wide range of correct and incorrect inputs. A correct program need only perform satisfactorily as long as the inputs are as specified. Reliability of programs is therefore a broader and more useful concept.

Procedure Development

Procedure development (manuals, instruction sheets, input forms, and HELP screens) can take place concurrently with program development. Procedures should be written for all personnel who have contact with the system. This includes the following:

1. *Primary managerial users.* This includes instructions for how to interpret a report and how to select different options for a report. If the user can execute the system directly, as in online queries, it includes detailed instructions for accessing the system and formulating different types of queries.

2. *Secondary data entry users.* This includes detailed instructions on how to enter each kind of input. It is more oriented to "how to" and less to "what" for different inputs (when compared with the instructions to primary users).

3. *Computer operating personnel.* These are procedures to be performed by computer operators and/or control personnel. Procedures include instructions for quality assurance, backing up system files, and maintaining program documentation.

Stage 3: Installation and Operation

The third stage of the application system development life cycle begins with conversion to the new application system. After the system is in use, changes and enhancements are made during the operation and maintenance phase of the system. Periodically, a post audit of the system may be conducted; based on this activity, the system may be modified, enhanced, or replaced.

Conversion

Conversion to the new application system begins after all programs and procedures have been prepared and individually tested. Three major activities prepare for actual conversion: acceptance testing, file building, and user training.

Acceptance testing is testing of the completed application and comparing it to specifications. The acceptance test should have been developed as part of the planning for the system. It verifies to the user that the system meets performance criteria and operational requirements. The testing includes user inputs, operating and control procedures, and outputs. Differences between what users expected and what the system delivers are identified and resolved.

File building refers to the collection and conversion of data to machine-readable form, and input of all new data required by the application.

User training may be relatively straightforward or a critical effort, depending on the degree to which the new application system affects existing jobs. If techniques such as job design are used, training will involve substantial reorientation of the users to their jobs.

If the system is to replace an existing one, conversion can be accomplished using a parallel run approach, or an immediate cutover. In a parallel approach the new system is run under actual conditions and the results are compared with the old system for reliability and accuracy. After the new system has shown consistent results for a reasonable period of time it becomes operational and the old system is dropped. The drawback to this method is that it is expensive; both machines and employees work double time. Machine time can be costly if new hardware is replacing old and both must be maintained. More important, employees are required to perform essentially two full-time jobs, one of them being new and unfamiliar. Moreover, if the system has not been sufficiently tested and errors are detected during conversion, costly delays and employee frustration can cause serious problems.

In an immediate cutover approach, there are very serious consequences if the new system does not work adequately or well. Therefore, the new system should be tested extensively under simulated conditions. In one approach to testing, representative users meet to walk through the operation of the new system. After a given cutover date, only the new system is used. The immediate cutover approach avoids the drawbacks of the parallel approach but requires more testing and walkthroughs.

Operation and Maintenance

Maintenance of an application can be classified as corrective, perfective, and adaptive. Corrective maintenance repairs defects. Perfective maintenance improves or enhances the system. Adaptive maintenance makes changes in response to changing needs for the application. Corrective repairs typically dominate the maintenance activity for the first few months of operation. Later, most of the maintenance is perfective or adaptive. Sometimes maintenance is performed by the system developers, but often it is the responsibility of a separate maintenance group.

Post Audit

A useful part of the system development life cycle for major applications is a review of the application after it has been in operation for a period, such as a year. An audit team with representatives from users, development, maintenance, operations, and perhaps internal audit review the operation, use, cost, and benefits of the application. Recommendations from a post audit include specific recommendations for dropping, repairing, or enhancing an application and suggestions for improving the development process on subsequent applications.

PROTOTYPING APPROACH TO APPLICATION SYSTEM DEVELOPMENT

The prototyping approach to application system development is especially useful when requirements are difficult to specify in advance or when requirements may change significantly during development. The prototyping approach is based on the simple proposition that people can express what they like or do not like about an existing application system more easily than they can express what they think about an imagined, future system. Unlike the linear traditional approach, prototyping employs small iterative steps to evolve toward a working system.

A Model of the Prototyping Process

Prototyping an application system is basically a four-step process, as described below and depicted in Figure 8-3. It is assumed that the feasibility assessment has been completed prior to the four-step process. There are two significant roles in the process: the user and the system designer.

Step 1: Identify the user's basic information requirements. In this stage, the user articulates his or her basic needs in terms of output from the system. The designer's responsibility is to establish realistic user expectations and to estimate the cost of developing an operational prototype. The required data

FIGURE 8-3
**Application System Prototype Development Model
(Adapted from A. Milton Jenkins)**

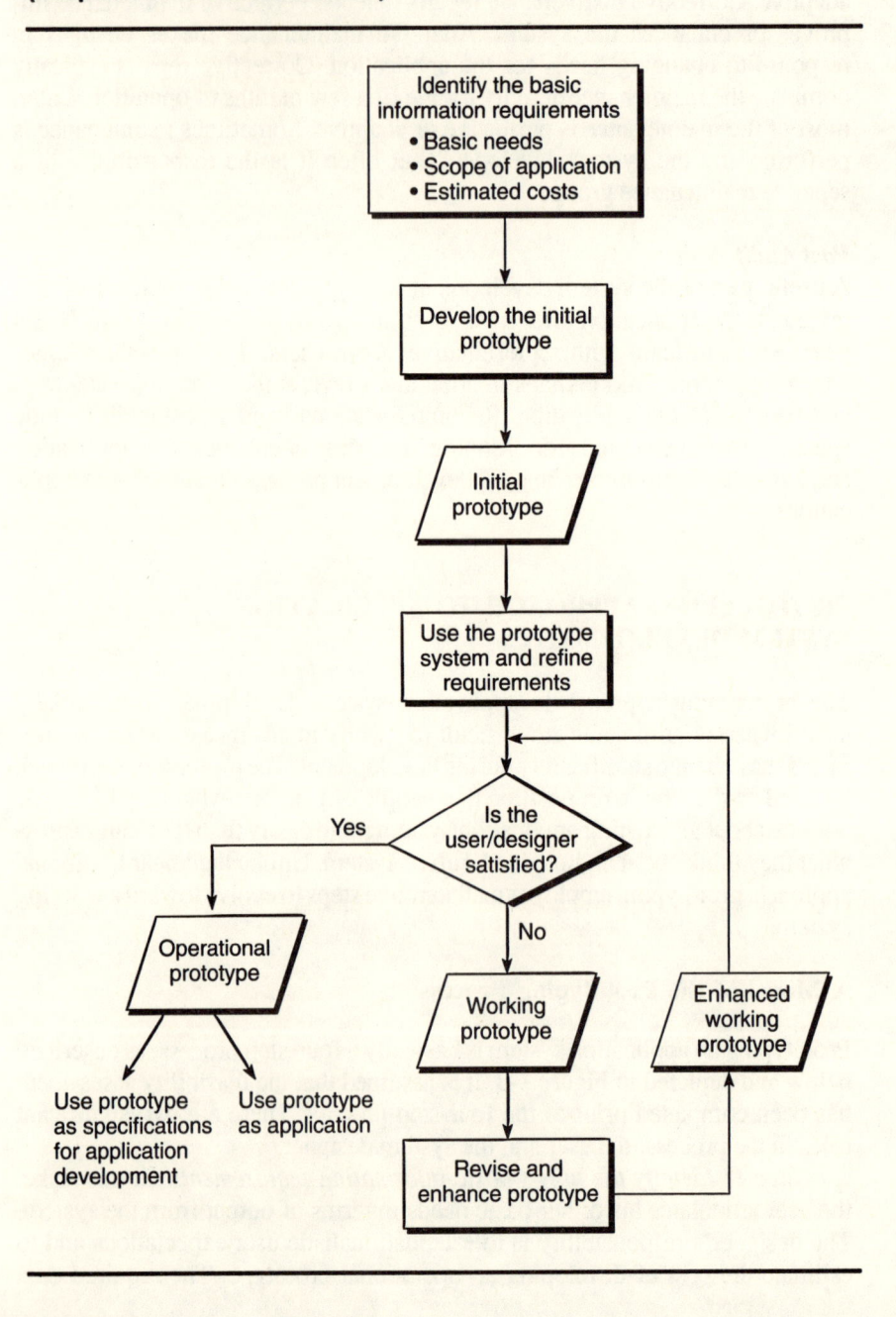

elements are defined and their availability determined. The basic models to be computerized are kept as simple as possible.

Step 2: Develop the initial prototype system. The objective of this step is to build an application that meets the user's basic stated information requirements. The system designer has the responsibility for building the application using very high level development languages or other development tools. Emphasis is placed on speed of building rather than efficiency of operation. The initial prototype responds only to the user's basic requirements; it is understood to be incomplete.

Step 3: Use of the prototype system to refine user requirements. This step allows the user to gain hands-on experience with the application in order to understand his or her information needs and what the system does and does not do to meet those needs. It is expected that the user will find problems with the first version. The user rather than the designer decides when changes are necessary and thus controls the overall development time.

Step 4: Revise and enhance the prototype system. The designer makes requested changes using the same principles as stated in step 2. Only the changes the user requests are made. The emphasis is on speed in modifying the system and returning it to the user.

> *Example.* In a variation of the prototyping approach, a package may be used as a prototype. After obtaining the software package on a loan or rental basis, the users can build a sample database with data from their organization and then run the system through several scenarios reflecting their business processes. This allows them to learn about the application, increase understanding of the tasks, and develop requirements. They may then choose to develop an in-house application or follow a package approach.
>
> This prototype approach was employed at a New Zealand manufacturer. A standard MRP software package was used to provide users and developers an increased understanding of how a formal planning and control system could be used. An external consultant helped build a prototype database that was used in a one-week hands-on training session about MRP concepts applied to the organization. Following use of the prototype system, the project team defined requirements for their planning and control information system.

As illustrated in Figure 8-2, steps 3 and 4 are iterative. The number of iterations may vary considerably. There may be two reasons for stopping iterative modification. First, the user determines that the prototype is not useful and the working prototype is discarded. Second, the user is satisfied with the system and it becomes an "operational prototype." It may be modified at a later stage, but at this point it is considered usable and may be distributed to other users. Alternatively, it may "seed" the idea of a new application and be used to provide initial specifications for the application development effort.

Evaluation of the Prototyping Approach

The prototyping approach, as outlined above, has several significant advantages in development of applications having high uncertainty as to requirements:

- Ability to "try out" ideas without incurring large costs.
- Lower overall development costs when requirements change frequently.
- The ability to get a functioning system into the hands of the user quickly.
- Effective division of labor between the user professional and the MIS professional.
- Reduced application development time to achieve a functioning system.
- Effective utilization of scarce (human) resources.

A major difficulty with prototyping is management of the development process because of frequent changes. Also, there may be a tendency to accept a prototype as the final product when it should only be the basis for a fully specified design. For example, a prototype may not handle all exceptions or be complete as to controls. It "works," but it is not complete.

SOFTWARE PACKAGE APPROACH TO APPLICATION DEVELOPMENT

Many firms lack the resources, expertise, and time to develop application software. Application packages represent a viable alternative to inhouse development when an appropriate solution is commercially available.

Conceptually, the package approach is an extension of the prototyping approach, since one or more implementations of the application exist and can be tested by the prospective users. However, a major difference is that the users are restricted to the features in the packages being reviewed.

The development methodology for the package approach follows the same definition phases as the traditional approach: proposal definition, feasibility assessment, and information requirements analysis. The requirements from the definition phases are typically supplemented with considerations about development and operation. For example, the application software may need to run on a specific operating system, database management system, or local area network. The requirements may also include considerations such as ease of installation, ease of use, stability of vendor, local availability of support and education programs, end user documentation, frequency of enhancements and upgrades, and nature of user groups.

Identifying and Selecting a Package

The requirements from the requirements definition phase form the basis for writing a request for proposal (RFP) that can be used to solicit proposals from software vendors. While an exhaustive RFP may seem desirable, it is usually more useful to focus on the critical "must have" and the important "desirable" requirements, because these will aid in differentiating potential software packages. A fairly short RFP (say 15 pages) should reflect these differentiating requirements. It helps in reducing potential package vendors to a small number for detailed evaluation.

Identifying potential package vendors for an application is a tradeoff between a broad search process that will identify many potential vendors and the need to deal with a small number in evaluating the proposals. For most situations, a selective distribution of the RFP is more productive.

Responses to the RFP can be evaluated against the requirements to reduce the number of contenders. After reducing the number of proposals for detailed evaluation to a small set, formal presentations are scheduled. As part of the formal presentation, each vendor should provide the company with a "test drive" of the package. The vendor is provided with a representative set of data and demonstrates the package using the data. This will provide a test of how well the package fits the organization conditions; it also allows some assessment of the required modifications and the difficulties of interfacing with existing systems. Representative users should be involved.

As part of the data collection for the selection decision, it is helpful to call and/or visit similar organizations that have installed the package. Their experiences will provide data on the quality of the vendor as a business partner. User groups will often provide lists of needed enhancements they have requested. These can be reviewed for important weaknesses.

The final selection is based on how well the package meets requirements and an assessment of the vendor as a business partner. It is virtually impossible to find a package that meets all requirements; decisions must be made about either relaxing some requirements or arranging for customized additions. As discussed in Chapter 7, it is important to minimize customization because unique features added to a package will add to the cost and difficulty of using vendor upgrades and support.

The selection of an application software package typically eliminates the need for conceptual design, physical system design, database design, and program development. Following vendor recommendations for hardware and systems software minimizes potential problems in operations, in using vendor support, and in utilizing future upgrades to the software packages.

Implementation of a Software Package

The procedure development phase is still required with a package. An application package should provide a major portion of the procedures, such as user manuals, sample input forms, online help screens, and training material. However, these must be supplemented by procedures for using and operating the package in the organization. Vendors sometimes offer assistance for this phase.

Conversion includes acceptance testing, file building, and user training. Training classes are usually available from the software package vendor. Vendor or consultant assistance may be utilized in the conversion to ensure that the software functions properly, business processes have a good fit, and common mistakes in the implementation process are avoided.

Maintenance of the application software package is generally provided by the vendor as part of a customer support program. The ongoing support includes upgrades to software and documentation, telephone hotline assistance, membership in a user group, newsletter, and perhaps electronic bulletin boards.

A post audit can provide useful internal feedback on the operation, use, costs, and benefits of the package. It can also result in suggestions for the software vendor.

SIMPLIFIED DEVELOPMENT APPROACH FOR END-USER COMPUTING

End-user computing is the development of applications by users (such as managers, accountants, financial analysts, sales representative, and so forth) rather than by professional information system specialists. The development is usually on microcomputers using generalized software packages that generate applications, such as a spreadsheet processor or database package. The applications may be ad hoc and discarded after one use, saved for repeated use by a single person, used by several people in a work group, or used across the organization.

> *Example.* An electronics manufacturer had monthly sales and operations planning meetings. To make the meetings effective, the manufacturing manager developed a spreadsheet model to analyze actual and planned sales, production, inventory, and shipments by product family by month. The spreadsheet became a critical tool in the meeting by providing summarized historical data and simulating the impact of future plans.
>
> This end-user approach to a sales and operations plan originally had important weaknesses. All data items were manually entered into the spreadsheet and the results were then manually keyed as input into the company's MRP system. The manufacturing manager was the only one who understood the logic and the application was not well documented. Its operation was constrained by the

manager's time availability. Company personnel revised the spreadsheet model to improve the design and to integrate it with the MRP system. Documentation was developed. The spreadsheet is now widely used by all managers.

The advantages of user-developed systems are impressive. However, standards, documentation, controls, testing, interfaces with other systems, and so forth may be neglected. In some cases, these omissions are not important; in other cases, they are a source of significant risk to the organization. Users developing their own systems may significantly underestimate the probability of errors and discount the need for and value of quality assurance and testing procedures, particularly if the systems are designed primarily for their own use.

Example. An example of unacceptable risk in end-user computing is the financial reporting section of the accounting function for a large multinational company. A PC financial modeling package was used to do the analysis and reports associated with its financial statements. More than 200 routines were written for this purpose. However, all the routines were written by one person; no one else in the accounting function understood the package or the programs. The programs themselves were apparently well done and contained documentation lines with them, but there was no external documentation explaining the purpose and logic of the routines and providing a listing. If the accountant/programmer had become ill, died, or resigned, the analysis and reporting activities could not have been performed properly.

Because of the advantages of user-developed systems, organizational policy should normally encourage this approach. However, policies should also establish that each user has responsibility for appropriate quality assurance and provide guidelines for quality. Development procedures, especially with respect to quality, should be based on the intended users of the application and the importance of the decisions from its use. Intended users may be the developer only, the developer plus other colleagues in the same department, or a variety of users across the organization. The need for formal development procedures increases as the scope of use increases. The importance of the decisions that will be influenced by the analysis may range from small to very large, and the need for quality assurance rises with the increase in importance.

For applications that will have continuing broad use either in a department or across the organization, an end-user computing development approach (Figure 8-1 on page 159) should be followed. The development process starts with some requirements that are not usually well formulated or complete. The development stage incorporates conceptual design and uses prototyping. It includes documentation and testing. Following development, there should be procedure development and ongoing operation and maintenance processes. Since the end-user systems tend to be small, the processes can be simplified.

Example. At one job shop manufacturer, the end-user system for forecasting and scheduling was developed by one person without documentation. It was tested by other members of the group who questioned the assumptions but did not test its logic. Only one person understood the program and there was no documentation. In this case, the controls on the development cycle were simply not adequate.

With respect to the importance or impact dimension of an end-user application, the user-developer should be able to explain its importance to analysis and decision making and describe the appropriate level of testing and review. Since one person typically does all of the design and development for an end-user developed application, testing during development has the weakness of the developer doing it (testing own work). The review is therefore a critical issue in quality assurance. Formal review procedures are not always necessary, but an explicit decision should be made as to the appropriate review given the users and use for the application. Alternative review procedures are no review, colleague review, outside analyst review, and formal review group. Applications that are very important may use more than one review including a formal review group; applications low in importance or impact may have no review or only colleague review. Very important applications also need better procedures for defining requirements and better documentation.

APPLICATION DEVELOPMENT METHODS AND TOOLS

An application development methodology provides a conceptual framework for defining the flow of work and the major decisions and actions. It also provides a useful framework for the selection and use of tools and methods. This is demonstrated by AD/Cycle (Application Development Cycle) supported by IBM. AD/Cycle addresses the integration difficulties with various tools and methods. A tool or method for use early in the development cycle may not fit with tools and methods used later. A software vendor with a good idea for a tool or method might find that potential customers would reject it because it was not compatible with other tools and methods they were using.

Selection of Methods

AD/Cycle defines a cycle for development and then uses it as a framework for tools and methods. IBM has defined standards for products to be used within the methodology. They produce products for the cycle, but they have made the system open to other products that meet the interface specifications.

A user of AD/Cycle may tailor the methodology and the tools and methods to individual needs. The approach is therefore very flexible. Users must purchase some basic IBM development software, but other software may be selected from any vendor who meets the interface standards. AD/Cycle is important because it reflects a more flexible approach to the development methodology and provides a way for utilizing development tools from other vendors.

Methods and tools can be manual or computer-based. Traditional methods such as charts, diagrams, matrices, and layout forms have been primarily manual. Recent developments have emphasized computer-based tools to support application development.

The Use of CASE Tools

Computer-aided software engineering (CASE) tools are intended to improve development productivity and quality. CASE tools that emphasize planning and modeling activities to define and document requirements are termed upper CASE tools. Lower CASE tools are oriented to program specifications and may include generation of program code.

CASE tools are software packages on developer workstations. They keep track of application requirements, draw diagrams for process flows and data models (and store them), record specifications, and may generate program code in COBOL, SQL (Structured Query Language) or other high level languages. Since all requirements and specifications are stored by the CASE tools, applications can be maintained using the tools. They may also be used in reverse engineering of applications.

An important element of CASE development tools is a repository of information about the application. The information is captured once and made available to any part of the development process. Information can also be easily modified. For example, the software to draw flow diagrams or data models improves productivity not only in the initial drawing but also in revisions.

The use of CASE tools is an important development in the application of computer-based tools to information systems work. They are in early stages of adoption but it is clear that they aid in documentation, development process and methods discipline, and improve coordination among developers.

IMPLEMENTATION OF INFORMATION SYSTEMS AS AN ORGANIZATIONAL CHANGE PROCESS

Successful implementation and use of a system are more likely if the process has gained management and user commitment to the project and to any changes necessitated by the new system. Generally, user participation in the system design process is advocated in order both to increase commitment and to ensure accuracy of requirements specifications.

Approaches to Overcoming Resistance

A significant problem with organizational change is resistance to the change by those affected. User resistance to new information systems can be a serious problem. If use is voluntary (for instance, use of a decision support system by primary users), resistance will be manifested by avoidance of the system. If use is not voluntary (for instance, data entry by secondary users), user resistance can cause significant problems in the way of disruptions, increased error rates, deliberate sabotage, or increased turnover. There are different approaches to overcoming user resistance, depending on the situation as well as the implicit theories of management and system designers. Three implicit theories to explain resistance are the following; each uses implementation methods that fit the theory.[2]

1. *People-oriented theory.* Resistance occurs because of factors internal to the users as individuals or as a group. Implementation will use education (training) of users, coercion through edicts and policies, persuasion, and user participation (to obtain commitment).

2. *System-oriented theory.* Resistance occurs because of factors inherent in the design of the system to be implemented. Implementation will use education of users (as to better technology), improved human factors in design, system modifications to conform to organizational procedures, and user participation (to obtain better design).

3. *Interaction theory.* People or groups resist systems because of an interaction between people and systems. Implementation will focus on fixing organizational problems before introducing a system, restructuring of incentives for users, restructuring of relationships between users and designers, and user participation (if appropriate).

Interaction theory brings new insight into the issue of implementation. According to this theory, the best prescriptions for an implementation strategy as well as system design will follow from a thorough diagnosis of the organizational setting in which the system will be used. One approach to system design and implementation which directly reflects interaction theory is *sociotechnical design.*

Sociotechnical Approach to System Design and Implementation

The goal of sociotechnical system design is to produce systems that are both technically efficient and have social characteristics that lead to high job satisfaction. It is most suitable for transaction processing systems where operating personnel will be affected; their direct participation in design is emphasized. In

---

[2]M. L. Markus, "Power, Politics, and MIS Implementation," *Communications of ACM,* 26:6, June 1983, pp. 430-44.

the sociotechnical approach,[3] users are asked to define human needs in their jobs (what they like and what they would like in an ideal job). This allows human objectives to be set for the application. A number of technical designs for the application are proposed and compared with the social objectives. Users are asked to propose modifications to the technical designs and even suggest alternatives. A cost-benefit analysis of each acceptable design as the starting point is done. Using the best sociotechnical design as the starting point, an analysis of tasks and organization of work and work groups is done. Followup diagnosis of job satisfaction and productivity allows the system to be modified if necessary.

With the sociotechnical approach, direct participation in system design by the users most directly impacted increases commitment to the system and ensures its technical quality. Experience with this approach suggests that productivity goals can be met without a tradeoff of human social needs and values.

EVALUATING QUALITY OF AN APPLICATION SYSTEM

There are four major sets of characteristics about the outcomes of development and implementation that help evaluate the quality of an application. The four sets of outcome characteristics occur in every application, although their importance may vary.

Technical performance. Does it work? This set of characteristics includes response time, operation, operational stability, capacity, error rates, uptime rate, and other performance aspects of the technology design.

User interfaces quality. Is it operational? This set of characteristics includes ease of use and user friendliness, such as the design of input and output screens, clarity and usefulness of help messages, and naturalness of flow of work required of the user.

Information requirements, completeness, and correctness. Do the outputs meet the user needs? The functionality of the system can be compared to the information requirements definition.

Organizational fit. Does it fit the business? This set of characteristics describes the application results with respect to how well they fit with objectives, culture, and business processes. It also relates to the fit with important stakeholders whose support is essential to system success.

> *Example.* The differences between success and failure can be small, as illustrated by an assembler of surgical kits for hospitals. The firm attempted to implement an integrated manufacturing software package to replace their in-house accounting system. Management wanted to integrate materials manage-

---

[3]Enid Mumford and Mary Weir, *Computer Systems in Work Design: The ETHICS Method*, Chapter 3, Halsted (Wiley), New York, 1979.

ment with the order entry function and avoid large costs involved in upgrading their existing hardware and developing the additional software. Several months after system cutover, the company went back to the old system and blamed the hardware reseller for the failure. Technically, the new system worked and provided the desired information. Yet the hardware configuration was inadequate to provide fast enough response times for order entry personnel (who had to configure the contents of the surgical kits) and production personnel (who had to record packing and shipment of kits). The users balked at the need to record the additional information (compared to their previous system) required to integrate order entry and materials management. While faster hardware (a network server and PC workstations in this case) would have solved the response problem, neither the company nor the reseller could come to an agreement on who should pay for it. Users wanted to minimize their job without realizing that the additional data entry efforts would benefit the entire organization. In this case, user involvement in development, some technical changes, and user education efforts could have made the difference between success and failure.

Example. The consequences of applications not having good organizational fit are illustrated by a producer of domestic beers. The manufacturer attempted to implement decentralized information systems at its breweries around the United States to replace the existing centralized systems. These efforts were undertaken by a new set of corporate executives who wanted to make each plant a separate profit center, with ownership of their own information systems. Eighteen months after starting implementation, the systems were still unused by the local plant personnel and the project was abandoned. Historically, the brewer had been a highly centralized company with corporate staff in charge of product recipes, product costing, master scheduling, purchasing, and accounting. Locally, each brewery only managed production to meet the master schedule. The attempts to decentralize other business practices were resisted by the corporate staff (who anticipated loss of responsibilities and even jobs). The local breweries were not staffed with personnel to manage local systems and to handle responsibilities for decentralized business processes. Finally, the team of corporate executives who championed a decentralized approach were replaced by others who favored a centralized approach.

LESSONS FOR MANAGERS

Four approaches or strategies for the development of an application are traditional, prototyping, package, and end-user. Each approach follows a system development life cycle (SDLC) that delineates the flow of work, decisions, and deliverables starting with project initiation and extending to the maintenance of the system after installation. Methodologies provide detailed procedures for carrying out the development approach. Methodologies may reflect a specific orientation (process, data, or behavioral views), but methods must finally yield all necessary specifications and procedures.

The traditional system development life cycle consists of three major stages: definition, development, and installation and operation. The phases in the life cycle provide a basis for system management and control by breaking the process down into small, well-defined segments. The traditional development approach tends to follow the development life cycle in a linear, step by step fashion.

The prototyping approach changes the processes for development of requirements and application design by building a prototype and working with the physical model to refine requirements and design. This approach changes some parts of the development cycle but other parts remain the same.

The package approach changes the traditional cycle because only the basic "must have" requirements need to be specified in order to select a package. The package establishes many of the requirements. There is no need to develop the application software, only to install it. To fit the package to the organization requires additional procedures and a conversion phase.

Small end-user applications need to be developed so they achieve accurate, complete results. The traditional system development cycle is not required and a simplified methodology for quality in end-user development is appropriate. However, the cycle employed should reflect the extent of use and importance of the outputs of the end-user application.

The implementation of an information system can be viewed as an organizational change process. The system designer may be viewed as a change agent to the user community. One common suggestion for improving the probability of successful implementation is user participation, which increases user commitment to the system and/or improve system quality. A sociotechnical approach, for example, uses participation to create a system that both is technically efficient and leads to high job satisfaction.

The approaches to development and implementation of applications produce applications that can be evaluated in terms of the outcomes from the development processes. The outcomes to be evaluated are technical performance, user interfaces, information requirements, and organizational fit.

CHAPTER 9

ACHIEVING CORRECT AND COMPLETE REQUIREMENTS

An information system should meet the needs of the organization it serves and the needs of users. The requirements for the information system are therefore determined by the strategies, goals, procedures, and behavior of individuals within the organization acting individually and collectively. Since this is so, why not simply ask the participants to describe the requirements for the information systems? This chapter will explain why asking directly may not be adequate. It will then describe alternative strategies.

Although the chapter is oriented to information system requirements, the issues in achieving correct and complete requirements are applicable across the functions in an organization. They apply to obtaining requirements for product and service design as well as requirements for business processes.

THE THREE LEVELS OF INFORMATION REQUIREMENTS

There are three levels at which information requirements need to be established in order to design and implement computer-based information systems:
　　1. The organizational information requirements to define an overall information system architecture and to specify a portfolio of applications and databases.
　　2. The requirements for each database defined by data models and other specifications.
　　3. The detailed information requirements for an application.
　　Some methods of requirements determination are more suitable for the less-detailed, broader-scope, organization-level information requirements, whereas other methods may be more suitable for the more detailed application information requirements. Some methods can be applied to requirements determination at both levels.

Organization-Level Information Requirements

The definition of information requirements for an organization is a key element in developing an information system master plan that is aligned with the organization's strategy and plans. Often termed *enterprise analysis*, the process of organization-level information requirements determination obtains, organizes, and documents a complete set of high-level requirements. The requirements are factored into databases and a portfolio of applications that can be scheduled for development. The overall information architecture is defined, and the boundaries and interfaces of the individual applications are specified. Strategic uses of information technology will usually be included in the organization-level requirements.

Database Requirements

Database requirements arise both from applications and ad hoc queries. The overall architecture for the databases to meet these requirements can be defined as part of organizational information requirements. Major classes of data are defined and associated with organizational processes that require them. There is very little detail in the requirements at this level.

The process of obtaining and organizing more detailed database requirements can be divided into defining data requirements as perceived by the users (programs or ad hoc queries) and defining requirements for physical design of the databases. User requirements are referred to as conceptual or logical requirements because the user views of data are separated from the organization of data in physical storage. User requirements may be derived from existing applications or by data modeling.

The requirements for physical database design are derived from the conceptual requirements, the hardware and software environments, and specifications related to use of the database. Logical data modeling is explained in Chapter 10; physical database design is beyond the scope of this book.

Application-Level Information Requirements

An application system provides information processing for an organizational unit or organizational activity. There are essentially two types of system application requirements: social and technical. The social or behavioral requirements, based on job design, specify objectives and assumptions such as work organization and work design objectives, individual role and responsibility assumptions, and organizational policies.

The technical requirements are based on the information needed for the job or task to be performed. They specify outputs, inputs, stored data, and information processes. The technical requirements include interface requirements between the user system and the application system such as data presentation format, screen design, user language structure, feedback and assistance provisions, error control, and response time.

WHY DETERMINATION OF INFORMATION REQUIREMENTS CAN BE DIFFICULT

There are four major reasons it may be difficult to obtain a correct and complete set of requirements:

1. The variety and complexity of information requirements.
2. The constraints on humans as information processors and problem solvers.
3. The complex patterns of interaction among users and analysts in defining requirements.
4. Unwillingness of some users to provide requirements (for political or behavioral reasons).

The chapter will focus on the first two difficulties. The part that follows in this section will illustrate the problem of requirements when the situation is complex. The next part will address the constraints on humans as information processors. The reasons for difficulty in arriving at correct and complete requirements for information systems suggest that there should be several general strategies for requirements determination that fit the conditions in a specific case.

The Effect of Complexity on Information Requirements Determination

The effect of complexity is illustrated by the problem of identifying strategic applications. Why is it difficult? Why not have a small group of high level and middle level executives identify strategic applications? If it were that simple, then strategic applications might not give competitive advantage because competitors would have thought of them and have implemented them at approximately the same time. The complexity of the situation arises from the number of alternatives that may be considered, and information technology acts to increase the number of alternatives.

1. The number of possible combinations of ways in which a company may be organized, offer goods and services, and differentiate itself from competitors. Information technology makes it possible to have more combinations.

2. The number of cause and effect relationships both inside the organization and with customers, suppliers, regulators, etc. Information technology introduces new cause and effect relationships, changes old ones, and enables reengineering of business processes.

3. The rapid changes in the capabilities and cost of information technology. Each new wave of technology innovation affecting performance and price opens up new opportunities for innovation. Past barriers are changed and new strategies become attractive.

4. The effect of new information systems and organizational changes frequently cannot be isolated within the organization. The effects can extend across the organization, often in unanticipated ways.

These complexity factors do not prevent an organization from identifying and implementing strategic information systems. They do suggest that it requires strong processes to aid identification efforts, a willingness to innovate, and an openness to creative efforts.

Constraints on Humans in Information Requirements Determination

Humans appear to be so versatile with respect to information use that human constraints or limitations are frequently ignored. Yet "asking" users to define their information requirements will not necessarily yield a complete and correct set of requirements. Understanding limitations of humans as information processors, human bias in selection and use of data, human problem-solving behavior, and the effects of background/knowledge of the users will help in understanding how to overcome these limitations in processes for determining requirements.

Humans make use of three memories in information processing: *external*, *long-term*, and *short-term*. External memory includes notes, documents, reports, and stored data. Long-term human memory is used to store the data that will be retrieved at a later time. Short-term human memory is small and actively used during human interaction and human data processing. The limits of short-term memory affect the information requirements obtained whenever the process being used to elicit requirements uses only short-term memory (e.g., an interview in which there is no use of external storage such as notes, reports, or documents). The user being interviewed cannot hold a large number of items in short-term memory for discussion or analysis purposes and is therefore limited in responses. The short-term memory limitation may also affect the number of requirements that users define as important. In various processing activities using short-term memory, the user may have selectively emphasized a few items of information and recorded these in long-term memory as being the most important. These few requirements may be the only ones recalled when a question is asked. These limitations of humans as information processors can be offset by appropriate methods of elicitation and documentation.

There is substantial evidence to show that humans are biased in their selection and use of data. The net effect on the determination of information requirements is a significant bias toward requirements based on current procedures, currently available information, recent events, and inferences from small samples of events. The analyst and user who understand these biases may compensate for them; a significant method of compensation is to provide a structure for eliciting of requirements.

The problem space for information requirements determination is how a particular analyst or user formulates a representation to use in working on information requirements. Methods for the determination of information requirements provide such a structure for the problem space.

Because of human cognitive limits, users and analysts involved in the process of requirements determination employ a somewhat simplified model of the organization and its information requirements. The completeness and correctness of the requirements obtained are thus limited by the model as well as by the training, prejudice, custom, and attitudes of users and analysts involved in the process. For example, analysts rated best on performance consider organizational and policy issues in establishing requirements; low-rated analysts do not.

The lack of background/experience in a given industry, functional area, or field of expertise can limit the ability of users to specify their requirements. They may not know their requirements or may have a piecemeal understanding of their needs. In many cases, consultants can be engaged as subject matter experts to assist in requirements determination, but then the consultant may lack the background/knowledge of specific organizational practices.

A method for determining information requirements should be able to assist users and analysts to formulate a useful model of the organization or problem for which requirements are being determined. It should aid in discovering requirements and overcoming limitations of humans as information processors, assist in overcoming biasing factors, and compensating for background and training differences of participants. It should provide assurance that requirements are satisfactory as to completeness and correctness. The relationship of system and application characteristics and human characteristics to the use of methods is illustrated in Figure 9-1.

STRATEGIES FOR DETERMINING INFORMATION REQUIREMENTS

There are four broad strategies for determining information requirements:

1. Asking directly
2. Deriving from an existing information system
3. Synthesizing from characteristics of the business processes
4. Discovering from experimentation with an evolving information system

FIGURE 9-1
Effects of Application Characteristics, Human Characteristics, and Information Determination Strategies and Methodologies on Information Requirements Obtained

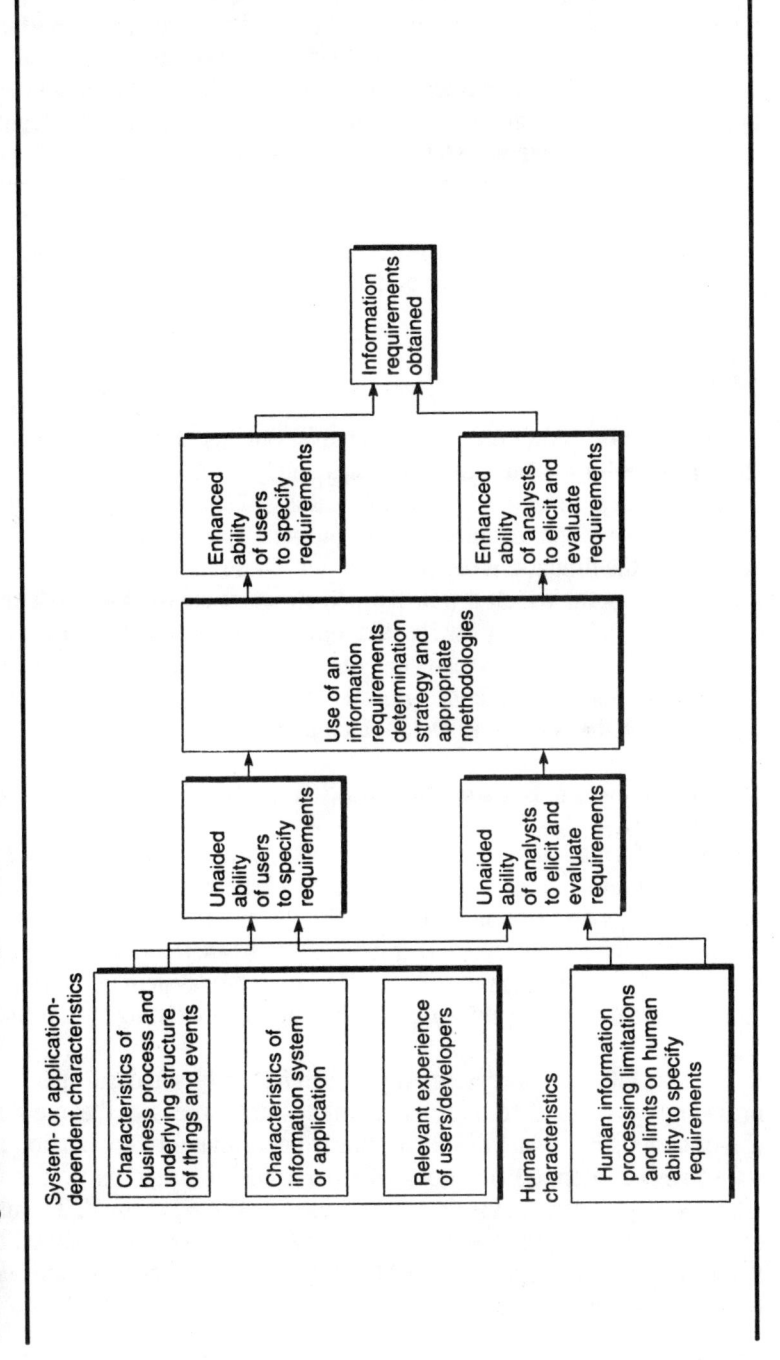

The set of four strategies is applicable both to determining organizational information requirements and to application requirements. For each strategy, there are a number of methods that are in use or have been proposed. Methods differ in the amount of structure provided. Some provide conceptual structure but little process and documentation structure; others provide detailed structure for all tasks and all documentation. In the discussion of strategies, some methods will be used as illustrations; no attempt will be made to provide a comprehensive list. Analysts and users may not follow one strategy exclusively but use a mixture of strategies depending on the application and difficulties encountered. In other words, the four strategies help to explain how information requirements may be done, but in practice there may be a mixed use.

Asking Directly

In a strategy of asking directly, the analyst obtains information requirements from persons in the business processes solely by asking them their requirements. From a conceptual standpoint, this strategy assumes that users can structure their model of the problem (problem space) and overcome or compensate for the limitations described earlier. These conditions may hold in very stable systems for which a well-defined structure exists or in systems whose structure is established by law, regulation, or other outside authority. There are a variety of methods for carrying out an asking strategy: a set of closed questions, a set of open-ended questions, brainstorming, and various group consensus methods (such as Delphi techniques).

Deriving from an Existing Information System

Existing information systems that have an operational history can be used to derive requirements for a proposed information system for the same type of organization or application. The types of existing information systems that are useful in deriving requirements for future systems are the system to be replaced, a system in a similar organization, and a proprietary system or package. In this strategy, users and analysts start with (anchor on) an existing system and adjust from it.

If the information system is performing fairly standard operations and providing fairly standard information for business processes that are stable, the use of an existing system as an anchor is appropriate. In application systems for some well-defined functions such as a bill of materials processor, data analysis of an existing system can be a useful primary method. The use of an existing package as the basis for requirements is a powerful method because the widely used packages will tend to meet the requirements that are necessary for a business process.

Synthesis from Characteristics of Business Processes

Requirements for information stem from the activities of the business processes. This suggests that a logical and complete method for obtaining information requirements is from an analysis of their characteristics. This analysis is therefore especially appropriate when the business processes are changing or the proposed information system is different from existing patterns (in its content, form, complexity, etc.), so that anchoring on an existing information system or observations of information needs will not yield a complete and correct set of requirements.

Several methods have been proposed for implementing a strategy for determining information requirements from analyzing business processes. Five examples illustrate methods for this strategy. The questioning or analysis process in each case begins with the needs, structure, objectives, etc., of the business process. When these components are established, they are the basis for deriving the information system requirements.

- *Normative analysis* methods are based on the fundamental similarity of basic business processes. For example, all billing applications perform a set of basic functions that can be prescribed in advance. These fundamental characteristics are the basis for a prescribed or normative set of requirements. Analysis then concentrates on tailoring the requirements to meet unique or innovative needs of a specific organization or application.

- *Critical factors analysis* methods derive information requirements from the critical factors for operating and managing an enterprise. There is therefore a two step process of eliciting the critical factors and then deriving information requirements. An example of critical factors analysis is the Critical Success Factors (CSF) method.[1]

- *Process analysis* is based on the idea that business processes (groups of decisions and activities required to manage the resources of the organization) are the basis for information system support. An example of a process-based methodology is Business Systems Planning (BSP). The BSP method is primarily appropriate for developing an information system master plan.

- *Ends-means analysis* is a technique for determining requirements based on systems theory. The technique separates the definition of ends or outputs (goods, services, and information) generated by an organizational process from the means (inputs and processes) used to accomplish them. The ends or output from one process (whether the process be viewed as an organizational, departmental, or individual process) is the input to some other process. For example, the inventory process and sales order process provide information to the production planning

---

[1] J. F. Rockhart, "Critical Success Factors," *Harvard Business Review*, March-April 1979, pp. 81–91.

process. Users are asked to define both ends and means for their function and the measurements for effectiveness and efficiency.

- *Input-process-output analysis* is a system approach. A system is defined in terms of its inputs, outputs, and transformation processes for receiving inputs and producing outputs. The approach starts in a top-down fashion on the system for which information is needed. The system is subdivided into smaller subsystems until information processing activities are defined as separate activities within a subsystem. The advantage of analysis based on inputs, processes, and outputs of systems is that it is systematic and comprehensive.

Discovering from Experimentation with an Evolving Information System

Traditional procedures for determining information requirements are designed to establish a complete and correct set of requirements before the information system is designed and built. In a significant percentage of cases, users may not be able to formulate information requirements because they have no existing model (either normative or experiential) on which to base requirements, they lack the background/knowledge with the area or lack an understanding of the possibilities of information systems. They may find it difficult to deal in abstract requirements or to visualize new systems. Users may need to anchor on concrete systems from which they can make adjustments.

Another approach to information requirements determination is, therefore, to capture an initial set of requirements and implement an information system to provide those requirements. The system is designed for ease of change. As users employ the system, they request additional requirements. After initial requirements establish an anchor, additional requirements are discovered through use of the system. The general approach has been described as prototyping; it was described in more detail in Chapter 8.

SELECTING A STRATEGY FOR DETERMINING INFORMATION REQUIREMENTS

Four strategies have been described for determining information requirements, with each strategy having a number of methods that may be employed. Selection of an appropriate primary strategy is contingent on characteristics of the environment in which the determination of requirements is conducted.

The underlying basis for selecting a strategy is uncertainty with respect to the requirements determination processes. The uncertainty is based on four factors: characteristics of the business process, the information system or application, the users, and the analysts.

The approach to selecting an information requirements determination strategy consists of four steps (Table 9-1). The steps represent a series of evaluations to establish a basis for selection. The evaluations are not precise, but do provide guidelines for judgment. The overall process of selecting a primary strategy is diagrammed in Figure 9-2.

Four elements in the development process affect the level of uncertainty in determining information requirements: the business processes, the application system, the users, and the analysts. As summarized in Table 9-2, for each of the elements there are characteristics that reduce expected uncertainty as to requirements determination, and there are opposing characteristics that increase expected uncertainty.

> *Example.* A manufacturing resource planning system includes content from some existing stand-alone information applications but does not directly replace an existing information system. The factors to consider and the way each factor increases or decreases information requirements uncertainty is indicated.

Supports mixture of programmed and nonprogrammed activities	Increases
Requirements not stable because they are dependent on experience and decision style of users	Increases
No well-defined model of business processes and their requirements	Increases
Users somewhat unsure of requirements	Increases
Analysts inexperienced in specific application because it is unique	Increases

The high level of uncertainty suggests a discovery, prototyping methodology in which requirements are identified iteratively as the application system evolves. An alternative is to use a package that normatively defines the basic requirements and adjust from these requirements.

> *Example.* Consultants employed to assist in defining information requirements, typically as part of a system selection process, use different strategies for eliciting information requirements from members of the organization. Some consultants use extensive interviewing, in an approach of asking directly or deriving from existing systems, to elicit requirements. This can take considerable time but has the advantage of detailed analysis. The process may be difficult in organizations without trained personnel or budget to support the investigation.
>
> An alternative approach followed by some consultants is to start with a normative model of the applications as found in available software packages. These requirements are used in an anchor-and-adjust approach to quickly identify the unique requirements of an organization. These critical requirements provide a focus for soliciting proposals and selecting an appropriate package.

FIGURE 9-2
Selection of a Strategy for the Determination of Information Requirements

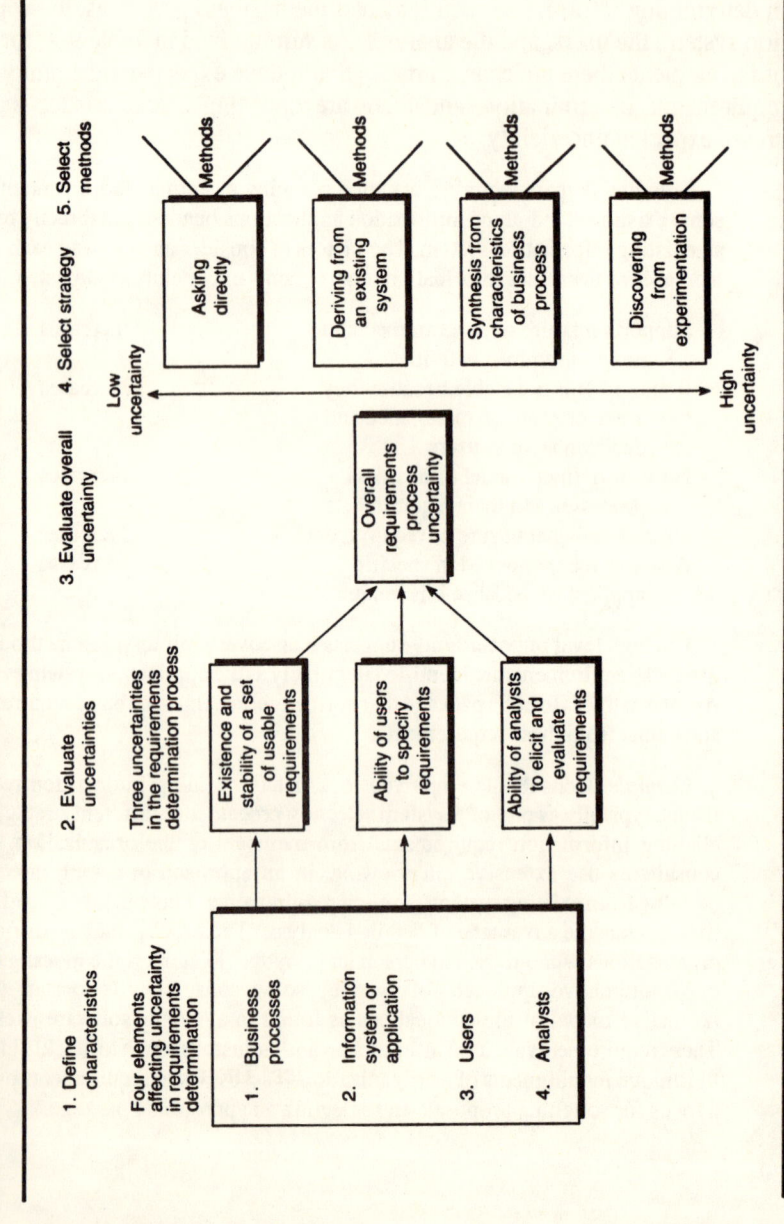

TABLE 9-1
Steps in Selecting a Strategy and Methods for Determining Information Requirements

---

1. Identify those characteristics of the four elements in the development process that affect uncertainty in the determination of information requirements:
   - Business processes
   - Information system or application
   - Users
   - Analysts
2. Evaluate the effect of the characteristics of the four elements in the development process on information requirements uncertainty.
3. Select a primary strategy for requirements determination based on the overall requirements uncertainty.

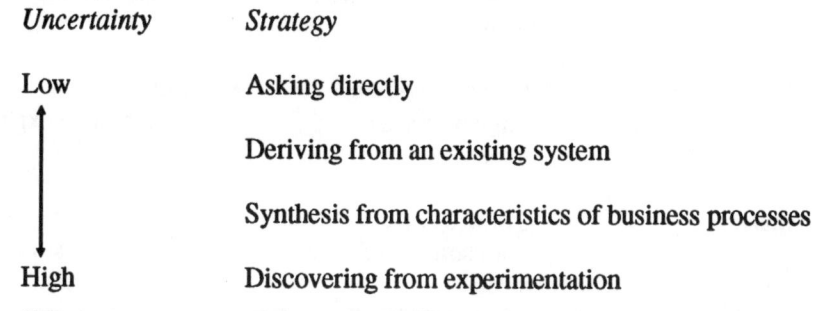

Uncertainty	Strategy
Low ↑	Asking directly
	Deriving from an existing system
	Synthesis from characteristics of business processes
↓ High	Discovering from experimentation

4. Select one or more methods from the set of methods to implement the primary strategy.

DETERMINING ORGANIZATIONAL INFORMATION REQUIREMENTS

In order to prepare or revise an information system architecture and information system plan, it is necessary to periodically examine the information requirements of the organization. A three-stage model for information system planning provides insight into the planning process and reduces confusion as to the position of competing methodologies. The model consists of three stages:

- *Strategic alignment.* The information technology strategy is aligned with the business strategy and business plan.

TABLE 9-2
Characteristics Affecting Requirements Uncertainty

Elements in development process	Characteristics that reduce uncertainty	Characteristics that increase uncertainty
Business processes	Stable, well-defined system not in process of change	Unstable, poorly understood system in process of change
	Programmed activities or decisions	Non-programmed activities or decisions
Application system	Traditional, simple set of requirements	Complex or unusual set of requirements
	Clerical support system	Management support system
	Basic, well-known technology	Advanced, new technology
Users	One or few users	Many users
	High user system experience	Low user system experience
Analysts	Trained and experienced with similar information system	Little prior training or experience with similar information system

- *Organizational information requirements determination.* Working from the strategic plans, the organizational requirements are identified in sufficient detail to identify major applications and databases.
- *Resource allocation.* The development resources are allocated to the various requirements and a schedule of development defined.

For requirements, the first two stages are important. The resource allocation stage is described in Chapter 11 in connection with organization and management of the information system function.

Requirements from the Strategic Alignment Stage

The objective of information system planning is to create objectives, goals, and strategies that align with (are derived from or a result of interactive planning with) the organization's objectives, goals, and strategies. A number of techniques are available for this. The most direct method is to derive the information strategy from the organization strategy document.

In some cases, there is no explicit business strategy, and the information system planner must attempt to formulate necessary plans without that information. One method is strategy set transformation.[2] The stakeholders for the organization are identified (owners, customers, suppliers, employees, etc.) and their major goals identified. The organizational goals and strategies for each group are then defined. These strategies and goals are used to distinguish information system strategies that provide the basis for information requirements.

> *Example.* An organizational objective of improving cash flow may be derived from the profitability goals of shareholders and creditors. An organizational strategy to achieve profitability may be an improvement in credit practices. An information system objective may be to improve speed of billing.

Performing the Organizational Information Requirements Stage

Once goals and strategy have been delineated, the next stage is to obtain organizational information requirements. Information requirements are required at the organization-wide level for information system planning, identifying applications, and planning an information architecture. More detailed information requirements are required for design of applications. Although the level of specification is different for the organization and application, many of the methods for obtaining requirements are the same.

The basic approach to defining organizational information requirements is to first identify major requirements for information and the classes of information needed for each subsystem (function, department, or major activity). This is done in sessions in which one or more persons associated with the decisions or actions identify the classes of information needed and the reasons for it. Having identified classes of information for each subsystem, a matrix of subsystems and information requirements can be constructed. By an examination of common needs by different subsystems, major databases can be delineated. Using the information requirements and reasons for them, applications can be outlined.

A major part of the process elicits information needed by asking questions about a business purpose or need. For example, questions such as the following start with the business need and then identify the requirements that follow from it:[3]

---

[2]W. R. King, "Strategic Planning for Management Information Systems," *MIS Quarterly*, 2:1, March 1978, pp. 27–37.

[3]B. Bowman, G. B. Davis, and J. C. Wetherbe, "Modeling for MIS," *Datamation*, July 1981, pp. 155–164.

- What problems do you have and what information is needed for solving them?
- What decisions do you make and what information do you need for decision making?
- What factors are critical to the success of your activity and what information do you need to achieve success in them or to monitor progress?
- What are the outputs (the ends) from your activities and what information do you need to measure effectiveness in achieving the outputs?
- What resources are used in producing the outputs and what information is needed to measure efficiency in use of the resources?

APPLICATION REQUIREMENTS

The four strategies for information requirements of asking directly, deriving from an existing information system, synthesizing from characteristics of the business processes, and discovering from experimentation with an evolving information system are applicable to application requirements. When a strategy or strategies have been selected, a full set of requirements covers process, data (see Chapter 10), and user interface considerations. This chapter will focus on the strategy selection and one part of the requirements, the interface requirements, of particular importance to users.

The Selection of an Application Requirements Strategy

The selection of an appropriate primary strategy (since more than one strategy may be combined) is based on the concepts presented earlier of uncertainty about the application-level requirements. The factors are:

- Business processes   Is there an agreed upon model of the business processes, is the understanding stable and is information stable? Are decisions programmed or non-programmed?
- Application   High-level versus low-level application, level of complexity, and number of users.
- Users/analysts   Experience with business processes and experience with application.

User Interface Requirements

Most computer-based information systems involve online interaction between the human user and the machine; a critical element of the design of these systems is the user interface. The interface consists of screens, keyboards, devices, languages, and other means by which the human user and the computer system exchange inputs and outputs. Many principles of good user interface design have been developed, focusing on user friendly systems and ease of use (much of it based on human factors engineering and ergonomics). Several guiding principles are that the system should be flexible, consistent, and under user control.

An important consideration in developing interface requirements is a clear understanding of the type of user. System developers will respond to somewhat different interfaces than non-developers. Novices need simple interfaces; experts desire more efficient interfaces. Ideally, the system should have facilities to accommodate both. A novice who is unfamiliar with both the system's specific syntax and generalizable knowledge about use of computers should be able to get explanations or assistance through the system. On the other hand, an expert who has internalized the system's syntactic structure or has considerable general system knowledge should be permitted rapid interaction and not be held up by explanations or details that are only required by the novice. The difference between occasional and frequent users are similar to novices and experts; however, users who have developed some skill and then not used the system for a time may need a different kind of help than novices. A last consideration is whether the user is a primary user employing the application for a primary business process or a secondary user doing data entry or other support functions.

The division of functions between person and machine, regardless of application, has shifted from emphasis on machine efficiency to enhancement of human effectiveness. The primary reason for this shift has been the declining cost of hardware relative to the cost of human labor. The distinction between the negative and positive effects of a computer system on individual quality of work life is related to the division of function between human and machine. A system that gives the user very little discretion in terms of selection of tasks or pace of work may have apparent cost advantages, especially if the skills required of the human operator are minimized. However, these cost advantages may be lost due to added costs of increased turnover of personnel and reduced job commitment. Therefore, whenever possible, a system should be designed so that the user controls the interaction rather than the system. In the long run, a system that is designed well from the user's point of view will result in increased overall performance. The sociotechnical approach to requirements (discussed in Chapter 8) is one method to achieve application designs that take advantage of the strengths of both humans and machines to achieve improved quality of work life.

Some considerations in the design of a user interface are listed to illustrate the range of that need to be addressed in requirements and design. They also need to be considered when selecting packages.

- *Screen design.* Clear and uncluttered. Provide information that is essential, preferably on a single screen. The placement follows both logic and culture. Place items together that belong logically together, place items in customary processing order, place most important items preferably at the left and arrange in importance from top to bottom.
- *Feedback and assistance.* The system should acknowledge every user request in some way. Additional assistance (such as system status) should be available upon request. If the request requires a long time to process, acknowledgment of receipt of the request may be appropriate. For instance, if a user submits a complex query to a large database and the processing time is expected to be fairly long (say 30 seconds), the system may respond, "Your query is being processed; there will be a short delay," or ". . . there will be about a 30 second delay." The user's psychological need for feedback is satisfied by the knowledge that the system has received the query and is not sitting idle.
- *System prompting.* This guides a user step by step through a task. It also may give the range of options available. Prompting is very helpful for novice users, but it may be frustrating to experienced users who have internalized the sequence of steps. Ideally, an experienced user should be able to "turn off" such prompting.
- *Help facilities.* Command assistance provides an explanation of how to formulate a specific command. For example, asking for HELP PRINT on one system obtains a brief explanation of the PRINT command and a list of parameters that can be specified with the command. General help provides a list of commands. When a user identifies the command needed, a command assistance HELP may be used. An online tutor help provides lessons on how to use the system.
- *Error detection and correction.* There should be a system response not only to every correct input but also to every incorrect input. A well-designed user interface should have four distinct dimensions of error control: error prevention, error detection, error correction (by user and/or by system plus agreement by user), and error recovery. An important feature of a well-designed system is the ability to "undo" something that has been done.
- *Response time.* Response time in an interactive system is the time that elapses between the user keying in a command and the system beginning to display a response. Response times are affected by the system's capacity, the number of other users (if it is a shared system), and the complexity of the user's request.
- *Commands versus menus.* With a command, the user enters command words. This tends to be very efficient for expert, frequent users. With a menu, the user is shown a list of options and is expected to choose the appropriate one. Menus may be arranged in a hierarchy. The advantage of menus is that they provide a clear, complete set of choices. They require less training than command words.

- *Forms.* In a forms-based interface design, the user fills in the blanks on a screen. Often color or foreground (bright) and background (dim) character printing differentiates system prompts from user-supplied information on the screen.
- *Icons.* Icons may be used in system dialogue instead of menus or command languages. A workstation display may show a menu of icons: a desk, an in box, an out box, a file cabinet, a wastebasket. The user moves the cursor to the icon representing the desired function and presses a key to select that icon; either the function is executed or a new set of icons is displayed.
- *Color.* Color can be used to highlight a particular aspect of a cluttered display, highlight a change, or separate information categories. Color is especially valuable in tasks involving identification, searching, and counting. There can be some problems with using color. Since it is very noticeable, it can distract a person by highlighting unimportant items or associating different items that are really unrelated. Color should generally be used carefully, consistently, and sparingly, since irrelevant colors can interfere with the ability to perform tasks.
- *Natural language.* The trend is to make computer commands as natural or as close to natural language as possible. The ultimate objective is for computers to understand natural language either keyed in or spoken.
- *Direct manipulation systems.* In this approach, the interface allows the user to manipulate the item of interest. A spreadsheet processor allows direct change to a cell by moving the cursor to the cell. Video games allow direct manipulation via a mouse or joystick.

LESSONS FOR MANAGERS

Information requirements determination is vital for information systems; it is also important as an example of a process needed for product, service, and process requirements.

There are three levels of requirements: organizational information requirements, application-level requirements, and database requirements. The difficulty of obtaining requirements stemming from complexity and the constraints on humans as specifiers of information requirements are explored. Four broad strategies for determining information requirements encompass groups of methods. These strategies are (1) asking directly, (2) deriving from an existing information system, (3) synthesizing from characteristics of the business processes, and (4) discovering from experimentation with an evolving information system.

The selection of a strategy is based on uncertainties with respect to determining information requirements. The level of uncertainty is associated with characteristics of the business processes, the information system or application, users, and analysts. The selection of a primary strategy for determining requirements points to a set of methods for use. An analyst may choose to use other strategies and methods to supplement the primary determination strategy.

In order to prepare or revise an information system architecture and information system plan, it is necessary to periodically examine the information requirements of the organization. A three stage model for information system planning provides insight into the planning process and reduces confusion as to the position of organization-level information requirements methodologies. The three stages are strategic alignment, organizational information requirements determination, and resource allocation.

The four strategies for information requirements of asking directly, deriving from an existing information system, synthesizing from characteristics of the business processes, and discovering from experimentation with an evolving information system are applicable to application requirements. When a strategy or strategies have been selected, a full set of requirements covers process, data (see Chapter 10), and user interface. Interface requirements are of special importance to users. The guiding principles are that interfaces should be flexible, consistent, and under user control. The type of user is a significant factor in interface design. The interface should incorporate principles of job design so that humans will have reasonably interesting, motivating jobs.

CHAPTER 10

MODELING DATA REQUIREMENTS AND USING DATABASES

The activities of organizations require data. Making sales, scheduling production, distributing products, billing, collecting amounts due, and assigning personnel are examples of activities that use data. An organization must have data, but what data items are important? There are both economic and physical limitations on the collection, storage, and retrieval of data. An organization must therefore make decisions about the data to be kept in its files and databases. How should data items be identified, and how should they be related? Data modeling is important because it is the process for defining data needs and data relationships.

Data items are of value only if they can be retrieved, processed, and presented to those who need them within the time allowed for the decision or action to which they apply. Data items that cannot be collected and maintained or cannot be located or processed in time have little value. The management of stored data, including storage and retrieval, is performed by database management software.

When a user formulates queries or retrieves data for a program or a report, the user employs a user view of the database organization. The user can visualize the data as being structured as tables, hierarchies, or networks. However, the physical storage of the data may be different from the user view.

Data items are not physically stored on a disk or other storage medium in a random or arbitrary fashion; they are organized and stored for efficient retrieval. It is not necessary for the user to understand physical storage structures and database organizations; however, it is helpful to have some broad understanding of physical database storage in order to avoid database queries that cannot be processed efficiently.

Data needs often extend beyond the databases oriented to numerical data; storage and retrieval often include other types of databases. Examples are databases storing text such as articles and reports, databases storing drawings and graphics, and databases storing analytical and computational models (model bases). These databases have unique storage and retrieval issues.

Much of the data used by an organization is a result of the transactions and other activities of the organization. However, an organization also uses data from external sources. In many cases, the external data is available from outside vendors. Databases maintained by outside vendors are an important source of data for analysis and decision making support.

DATA CONCEPTS

There are a few data concepts that should be understood before proceeding with the topics in the chapter. These are the important concepts of entities, attributes, and relationships; data items, records, and files; sequencing of data; traditional types of files; and databases and database management systems.

Entities, attributes, and relationships are different and more abstract terminology than commonly used business terms. However, these abstract terms are very useful because they provide a way to think about data that breaks with traditional views tied to media and devices. In this section, the more abstract terms will be defined first followed by common, traditional terms. The relationship between the abstract terminology and the common everyday terms will be explained.

Entities, Attributes, and Relationships

Organizations are not able to collect and store data about everything. They identify objects of interest and collect data about them. The objects of interest are those things that the organization must deal with in some way, such as in buying, selling, producing, hiring, and so forth. They are subjects of transaction processing, reports, analyses, and decisions. These objects of interest are termed entities.

Entity. An entity is any type or category of objects about which data is collected. An entity may be a thing, person, abstract concept, or event. It can also identify a role of objects such as customer, employee, or component part. For production scheduling, products and orders are entities, i.e., they are objects of interest and things about which data is collected. An example of an event is a production run. The instances of a category or type are termed entity instances (although different terminology is sometimes used). If PRODUCT is an entity, then PRODUCT-A and PRODUCT-B are entity instances.

If an organization finds it useful to keep files about something, the file is probably for an entity (PRODUCT, CUSTOMER, EMPLOYEE). The individual records in the file correspond to entity instances. For each entity, there are characteristics that describe entity instances. A part is described by its part number, description, cost, etc.; an employee is described by employee number, name, social security number, date hired, etc. There are many characteristics of parts and employees that are not of interest to an organization. In fact, different organizations may decide on different sets of characteristics in which they have an interest. These are termed attributes.

Attribute. An attribute is a characteristic of interest about an entity. Each entity instance has a value for each of its attributes. That is, the values of the attributes (attribute descriptor) describe a particular entity instance. Thus, an instance of the entity is represented by the set of specific values for each of the attributes. The list of attributes for an entity should include all that are of interest to different parts of the organization. For example, in addition to part number, description, and costs, the production scheduler may be interested in attributes of replenishment order policy, lead times, lot sizing modifiers, and planning responsibility.

Each entity has at least one attribute whose value uniquely distinguishes the instances of the entity. In other words, the question of what attribute(s) distinguish one employee from another is a question about the identifier(s) for the entity.

Identifier. The identifier may be a natural attribute such as a person's name but is usually an artificial attribute such as an employer number that is created for that purpose. Most data items cannot be identifiers because they do not have unique values. The customer name may be unique for a business customer but not for individuals because more than one person may have the same first and last names.

Entities do not stand alone. There are associations or relationships between them. In the modeling approach to understanding data, relationships can be between two entities (binary) or more than two (n-ary). Some issues in modeling data are whether the relationship must exist in all instances (must every PARENT have a relationship to a CHILD) and whether there can be more than one instance (more than one CHILD with a relationship to a PARENT).

Relationship. A relationship is a correspondence or association between entities. Each entity in a binary relationship both describes and is described by the other, i.e., relationships are bidirectional. "Has" characterizes the relationship from department to employee; "works for" characterizes the relationship from employee to department. Each direction of a relationship has a minimum and maximum number of related instances. Frequently, for example, a department "has" one or more employees (minimum 1, maximum 1) and each employee "works for" exactly one department (minimum 1 and maximum 1).

The three concepts of entity, attribute, and relationship provide a powerful way to describe the objects of interest about which data should be collected and stored. The entities describe what things are of interest. Attributes describe the characteristics of the entities that should be stored in some way. Relationships define the fact that entities are related to each other; the data should be organized so the connections can be made for reports and analyses.

Files, Records, and Data Items

An organization keeps files describing things and events that are important to the organization. There is typically a sales file (about sales events), an employee file (about people in a role of employee), a customer file (about people or companies in a role of customer), a product file (about things made and sold), etc. In other words, the traditional concept of a file corresponds to the more abstract concept of an entity. Entities are categories or groupings of objects for which an organization has reason to keep a file.

Within a file are records. In fact, a file can be defined as a collection of records of a given type. Each record in the file describes one instance or occurrence of the object (entity) of interest. There is a record for each sale, employee, customer, or product. Each record has within it a number of data items. These correspond to the concept of attributes. The data items of employee name, employee number, salary, etc., are attributes of employee. One (or more) of the attributes is the record key; this is the same as the entity identifier. Data items can also be used to represent relationships. Keeping the employee's department number in the employee record represents the relationship between employees and departments.

A data item (or attribute) is assigned a name in order to refer to it during storage, retrieval, and processing operations. Associated with each data item is a set of possible values (a domain). The set of possible values can be defined in a general way by the value class from which they may be taken (such as numeric, alphanumeric, or date). The possible values may also be defined by enumeration, by limits, or by an algorithm. For example, the domain for marital status is single or married.

> *Example.* Products have many attributes that concern planning. The basis for a replenishment order, for example, is typically limited to a few choices that can be enumerated. The replenishment lead time reflects an algorithm that adds the fixed lead time, the variable run time (which is lot size sensitive), and inspection lead time. Limits may be placed on the replenishment order quantity, such as a lot size minimum and maximum.

Data item has some physical storage connotations. It is the elementary unit in data storage. A data item is sometimes referred to as a *field*, but that term is used more precisely to refer to the set of storage locations assigned to a data item (or the spaces on an input or output medium to be occupied by the data item values).

Two or more data items may be assigned a name for data processing purposes if they are sometimes referenced as a unit. This depends on how the user views the data (user data model). For example, there may be two elementary data items for FIRST NAME and LAST NAME, but the data name NAME may be assigned to the entire name composed of first and last names. In a search or retrieval operation, FIRST NAME will obtain only the first name; NAME will retrieve the combination of first and last names.

Sequencing of Data

There are a variety of useful sequences for presenting data depending on the purpose of the report being prepared. They have no necessary relationship to the physical sequence in which the data records are stored. The sequencing of data into the sequence needed for the output is termed *sorting*, a significant activity in data processing. For sorting, one or more attributes or data items are designated as the sort key, the item whose values determine the sequence of records. By designating a primary sort key and a secondary sort key, the records may be sorted into groups and then each group also placed in sequence. The process may be continued with more sort keys.

> *Example.* Sales reports require many different sequences and subtotals to satisfy the requirements of sales managers. The historical sales data may be sequenced and subtotaled by product, product type, customer, customer type, location, sales representative, and so forth. Totals may represent units or value and be categorized by time period, such as monthly and year-to-date totals. With a sequence, such as a list by customer type, a secondary or tertiary sequence may be used (such as by product type and sales representative).

Traditional Types of Files

Creation and maintenance of stored data is a major part of the workload of an information processing system. In traditional data processing prior to database technology, the emphasis was on files and the relationships among files. Since many of the concepts and terminology still exist, the major types of files will be reviewed. These are master files, transaction files, and report files.

Master file. This is a file of relatively permanent information about entities. It contains identification, historical, and statistical information. Master files are used as a source of reference data for processing transactions and often hold accumulated information based on transaction data. For example, an employee master file will contain identification and pay rate data as well as gross and net pay to date. A customer master file will contain data about current balance and past due amounts.

Transaction file (or detail file). This is a collection of records describing activities or transactions by the organization. It is developed as a result of processing transactions and preparing transaction documents; it is also used to update the accumulated data in the master file. An example of a typical transaction file is a payroll file created by the preparation of a weekly payroll; it is also used to update the year-to-date data items in the employee master file.

Report file. This is a file created by extracting data to prepare a report. An example is a report of all customers, by name, with past due balances over a given amount. The ease of handling special requests for reports depends on the availability of report generator software that efficiently extracts, sorts, and formats data for reports.

> *Example.* An organization stores master file information about products and customers and transaction files about customer orders and line items. In order to generate sales reports about order backlog, a report file about customer orders must be extracted. The report file includes information from the item master (e.g., product type), the customer master (e.g., customer type), the customer order header (e.g., the customer and sales representative), and the customer order line items (e.g., the products ordered and requested shipment dates and quantities).

DATABASES

The concept of a file as a set of related records historically resulted in physically separate files with "owners" for each file. For example, there was a personnel records file with the personnel department being responsible for input and correctness of the personnel records, an accounts receivable file with responsibility (ownership) by the accounts receivable section of accounting, etc.

The ownership of and responsibility for separate files can be a useful organizational control on the quality and use of data. However, it tends to restrict data access and results in duplication of data, lack of data sharing, and lack of data compatibility. If similar or identical data items are used in separate files, they are frequently updated separately at different updating intervals. There may be different quality control procedures, so that the data item values for identical entities may not agree. It is difficult to physically assemble data items when they exist on several separate files. It is also difficult to establish data security.

The solution to the problem is a single database that contains all related data files. A high uniform level of quality is obtained by quality assurance procedures applied consistently and by coordinated updating. All applications can access the data; all users of the data receive the same information with the same quality and recency. The logical concept of a database requires software to manage it (a database management system) and a special organizational authority over it. The *database administrator* is the person who has authority over definition and use of the database.

A *database management system* (DBMS) is a software system that manages the creation and use of databases. All access to the database is

FIGURE 10-1
DBMS as the Way to Access Data

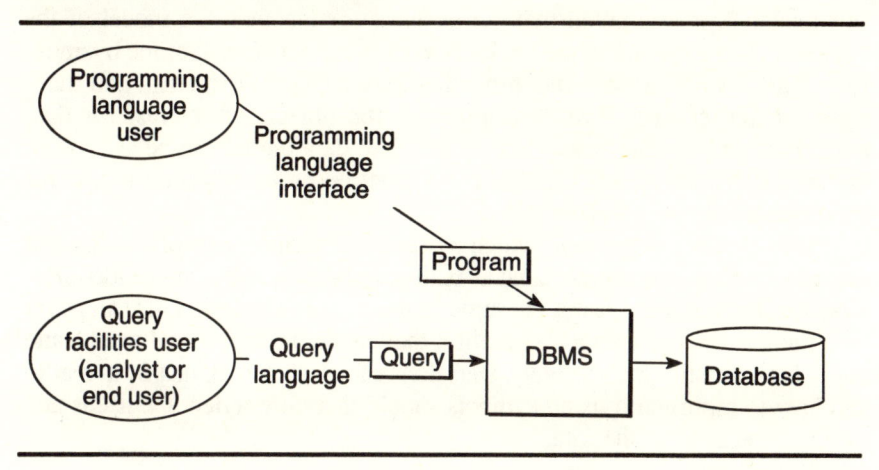

through the database management software; access language facilities are provided for application programmer users and end users who formulate queries. Thus, application programmers define a user view as a logical model of the data to be processed by the application program. The programmer writes instructions using a programming language interface to the database management system, which handles the translation to the internal schema of physical storage. All data validation and authorization checks of user authority to access a data item are handled through the DBMS. A person wishing to access the database for a query or special report uses a database query language to formulate the request and format the output. Thus, the database management system may be viewed as the only "door" to the physical storage of data in the database. This is depicted in Figure 10-1.

A *data dictionary* is used with a database. It contains the names and descriptions of all data items in the database. It may also contain definitions of relationships, integrity rules, and data processing procedures associated with the data items.

Report and application development facilities are often part of the database software. One example is a report generator that assists users in extracting information from a database and sorting and formatting it for a report. Another example is an application program generator designed to operate with the database software. It includes a program to generate the screens displayed to users, generate data retrievals, and handle logic associated with the application.

DATA MODELING

In Chapter 3, it was noted that the business architecture is a model of the business. The structure of the business system reflects four factors: business functions, coordination and communications, objects of interest, and management and control. The description of the objects of interest for data collection and storage is the data model. The data model can be an overall model for the enterprise, a model for a function or activity, or a model for an application.

Data consists of symbols which represent, describe, or record reality, but the data symbols are not the same as reality. In other words, a name identifies a person, but the name is not the same as the person. Data symbols can never be a complete representation of reality; they describe objects and events and their characteristics incompletely. Decisions about what to extract from reality and how to represent it using symbols should therefore reflect the needs and views of the users of the data.

> *Example*. An organization may ask employees about prior work experience, code their responses, and store the data items because personnel administration views prior work experience as important in understanding employee ability. Another user of employee data (such as the employee's medical plan insurer) may be interested in the characteristics of childhood illnesses because of their importance in employee immunity to certain diseases.

Logical and Physical Data Models

A data model is an abstract representation of data. It expresses the way entities are defined and related. The model can use a variety of representations. Examples are graphs, diagrams, tables and mathematical formulas. The objective is to represent the essential elements of the data without the detail.

There are two major classes of data models: logical data models and physical data models. These two classes reflect the fact that efficient physical storage and retrieval of data must be designed around the physical characteristics of storage media and devices, but users of data should be able to describe, think about, and use data without being concerned about its physical storage.

The user-oriented ways of describing and understanding data are termed logical data models or user views; the models that describe physical storage of data are physical data models or physical views. The two data models reflect a separation of what data is used from how data is stored and accessed. Ideally, changes in storage technology should be possible without affecting applications using data. This separation of the physical and logical data models is termed *data independence*.

The logical data model aids users and designers in specifying data requirements and relationships among data items. The logical model is conceptual; it

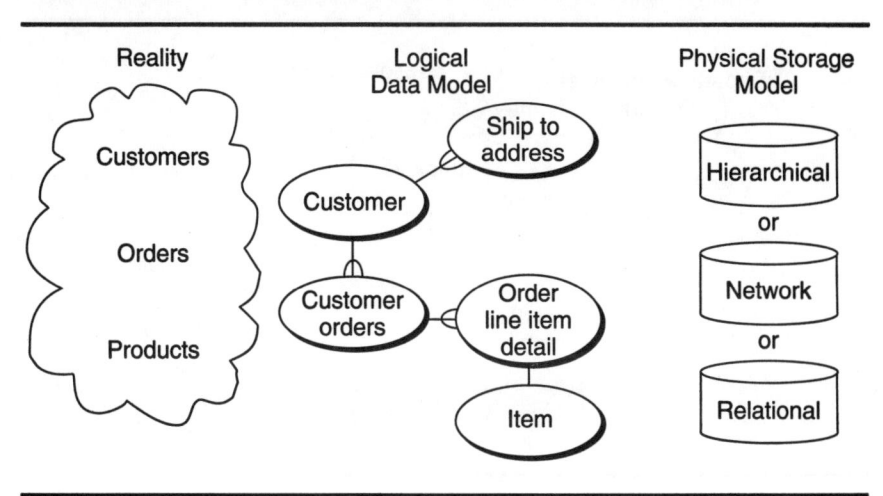

FIGURE 10-2
Relationship of Reality, Data Models, and Physical Storage of Data

Reality	Logical Data Model	Physical Storage Model
Customers, Orders, Products	Customer — Ship to address; Customer orders — Order line item detail — Item	Hierarchical or Network or Relational

mirrors the way users describe reality. It has also been termed a *semantic data model* because it focuses on the meaning of the data. The user or analyst is responsible for defining logical data requirements; the developer of the database system is responsible for defining the physical storage of data in such a way that the logical requirements can be met.

The overall flow from reality to logical views of data to physical storage models is shown in Figure 10-2. The complexity of reality is organized and simplified by mental models (that depend on users and user objectives). The mental model is likely to be imprecise, and it is necessary to describe data requirements by some type of formal, logical representation. This logical, user-oriented description of requirements is mapped into or related to a physical storage model that describes the structure of data for storage.

A knowledge of how data items are organized and stored in physical storage is not required for users; however, it is often helpful for users to have some knowledge of physical data storage in order to understand and respond to constraints in logical representation that may be imposed by physical storage.

This section has used the terms logical and physical data models. In the literature on database systems, other terms are also used. The term *schema* is often used as a synonym for view, model or diagram. Three major schemas are the external schema or user view (the way the user defines the data), the conceptual schema that is the overall logical model, and the internal schema that is the physical storage model.

FIGURE 10-3
Simplified Segment of Data Model

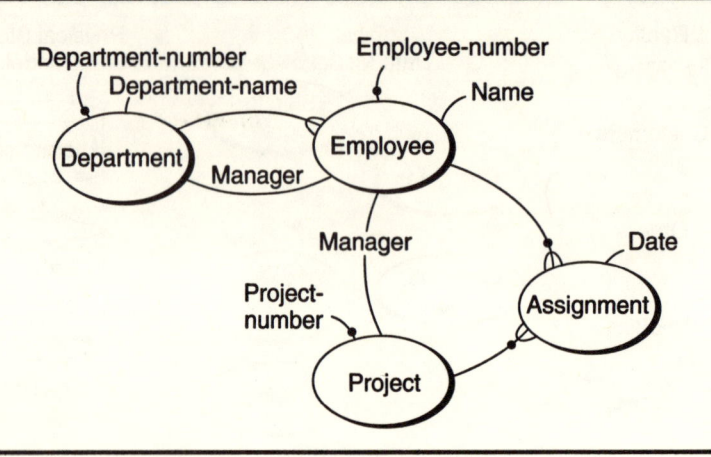

[Diagram showing entities: Department (with attributes Department-number, Department-name), Employee (with attributes Employee-number, Name), Project (with attribute Project-number), and Assignment (with attribute Date). Department and Employee are connected by a Manager relationship. Employee and Project are connected by a Manager relationship. Employee and Project are connected through Assignment as an intersection entity.]

Formalisms for Logical Data Modeling

The goal of logical data modeling (semantic data modeling) is to accurately and completely represent the data requirements of an application, a function or activity, or an enterprise. There are a variety of techniques and notations for preparing a data model. The most widely used is referred to as E-R modeling or Entity-Relationship modeling. Other data modeling formalisms are quite similar in objectives and outcomes. They all handle the four basic constructs of entity, attribute, relationship, and identifier. A modeling formalism will be used in the examples that is similar to the E-R model but allows only binary relationships.

A graphical representation is usually used during development of the data model. Figure 10-3 is a simplified example of a segment of a logical data model. There are four entities: department, employee, assignment, and project. In other words, the things that are objects of interest are departments, employees, projects, and assignments (intersection entity) that connect employees and projects. Each of these entities has several attributes. The attribute that is the identifier (or key) for the entity is marked with a black oval. The identifier for employee is employee-number and the identifier for project is project-number. Another attribute of employee, in the example, is name. The arc between entities shows the degree of relationship; a single line indicates one; the chicken foot lines indicate a many relationship. The relationship between department and employee says that a department can have many employees, but an employee belongs to only one department. Also, a department has only one manager and only one employee is manager of a department.

Preparing a Data Model

The value of preparing a data model is in identifying all objects of interest for which the organization should maintain data, the attributes that are of interest, and how entities are related. The model shows whether a proposed data analysis is supported by availability of data. In other words, if a proposed data analysis will depend on or make use of entities and relationships shown in the data model, the data can be retrieved and analyzed because the physical data model will reflect the logical data model. If a proposed analysis needs entities or attributes not in the logical model, they will not be available. If a proposed analysis will depend on entity relationships that are not modeled, it may be very difficult to obtain the data from the physical database; if it is possible, it will require significant processing to establish the data relationships.

> *Example.* In Figure 10-3, the relationship between department and projects is not modeled. A query about the projects for which the department is responsible is not possible.

Advocates of data modeling claim that the objects of interest for an organization, if carefully modeled, are quite stable; the processes for analysis and reporting are, in this view, more likely to change. In other words, a good data model will document how the organization (or function or application) views its world. If this is captured, then any analysis or reporting that is desired will have data available for it. Only if the view of the world changes will the data model change. The process of preparing a data model can be aided by computer-aided system engineering (CASE) tools explained in Chapter 8.

The details of data modeling are beyond the scope of this book. A simple example will, however, provide the basis for insight into the process[1] and a starting point for further study.

Assume there is a process to mix bulk chemicals to produce a batch of products to be sold in one, two, and five gallon cans.

1. Start with an analysis of existing documents. A simple document shown in Figure 10-4 is used to authorize a production batch.

2. Analyze activities to identify other objects of interest associated with the function that were not represented on the documents.

3. Categorize the headings of the documents into one of three classes: entity identifier, attribute, or calculated value. Name the entities and attributes. Do the same for objects of interest not on the documents. Start the data model diagram with the entities. The completed data model is shown in Figure 10-5.

---

[1] This is based on the work of Salvatore March. See, for example, his article, "Logical Data Modeling," in *Macmillan Encyclopedia of Computers.* New York: Macmillan, 1992.

FIGURE 10-4
Document to Authorize Production

Authorization for Production Batch

Date_____   Batch number_____

Product number _____

Product units _____

Yield per formula _____ Units _____

Production batch quantity _____

Line number	Raw materials number	Raw material units	Raw material description	Formula standard quantity	Batch standard quantity	Actual use
01						
02						
03						
04						
25						

Actual quantity produced_____

---

4. Establish relationships among entities. Show these on the diagram. Identify the minimum and maximum degree of relationship (one or many). A many-to-many relationship is not allowed, because this would result in ambiguous relationships. An apparent many-to-many relationship is usually resolved by an intersection entity that clarifies the relationship (not explained here).

5. Assign attributes to entities. Determine the attributes needed to calculate the calculated values and associate each with the appropriate entity.

6. Mark the identifier for each entity. This is the attribute that uniquely identifies an instance of the entity. (In Figure 10-5, the identifier attribute is marked with a black dot.)

There are some additional considerations in making a well-designed data model. Examples of these are how to model a relationship that applies to some but not all instances of an entity, how to model attributes that apply to some but not all instances, and how to deal with many-to-many relations with an intersection entity.

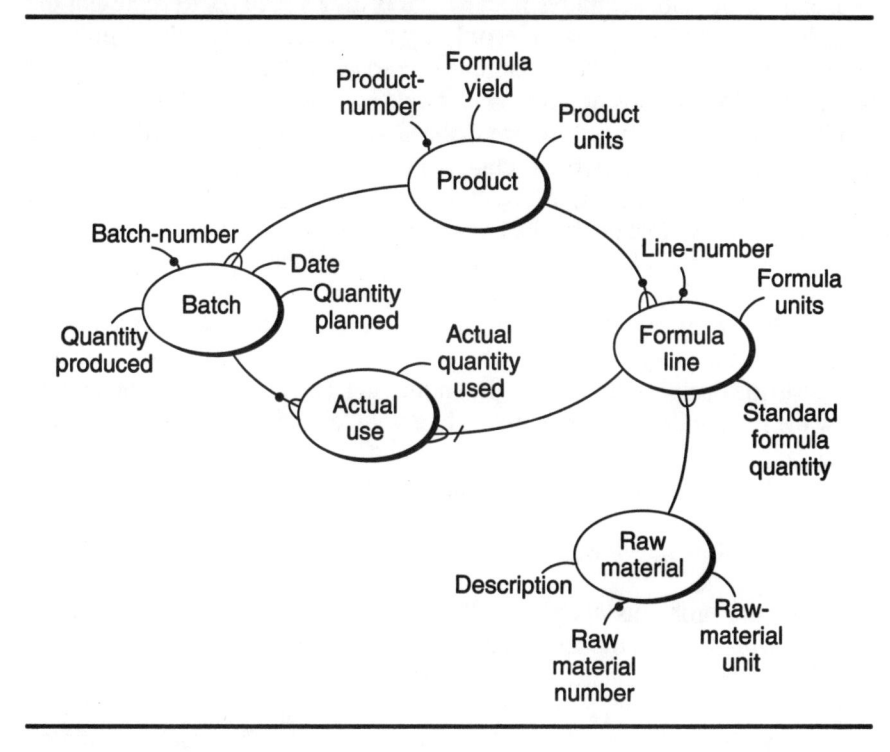

FIGURE 10-5
Simplified Data Model for Document in Figure 10-4

CONCEPTUAL DATABASE ORGANIZATIONS

Database management systems handle all of the physical details of storage and retrieval. Although the user need not know how the DBMS stores the data, the user does need to have a conceptual model of database organization in order to formulate queries and use programming facilities to access data. There are four models of how a database is organized. These models have corresponding physical implementations, but a database may provide facilities to allow the user to utilize one model for formulating queries while the physical implementation utilizes another. The models are hierarchical, network, relational, and object-oriented. They will be described as conceptual models to guide the user rather than as physical implementation models.

Hierarchical Database Model

A hierarchical model employs hierarchical or tree structures to represent the relationships among entities. A record may have multiple records subordinate to it, which in turn may have multiple records subordinate to them. In other words, multiple records of a particular type "belong to" (are subordinate to) a single record of another type higher in the hierarchy. "Parent" records can have several "children" records, but a "child" can have only one "parent." A hierarchy essentially describes a complex object. Figure 10-6 shows a simple schematic of a hierarchical tree structure for the five entities in the data model in Figure 10-5.

Many natural relationships among entities can be represented well in a hierarchical model (e.g., multiple employees belong to a single department, a product has many parts which in turn have parts). In other words, the hierarchical model of a database is very natural for any business situation in which people in the business think about the entities in terms of a hierarchy and might draw the relationships as a hierarchy chart with high levels divided into lower levels, etc. In some cases, all entities do not fit easily into the hierarchy. In Figure 10-6, the RAW MATERIAL entity is not in a hierarchy.

Network Database Model

Some of the problems encountered with a hierarchical data model can be avoided with network model. A hierarchical structure has one superior record for one or more subordinates. A network structure allows a given entity to have any number of superiors as well as any number of subordinates. The relationships between entities are represented by what are termed as sets. A common

FIGURE 10-6
Schematic of Hierarchical Database Model

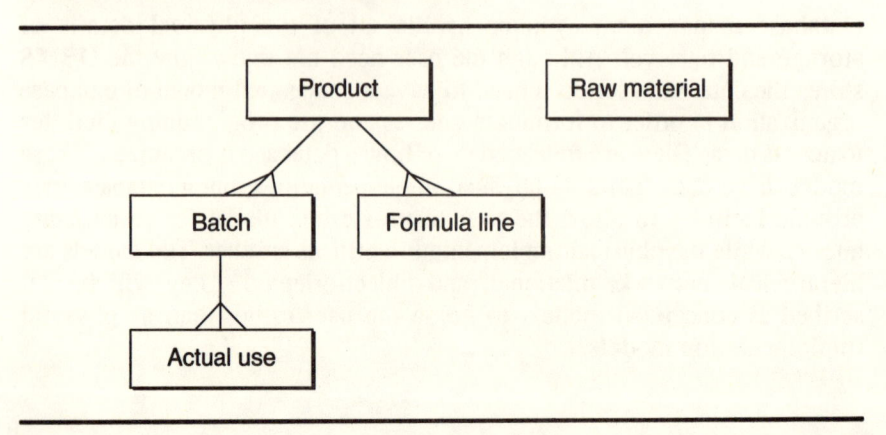

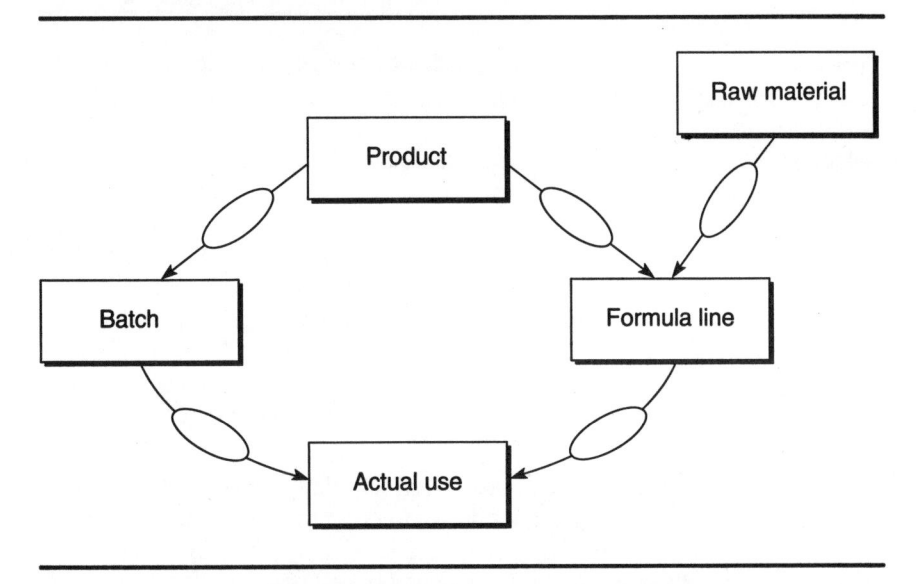

FIGURE 10-7
Schematic of Network Database Model

approach is to link related records via pointers. In terms of objects of interest, networks support explicit definition of relationships. A network structure is depicted schematically in Figure 10-7 for five entities in the data model in Figure 10-5.

Although many of the problems inherent in a hierarchical model do not exist with a network database model, a major disadvantage of a network model is that it tends to be more complex for a user. A user of a network model must have explicit knowledge of the relationships represented, including the sets, in order to formulate a query.

Relational Database Model

In the relational model, the database is conceived as a set of tables that define simple objects (do not contain relations or hierarchies). In each table, the rows (called tuples) represent unique entities or records and columns represent attributes (data items). Each table is termed a *relation*. Relationships are represented by common data values in different relations (tables). Relational data structures are based on a formal theory of relational algebra which uses very specific terms to refer to the concepts underlying the structure. Figure 10-8 shows a schematic of the tabular logic of the relational database structure for the five entities (each a relation) in Figure 10-5.

Operation	Explanation
Projection	Select specified columns from a table to create a new table.
Selection	Create a new table by selecting rows that satisfy conditions.
Join	Create a new table from the rows in two tables that have attributes satisfying a condition. For example, a new table with all batches for a given product is obtained by joining the PRODUCT and BATCH tables.

The use of common data values to reflect relationships is shown in the diagram; the other attributes are not drawn in order to simplify the figure.

The logic associated with formation of requests is fairly natural. In processing tables there are three fundamental operations.

Object-Oriented Database Model

The relatively new object-oriented database model is based on the same concepts as object-oriented programming described in Chapter 7. A database object encapsulates data and methods associated with an entity. This means that an entity will have associated with it not just attributes but also methods. The PRODUCT entity, for example, might have a method for parts explosion. A query message to PRODUCT could ask for the entity to provide a parts explosion.

From the user standpoint, an object-oriented database model can be simple and convenient. Methods that are likely to be used are stored with the entity. The user does not have to think about how to formulate a query to direct the database management system to perform the actions. In current query systems, it is necessary for the user to formulate the query in order to direct the system to do a parts explosion (for example). A user who expects to repeat such a query will develop a standard method and write a macroinstruction or template to reduce effort. In a sense, the object-oriented database model incorporates the template with the entity itself.

Object-oriented databases are a fairly new concept. They are fairly difficult to physically implement. However, the advantages of this model suggest it will receive increased use.

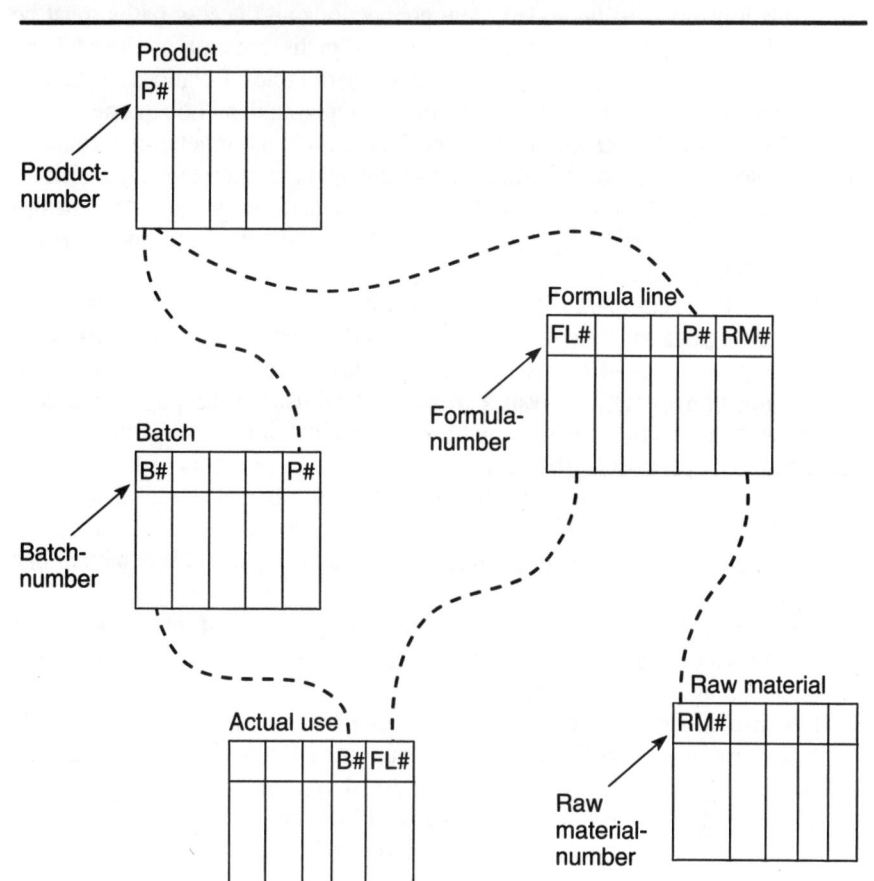

Modeling Data Requirements and Using Databases **215**

FIGURE 10-8
Schematic of Tabular Logic of Relational Database Structure

[Diagram showing five related tables:]

- **Product** table with key **P#** (Product-number)
- **Batch** table with key **B#** (Batch-number) and attribute **P#**
- **Formula line** table with key **FL#** (Formula-number) and attributes **P#**, **RM#**
- **Actual use** table with attributes **B#**, **FL#**
- **Raw material** table with key **RM#** (Raw material-number)

Dotted lines indicate how relations (tables) are related by common attributes (keys and foreign keys) in the tables. See Figure 10-5.

Issues of a Physical Database Model

The issue of a conceptual database model can be separated from the physical implementation. The logical or conceptual model should fit the way the users think about the data. The physical model may be the same as the logical database model but may be different to reflect physical implementation considerations and performance issues.

The relational database model has several advantages. In a hierarchical or network model, the connections and relationships are in the data structure. If a new relationship is to be added, new connections and access paths must be established. In a relational database, access paths are not predetermined. Creating new relations simply requires a joining of tables. Relational databases are therefore the most flexible and useful for unplanned, ad hoc queries.

The preestablished relationships of the hierarchical or network structures require more complex data definition and data manipulation languages. Maintenance is more difficult. The relational model data definition and data manipulation languages are simple and user-oriented. Maintenance and physical storage are fairly simple.

Given these comparative advantages, why are all databases not relational? For many applications, there are issues of performance related to transaction processing and pre-defined, frequent retrievals. If retrievals for transaction processing or repeated analysis can be preestablished, the physical access paths can be much more efficient with a hierarchical or network structure than general table operations. Therefore, if there are large numbers of records (say more than a million), and/or performance requirements are critical, or if transaction volumes are large, and ad hoc queries are very infrequent, the hierarchical or network models are more efficient physical implementations than the relational model.

Proponents of relational structures point out that, even if the nonrelational system provides superior run time performance, the value of that benefit has to be balanced against the amount of time it takes to get the system operational and the time for maintenance. Some experts advocate two types of DBMS: a high performance DBMS and a decision support DBMS. A high performance database structure is advocated for operational systems with high transaction processing rates, large amounts of data, and high online availability requirements. A relational database structure is advocated for applications focusing on ease of use, ease of change, short development cycle, database scan capabilities, and reporting capabilities.

PHYSICAL DATABASE ORGANIZATION

Physical data models describe how to put data items into storage locations so that they can be retrieved. Traditional data processing has used file organizations; the trend is toward more complex physical organization required for databases. Efficiency in processing is a dominant factor in file organization, whereas database organization is also influenced by other factors such as availability, evolvability, and integrity.

A short survey of some physical implementation concerns and methods is useful background for a user. Although the user need not be concerned with the details of data storage and access mechanisms, some understanding will help a user to appreciate why some queries are almost instantaneous and others can take significant time.

Concerns in Database Organization

The organization of data is influenced by a number of factors, but by far the most significant factor is the very large difference between the time required to access a record and transfer the data to primary storage (or to write a record) compared with the time to do the processing once the record is in primary storage. The magnitude of this relative difference for disk drives is from 1,000:1 to 100,000:1.

Given the significant differences in these times, an important factor in information system file design is a physical organization that will support the kind of record access needed yet be efficient in terms of access times.

Five types of operations are required for a database. These are database creation, locating a record, adding a record, deleting a record, and modifying a record. Database physical designs differ in efficiency for these operations. The choice of physical implementation will therefore be influenced by the physical storage device being used and the mix of operations.

The physical storage and access design is likely to use sequential, hashed, indexed, or multikey access methods. Each of these will be described briefly. It may be helpful to understand the concept of a pointer in connection with physical access methods. No matter what the organization and access method, records are stored in locations that have addresses. A separate data item in the record (or in an index) may be used to indicate (point to) the storage location of a related record.

Sequential Access Method

In a sequential access method the entity instances or records are stored and accessed in order by the identifier or record key. There is a single sequential access path for obtaining records. For example, if the identifier of the customer record is customer number, the record for customer 35012 will precede the record for customer 35013 in the record sequence. Sequential file organization is consistent with many periodic business processes such as weekly payroll, monthly billing, etc. It also works well with magnetic tape in which records can be accessed only sequentially. If disk direct access storage is used for sequential organization, it is not necessary for the records on a disk to be physically stored in sequence, since each record may contain a pointer data item with the address of the next record in the sequence.

Hashed Access Method

Since storage technology permits many external access paths to stored data, it is not necessary to read records sequentially. Records can be accessed in random order. The major difficulty is determining the storage location where a record is stored. Thus, some relationship must be established between the record key and the storage location; this will determine where an individual record is initially stored and subsequently accessed. In other words, the task is to take a set of record keys and find a formula to map them into a set of disk storage location identifiers. An arithmetic procedure to transform the record key into a direct access storage address is termed hashing or randomizing. A hashing procedure takes part or all of the record key and performs an arithmetic procedure to produce a random number falling somewhat uniformly in the range of the assigned storage identifiers.

The advantages of the hashed direct access method arise primarily in situations where the records need to be located quickly such as in online inquiry and online updating. A difficulty with the hashed organization is that hashing may result in two or more record keys yielding the same address. This is handled by overflow procedures, which is not a problem unless most of the storage locations are used.

Indexed Access Method

In the indexed direct access method, determining the storage location is a separate operation from accessing the record. An index contains a list of record keys and the physical address of the record associated with each key. To find a particular record, the index is searched for the record key and the index entry points to the record.

A common indexed organization is the indexed sequential organization. Records are stored on the disk sequentially by record key so that sequential processing may be performed, but indexes are also maintained to allow direct retrieval based on a key value. The indexed sequential organization allows records to be processed relatively efficiently in either sequential or random order, depending on the processing operations.

Multiattribute Access Method

The three access methods described so far not easily support access to a record through multiple attributes or multiple keys. The concept of using indexes for locating records in the database may be extended to the creation of indexes for many data items in the records. An index may contain all possible values for a particular data item (or ranges of values) and a pointer to every record that contains that value for the data item. This concept is called an *inverted index*.

Inverted indexes are very efficient for information retrieval by multiple attributes. The index is searched for the attribute values desired rather than having to search the file itself. Multiple indexes may be compared for retrieval on multiple fields. Search routines find the appropriate value in the two indexes and select all record addresses that are common to both. The records meeting the criteria are accessed based on the addresses in the indexes.

A list organization may be used in place of inverted indexes to link together all fields with the same content. In the inverted index, a record address is stored which points to the appropriate record in the file. In a list organization, the pointers are moved to the records themselves and stored as separate data items. A record may be part of several logical list files because there may be many pointers in the same record. The pointers allow a logical retrieval and processing sequence to be imposed on the file regardless of the physical sequence of the records in the file.

ISSUES IN ENTERPRISE DATABASES

In the literature, enterprise database planning is proposed and many organizations have projects along this line. The reasoning in favor of enterprise database planning is that the objects of interest for an organization are not easily partitioned for departments or functions; they are likely to be needed across several departments or functions. In fact, it may not be possible to know in advance where or how data will be needed.

The enterprise database planning concept has intuitive appeal but has some operational problems. These problems relate to the ability of a central database planning effort to capture the data model for an organization and deal with the inherent complexities. By the time a central group has collected all of the data model information and coordinated it, the organization may have changed. People's understanding of objects of interest may have changed either by greater awareness or changes in the business. Also, such a large data model becomes very complex, and the effort becomes difficult to manage.

The creation of an enterprise database serving all needs of the organization again has intuitive appeal but operational difficulties. When databases are associated with some primary users, those users tend to take responsibility for its completeness and accuracy. When there is an organization database, who is responsible? A central data administration group can take some responsibility, but user responsibility for completeness and accuracy is diminished. A large central database reduces problems of coordination for updating and correcting of the database; however, it also introduces significant security and downtime issues. If a single enterprise database is used, the dangers from failure or security violation are increased.

An alternative is to create separate data models and databases, i.e., to distribute the databases. The databases can be designed around locations or functions. For example, the vendor database used by purchasing may be organized as a separate database. Plants at two different locations may have local databases covering their operations. It is still necessary to communicate with the separate databases, but the data transferred may be relatively small.

Having distributed databases raises issues of coordination because the databases may have common information that must be updated at all locations. If other locations can access and read from the distributed databases but not update or change, the timing and coordination issues are reduced. If, on the other hand, updates are allowed, there must be strict procedures.

OTHER KINDS OF DATABASES

The discussion to this point has been oriented to databases that contain numeric data (with limited text associated with it). Databases can be used for non-numeric data. Databases can store anything that can be digitized (represented by digital codes). As explained earlier, text can be represented by codes for letters and symbols, graphics and pictures can be represented by codes for pixels, voice can be represented by codes for the waveforms that represent speech. In other words, in addition to numeric data, databases can store text, graphics and pictures, voice messages, and multimedia data. A special type of database is a modelbase that stores computational and analytical models

Text Databases

Databases that store primarily text are used for in-company information such as letters, memoranda, and reports. Text databases are widely used for information retrieval of articles, reports, books, etc.

In terms of technology, text databases may be stored on regular magnetic media, but the storage capacity of magnetic disks is fairly small compared to the size of texts. Therefore, optical disk storage is often used for this purpose.

Retrieval from text databases can take several forms: searching for keywords that have been placed in indexes, searching abstracts of documents, or full text search. The search is defined in terms of search words. Combinations of words can be specified by AND and OR conditions and exclusions can be stipulated by NOT commands. For example, all documents that have the words MRP and Material Requirements Planning in them but do not mention TQM or Total Quality Management would be specified by a command with the search conditions: MRP OR Material Requirements Planning AND NOT (TQM OR Total Quality Management).

Most word processing packages contain text search commands to search a document or to search all documents in a directory. For example, a person may have forgotten the file name for a letter stored in a directory. Using a text search command, all of the documents in the file will be searched for words that are contained in the document.

Graphics, Picture, and Document Image Databases

Graphics, pictures, and document images may be stored because they can be digitized as pixels. In doing a database search, however, the search is done on a title, description, date, author, or other text information associated with the stored representation.

An important type of database is a geographic database that maintains maps, photographs, satellite pictures, and other geographic data. Associated with the maps are data about the areas such as census data. Maps can be retrieved and processed to produce selected portions with overlaid data and other similar features.

Voice and Multimedia Databases

Voice and multimedia presentations can be stored by digital encoding of voice. Searching is done by using indexes that store titles, descriptions, times, and so forth.

Modelbases

A user of information technology may have a need for a large collection of models for computation and analysis. These can be viewed as a file of programs or routines. However, it is also possible to create indexes of descriptors that categorize the models in terms of problems to which they apply, methods, constraints, and so forth.

ONLINE DATABASES FROM EXTERNAL SUPPLIERS

A large variety of text databases are available for use with one's own system. Examples are dictionary, encyclopedia, and census data. In addition to databases that may be purchased for use, there are vendors that sell access to online databases.

The access to online databases is through a communications line to the vendor. The cost can range from a few dollars to several hundred dollars per hour. The savings to the user may, however, be very substantial in terms of breadth of search and being able to do it from the office. The following are examples of online databases:

- Financial records of thousands of firms.
- Medical and social science literature.
- The *Federal Register* and other government agency reports.
- Full text of *The Wall Street Journal*.
- Periodicals and newspapers.
- Standard library reference books.
- Trade, industry, and professional newsletters.
- Comprehensive list of academic and professional publications.
- Doctoral dissertations—titles and abstracts.

As an example, a restaurant supply company interested in exploring the use of improved inventory management procedures might do a search to find articles and reports on inventory management procedures in restaurant supply companies. This is a very specialized request that would be very expensive to undertake manually. Only a few citations may be found, but they are likely to be valuable. Some vendors will supply the full text of the articles either online or as a separate copy service.

LESSONS FOR MANAGERS

The database is a vital part of the information system of an organization. Technology for managing data is critical. A manager needs to understand basic concepts of data and data modeling. Physical implementation is handled by a database management system, so detailed knowledge of physical storage is not necessary. Some understanding of physical access mechanisms is useful, however, in order to appreciate the limitations of database access.

Organizations capture and store data about objects of interest. These are termed entities and correspond roughly to objects for which organizations maintain files. Each entity instance (like a record) has attributes or characteristics that describe and differentiate it. Record sequencing is important for business data processing and report preparation. Sequencing is based on attributes of records and sorting operations. Traditional data processing files are still applicable to many transaction systems. A master file for relatively permanent data, transaction file or detail file for transactions, and report file that is derived from the other files and sequenced for report preparation.

A data model is an abstract representation of data. It defines the way data entities are organized and related. The objective is to represent the essential elements of the data without the detail. Data modeling is the process of creating a data model. There are a variety of formalisms for doing data modeling, but the entity-relationship approach is most common.

Rather than having separate files for the different records in an organization, databases are used for related sets of data. A high uniform level of quality is obtained by quality assurance procedures applied consistently and by coordinated updating. All applications can access the data; all users of the data receive the same information with the same quality and the same recency. The logical concept of a database requires software to manage it (a database management system) and a special organizational authority over it (database administration).

Four different concepts of database organizations are hierarchical, network, relational, and object-oriented models. Each of the models has advantages and disadvantages for users in conceptualizing and formulating queries to obtain data. The database management system handles the physical implementation of database organizations. It is useful, however, for users to have an awareness of access methods for obtaining records from a database. The common methods are sequential, hashed, and indexed access. Multiattribute access methods are also used.

Databases are also used for non-numeric data. Databases can store text, graphics and pictures, voice messages, and multimedia data. A special type of database is a modelbase that stores computational and analytical models.

CHAPTER 11

ORGANIZATION AND OPERATION OF THE INFORMATION MANAGEMENT FUNCTION

The organization and operation of the information management (or MIS) function are based on the fundamental principles of organization and management. After a history of rapid evolution, the function has emerged with a strong organizational mission. The chapter focuses on several major organization and management alternatives for the function. The chapter describes how the information system master plan can be used to coordinate information technology activities. The MIS function essentially runs a factory to process information and provide services. This requires management of computer operations and control of information processing costs. It also involves an assessment of the MIS function.

THE INFORMATION MANAGEMENT FUNCTION

During the past 30 to 40 years, there has been a major change in the business role of information management. A new organization function has emerged. Information management has become important to the vitality and competitiveness of organizations. The phenomenon is found in small, medium, and large organizations, although the size difference affects the way information management is organized and operated.

The Evolution of the Information Management Function in Medium to Large Organizations

There has been a dramatic increase in the scope of the information management function from the mid-1950s to the early 1990s (Figure 11-1). As a broad perspective, a series of changes has been observed in organizations large enough to create separate organizational units to manage information processing.

FIGURE 11-1
Increasing Scope of Information Management

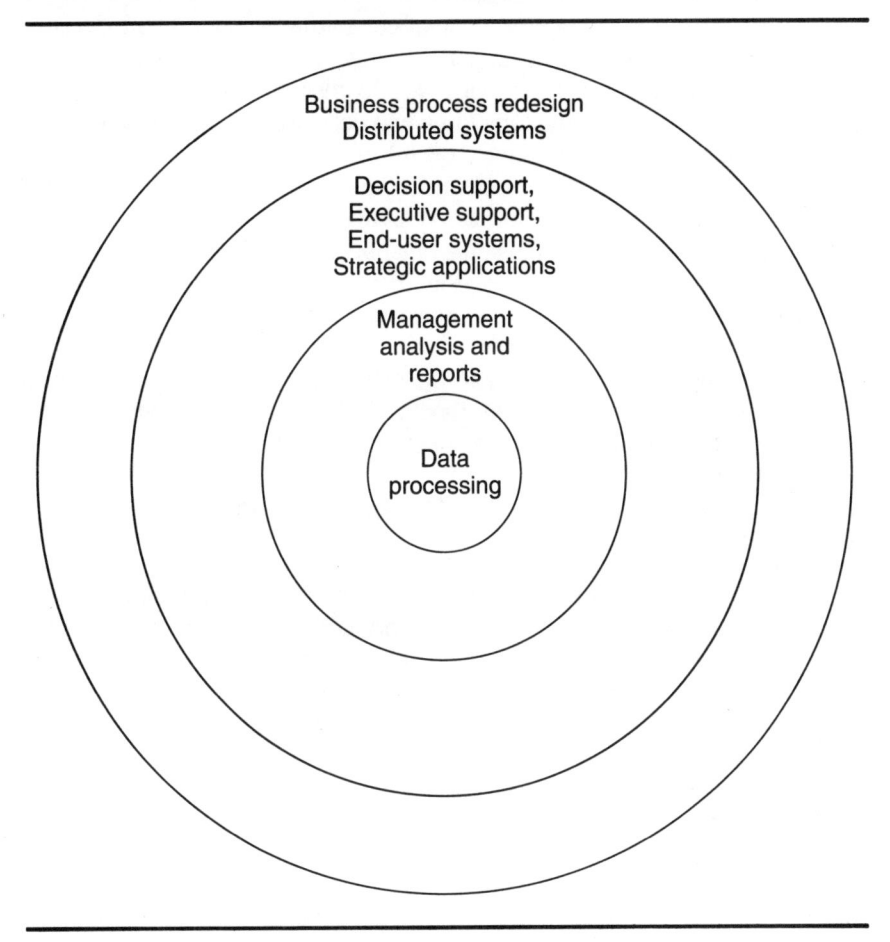

- Business process redesign
  Distributed systems
- Decision support,
  Executive support,
  End-user systems,
  Strategic applications
- Management analysis and reports
- Data processing

In the 1950s and 1960s, computers were introduced in most medium and large organizations. Many of them had previously used punched card equipment; and the computer processing function was considered a successor. A frequent name for the function was data processing. The function was almost always centralized. The systems tended to be oriented to batch processing of transactions and preparation of business documents and reports.

In the 1970s, many organizations began to add applications to support management activities and various types of analytical and decision-oriented applications. The function, in some organizations, was renamed the MIS or information systems department. Centralization was still the dominant mode, but some decentralization occurred.

In the 1980s, the management use of computing increased with decision support systems and executive support systems. There was emphasis on strategic uses of information technology. Minicomputers and microcomputers supported a trend to end-user computing and decentralization of many activities. The function was often renamed the information management function to reflect the pervasive role of information in the organization and the alignment of business architecture and information architecture. The Chief Information Officer (CIO) was established in some organizations.

The 1990s are continuing previous trends to decentralize many information management activities and to downsize the centralized computer facilities. The distribution of hardware, software, and databases has increased end-user computing applications and the need for a smaller but higher-level corporate information management function. The emphasis on business process redesign has placed new responsibilities on information systems personnel.

The Evolution of the Information Management Function in Small Organizations

In small organizations without sufficient size to have a separate information management department, there are still information management activities to be organized and managed. There is still an information management function even though, organizationally, it may be part of accounting or some other unit.

Many small organizations started to use computers in the 1960s by buying basic transaction processing and reporting through a service bureau that used standard packages for typical activities such as billing, payroll, and inventory accounting. One person was usually sufficient for managing the relationship with service providers.

In the late 1970s and early 1980s, the technology became much less costly and much simpler to operate. Small computer systems (such as minicomputers) were very reliable and required few staff to operate. Microcomputers were introduced as computers for individuals but, by the end of the 1980s, they were sufficiently powerful for multiple users in a department or across the entire company. Packages were available for these systems and many vendors provided turnkey systems that required a very small internal staff.

In the early 1990s the use of turnkey hardware/software solutions has been continuing, especially in small businesses. Users within small businesses are using microcomputer software packages for end user computing in much the same way as users in large organizations. The use of turnkey systems still requires an internal MIS person with management responsibility for planning system needs, dealing with vendors, and supervising operations. There is also a need to support end users.

Why Organizations Have a Separate MIS Function

Why should there be a separate information management function (in whatever form it takes in the organization)? The question is at the heart of organization design. Why is there a separate production, scheduling, purchasing, or accounting function? Why not let each person or department in the organization handle their own scheduling, purchasing, or accounting? The major reasons are the benefits of specialized knowledge for specialized activities and the need for coordination. If an activity is specialized, there are benefits from hiring specialists in the domain and assigning the specialized work to them. As an example, accounting activities beyond simple transactions and reports require specialized knowledge of rules, standards, and procedures. To train everyone as a professional accountant would be too costly, so an accounting department is formed.

The second compelling reason for separate organizational functions is coordination. Personnel throughout the organization use or depend on activities performed by others. The tasks they perform require agreement on procedures, standards, and allowable operations. For example, if every person, even if trained in accounting, developed his or her own chart of accounts for coding transactions, there would be confusion. If every person made his or her own interpretation of accounting rules for depreciation, it would be almost impossible to prepare financial statements.

Whenever specialists, such as information systems personnel, provide services for others (who otherwise would do it for themselves), there are costs and benefits. Extra costs are incurred in order to communicate requirements to specialists such as information systems specialists and to monitor their work. In the case of an application, for example, costs are incurred because the user must provide requirements to and monitor the work of analysts and programmers who develop the system. The issue is whether these costs are less than the benefits. The issue is not unique to information systems; the same discussion can be held relative to other specialists.

ORGANIZING THE INFORMATION MANAGEMENT FUNCTION

The information management function requires an organization to manage the activities and perform technical support, application development and implementation, and operations. There are a number of specialized MIS positions in a large company; for a small company, the positions will be limited. The organization structure can be a functional or matrix one. The information system operations and development can be either centralized or decentralized.

Activities within the Information Management Function

Within the information management function, there are a variety of activities to be performed. These require different technical, managerial, and people skills. The activities may also differ in the motivation they provide for those who perform them. There are four broad classes of activities to be performed:

1. Management of the information management function.
   —Planning the information system infrastructure
   —Planning, budgeting, and scheduling the work of the function
   —Organizing the function and its activities
   —Staff selection, training, assignment, and evaluation
2. Technical support.
   —Tracking new technologies and standards
   —Technical innovation experimentation and evaluation
   —Selection of new or replacement computer hardware, software, and communications services
   —Technical training of staff and users
   —Technical support for users of systems and services
3. Development and implementation of applications (described in Chapter 8).
   —Track developments in software packages and development tools
   —Define, develop, and maintain applications
   —Implement applications
4. Operations.
   —Operate computer facilities operations
   —Perform security, backup, and recovery operations
   —Install and maintain system software
   —Operate and service communications facilities

Organization Structure

The information management function may have an organizational structure based on functions to be performed or a matrix of responsibilities. Each of these structures has advantages and disadvantages.

The most common organizational structure for information systems is a functional organization. Personnel are grouped by the function they perform such as application system development and operations. Figure 11-2 shows a typical functional organization structure for a large organization. There are three managers reporting to the executive for information management: a systems development manager, an operations manager, and a technical services manager. Within systems development, a functional organization will have managers for separate development functions such as systems analysis

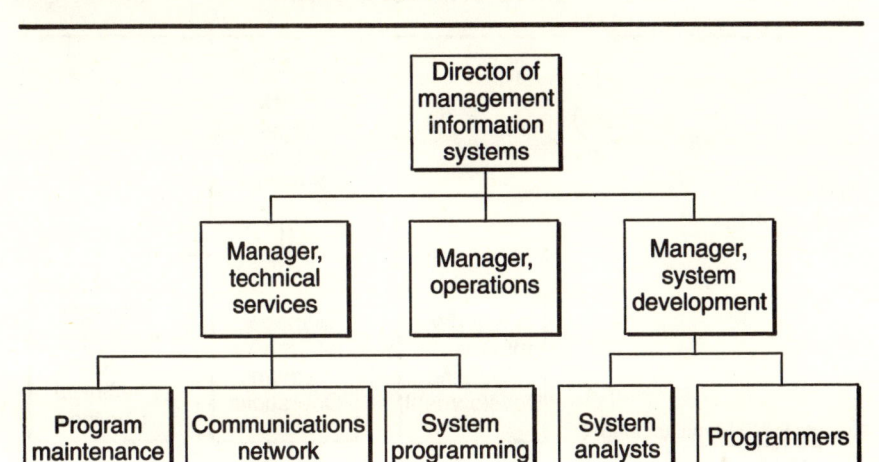

FIGURE 11-2
Functional Information System Organization

```
                    Director of
                    management
                    information
                      systems
        ┌───────────────┼───────────────┐
    Manager,         Manager,         Manager,
    technical       operations         system
    services                        development
    ┌───┬───┬───┐                    ┌───┬───┐
 Program  Communications  System   System  Programmers
 mainte-  network        program-  analysts
 nance    services       ming
```

and applications programming. Under technical services, there may be managers for program maintenance, communications network services, and systems programming. Under operations (not shown), a possible functional breakdown is input and output control, computer center operations, security, and capacity management. One advantage of a functional organization is specialization of personnel. One disadvantage is the narrow view promoted by technical specialization.

The matrix organization applies when the information management function is dispersed among different organizational units. Each information systems professional reports to the management of the organizational unit it supports; it has a "dotted line" relationship to a corporate information systems executive who provides technical direction, coordination, standardization, and other support services. The matrix organization can be applied to all parts of the information systems function or only to some. For example, Figure 11-3 illustrates a matrix organization in which each major business function has its own application development staff; a manager of application development for a function reports directly to the manager of that function and reports on a dotted line basis to the corporate information systems executive. In this example, only application system development is decentralized; the functions of system operations and technical services are centralized.

One advantage of this matrix organization for system development is responsiveness to user requirements. One disadvantage is the narrow view

FIGURE 11-3
Matrix Structure for Information System Development

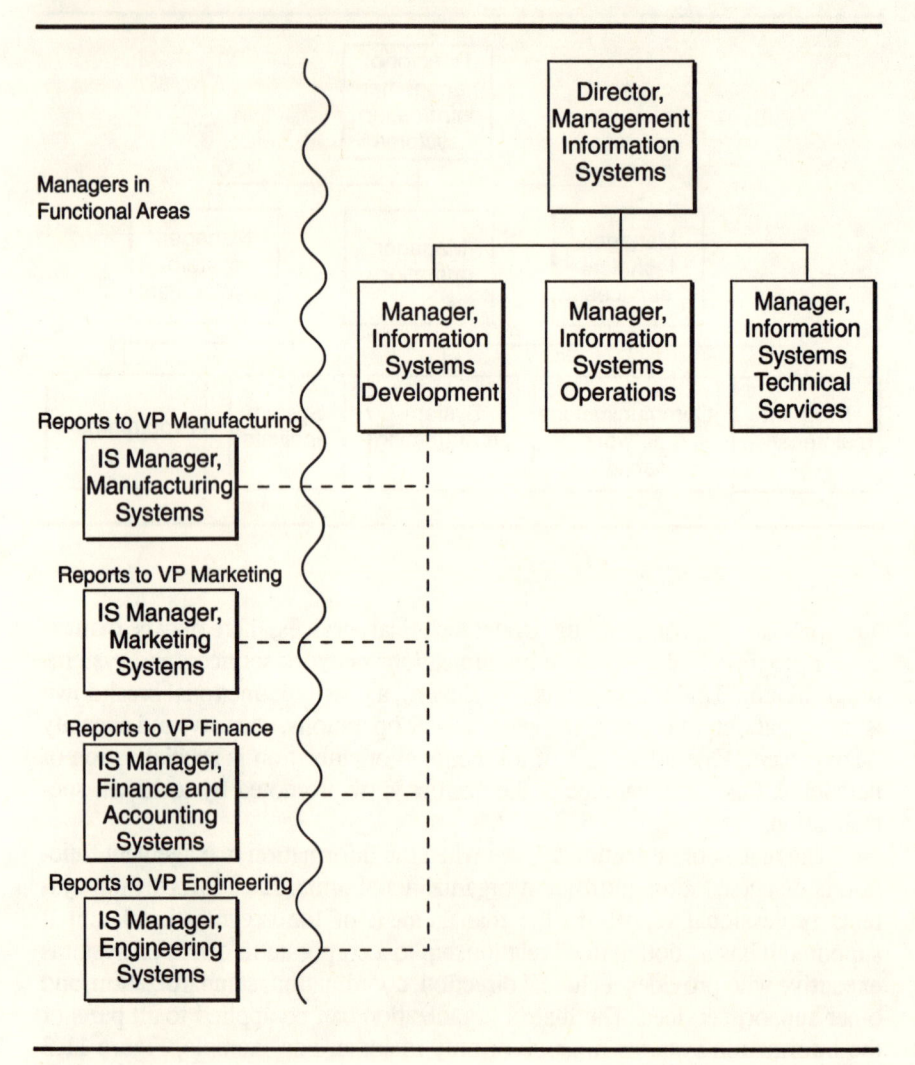

```
Managers in
Functional Areas

                                    Director,
                                   Management
                                   Information
                                     Systems
                                        |
              ┌─────────────────────────┼─────────────────────────┐
              |                         |                         |
          Manager,                  Manager,                  Manager,
         Information              Information              Information
           Systems                  Systems                  Systems
         Development               Operations               Technical
                                                             Services

Reports to VP Manufacturing
  ┌──────────────┐
  │ IS Manager,  │
  │Manufacturing │──────────────┤
  │   Systems    │
  └──────────────┘

Reports to VP Marketing
  ┌──────────────┐
  │ IS Manager,  │
  │  Marketing   │──────────────┤
  │   Systems    │
  └──────────────┘

Reports to VP Finance
  ┌──────────────┐
  │ IS Manager,  │
  │  Finance and │──────────────┤
  │  Accounting  │
  │   Systems    │
  └──────────────┘

Reports to VP Engineering
  ┌──────────────┐
  │ IS Manager,  │
  │ Engineering  │──────────────┤
  │   Systems    │
  └──────────────┘
```

promoted by functional specialization. The matrix organization approach is frequently employed for information system development projects in which information system staff and users report to their functional area supervisors and to the project manager.

MIS Positions in a Large Organization

While some of the work of systems professionals has been shifting to users, recruiting and retention of technically trained employees is still a major management task. Not all of the following positions will be found in every installation. Certain duties will be combined or not performed in smaller installations. In some cases, organizations have combined positions for performance purposes. The most common example is combining the duties of analyst and programmer into a programmer-analyst position. The rationale is that this provides continuity for system development and reduces communication difficulties inherent in two separate positions.

One reason for the diversity of positions is the range of skills, training, and aptitude required. For example, successful analysts tend to have different aptitudes and require different training than programmers. They also need a broader organizational perspective. Analysts need to deal with people as well as systems; programmers deal with programming languages, compilers, and

TABLE 11-1

Position	Description
Information analyst	Works with users to define information requirements. Requires ability to work with people and understanding of organization, management, and decision-making functions. Requires more organizational knowledge and analytical skills than technical skills.
System designer	Designs computer-based processing system (files, program specifications, etc.) to provide the information specified by the information analyst. Requires higher technical capability than information analyst. Knowledge of programming is helpful.
Systems analyst	Combines duties of information analyst and system designer.
Application programmer	Designs, codes, and tests programs based on specifications from system designer. Requires ability to design, code, debug, and document computer programs.
Maintenance programmer	Works on the maintenance (repairs and enhancements) of existing application programs.

TABLE 11-1 (*cocluded*)

Position	Description
Program librarian	Maintains library of programs and documentation. Schedules changes to production applications after completion of testing and maintains records of changes.
Data communications specialist	Designs systems for data communications support. Requires expertise in data communications hardware and software and distributed processing.
Database administrator	Administers and controls the corporate database.
User liaison	Coordinates communication flows between users and systems analysts, primarily for long-range planning and the definition stage of application development.
Office automation coordinator	Provides assistance in development of office applications. Requires knowledge of all hardware and software related to office automation.
Information center analyst	Provides guidance and training to users in solving user-defined problems, particularly using personal computers and software.
Operator	Operates the computer equipment.
Data control clerk	Establishes control over jobs and input data to be processed. Checks controls on processing and distributes output to authorized recipients.
Data entry clerk	Enters data into machine-readable form for processing, using data entry devices or online terminals.
Security coordinator	Establishes system security procedures, monitors security, and investigates security violations.
Systems programmer	Maintains specialized software such as operating systems and data management systems. Writes specialized system-level routines. Requires technical proficiency in hardware and software, usually specialized by the particular type of hardware in use.

documentation systems. This does not mean a person cannot be both a good analyst and programmer, but it does suggest that different recruiting criteria and different training are necessary.

MIS Positions in a Small Company

Smaller organizations typically require only a few job categories in the information management function. In a small company using a turnkey system with package software, only one fulltime system administrator is typically required. The system administrator operates the computer facilities, performs backup and recovery procedures, coordinates with vendors regarding upgrades and user questions, provides support and training to end users, and performs limited software development (such as preparing custom reports).

If the company has only one person who knows how to perform these activities, there is significant risk to the information capabilities of the organization if the person quits, dies, or has a severe illness. Also, from an internal control standpoint, it is not desirable to have the operations performed by only one person. The solution in a small company is to train an assistant system administrator who can perform all duties of the system administrator but has other responsibilities (such as accounting duties). The assistant system administrator performs the duties on a regular basis in order to maintain competence and to provide some internal control by having another person perform the activities.

As an MIS function grows in size, additional personnel, such as an operator and an analyst/programmer, may be added. The MIS manager has increased supervisory duties and becomes more involved in planning, budgeting, selecting and training personnel, and scheduling work.

Major Alternatives in Centralization/Decentralization

There are a number of different ways to organize the MIS function in larger companies. A key issue is whether information management should be organized as a centralized function or dispersed in functional departments (or in business units for a multisite operation). Four major alternatives can be considered:

1. Centralize all facilities and expenditures under a corporate information management function.

2. Have both centralized and decentralized facilities but have overall control and direction by a central information management function.

3. Have a centralized information management function for corporate systems and corporatewide planning and control, but have decentralized facilities under departmental or divisional control.

4. Have only decentralized facilities with a small corporate coordination function.

The rationale for centralized facilities and control is lower cost of shared facilities, increased value from coordinated applications, improved management by having specialists, and standardizing the use of information technologies. The rationale for decentralized facilities and control is more responsive service.

There can be various combinations of centralization or decentralization for system operations and system development, especially in a multisite operation. In order to standardize the use of information technologies in multiple sites, many companies centralize overall control and direction. Two examples of failures with centralized direction illustrate some of the potential difficulties.

> *Example.* The corporate MIS function at a major consumer products manufacturer dictated the choice of certain information technologies by all divisions. In particular, only one local area network software package could be used. The intent was to standardize the operating platform so that applications software could be exchanged between divisions. Unfortunately, the selected LAN platform did not conform to the de facto industry standards. Very few software packages were certified to run on the LAN platform, which constrained the options available to the divisions. The standardized LAN platform was finally abandoned.

> *Example.* The corporate MIS function at a multinational pharmaceutical products manufacturer also tried to standardize the operating platform used by all divisions. First they tried to standardize on a vendor's line of minicomputer hardware, but that approach failed when the price/performance of microcomputers and LANs made the minicomputer platform too expensive, especially for smaller divisions. Then they tried to standardize on a specific relational database management system, but that approach failed because the limited availability of manufacturing software packages running on the database management package forced many divisions to develop their own applications. The expense and schedule delays of in-house development efforts forced them to change their approach. They are now attempting to standardize by limiting divisions to two major alternatives in applications software packages. The choice of a package limits the choice of hardware and database management system, since each package is certified as portable across only a few operating platforms.

Alternatives for System Operations

The organization of system operations must consider the hardware location, control over processing, and location of data. Economies of computer equipment and communications do not favor any one organizational alternative; rather, the alternative selected will generally reflect other factors such as the fit with the organization and its responsibility structures, the ability to provide adequate technical support for operations, and the nature of the application being supported. For example, system operation for a mission-critical, businesswide application will be different than operation of a limited impact, infrequently used decision support application.

A list of alternatives for hardware location and control suggest the range of options available to a company. The list is arranged in approximate order from highly decentralized to highly centralized.

- Distributed computer hardware with no central control over configurations and no communications among departments.
- Distributed computer hardware with central control over equipment configurations but no central processing.
- Distributed computer hardware with a communications network for communicating among hardware at different locations.
- Distributed computer hardware for local processing and a central computer for larger jobs.
- Distributed computer hardware connected by a communications network controlled by a central computer that allocates jobs to local computers.
- Centralized computer hardware with remote job entry and remote terminal access for job management.
- Centralized computer hardware with remote terminal access only for input and output.

Another aspect of system operations that can be centralized or decentralized is data. As with hardware, there are a number of alternatives for achieving centralized or local storage and control. They are arranged below in approximate order from decentralized to centralized.

- Each distributed computer has its own files and databases, and there is no interchange or central control of data.
- Each distributed computer has its own files and databases, but there are organizationwide standards.
- Each distributed computer or file server has files and databases, but the data can be accessed by other computers.
- There is a centrally controlled network of distributed files and databases (either segmented or replicated databases). A file or database is assigned to a local computer and data records are transferred to other computers as needed.
- There is a central database with data downloaded to local computers for local use; database updates are sent to the central computer for updating of the central database.
- A central computer has all files and databases.

Centralization-Decentralization of Application Development

In a decentralized environment, development personnel are assigned to user organizations. This has the advantage of making the personnel more responsive to user needs. They can interact with operating personnel much better than systems analysts coming in from a corporate group. Managers tend to be more responsive to information processing if they have someone on their staff with whom they can work. Some offsetting disadvantages are the fact that systems analysis personnel who operate in decentralized units tend to have reduced support for cross-fertilization of technical ideas, technical training, or the opportunity for specialization that occurs in a centralized group. Development of technical expertise and a career path in information systems are difficult. Standards are also more difficult to enforce than when a centralized group is used.

If systems analysts remain in a centralized group, project organization may be used to gain some of the advantages of decentralization. Having a user as a member of the project team is commonly suggested as a way to increase user input and user responsibility for the final product.

Companies with a large development staff can organize their analysts into permanent project teams responsible for all projects in a particular functional area or division. This arrangement has advantages and disadvantages similar to those of the decentralization alternative. The responsibility for hiring and reassigning staff remains with information systems management, so training and provision of career paths may be facilitated.

Another common mechanism for maintaining a centralized development group while improving responsiveness to user needs is the role of a user liaison. A person in this position typically reports to a centralized function but may have "dotted line" responsibility to the user group for which he or she is responsible. The reverse is also possible. The user liaison's most important task is translation of user requests into system specifications and MIS messages into terms understandable to the user.

ORGANIZATION AND MANAGEMENT OF END-USER COMPUTING

End-user computing represents a significant shift to decentralization of information systems resources. The shift has been encouraged by the availability of low cost microcomputers and software that can be acquired by departments or individuals as part of their budget authority. End users can develop, purchase, and operate applications on microcomputers that fall outside of any centralized control. However, this decentralized approach typically encounters one or more of the following problems.

- The microcomputers may be incompatible. At first, this may not be a problem, but as use expands, there is a need to transfer software and data among computers.
- The microcomputers may need to access data in the main computer, but this requires special software and introduces new data control problems. A variety of microcomputers makes this more difficult.
- A variety of software packages and databases makes integration difficult.
- A variety of software packages and microcomputers makes training difficult and inefficient.
- A variety of vendors for hardware and software systems increases maintenance and trouble-shooting difficulties.

Because of these difficulties, many organizations have established a policy on microcomputers. A limited set of hardware, software, and vendor options are established. These options are supported by the training, consulting, and maintenance staffs of the computer center or an information center established to support end-user computing.

The technical support for users consists of four types of activities.

1. *Acquisition, upgrading, replacement, and setup for hardware, software, and network facilities.* The facilities for an individual user need to fit within the overall company technical infrastructure. Standards for hardware and software reduce confusion and incompatibility. They also reduce training, maintenance, and technical support costs. The setup support also allows company standards such as documentation, backup and recovery, and portability to be implemented.

2. *Formal training.* This may be provided in-house or by contractors. Support for this activity reduces training costs and ensures coverage of vital topics such as quality control in use of facilities.

3. *Applications support.* Day-to-day applications support is usually best handled by one or more functional area experts (users who work in the function and have some technical skill). The questions usually are best understood and answered within the context of the application being performed. The role of the information systems function is to support the functional area experts.

4. *Technical support.* There are questions that require significant technical skill regarding the operating system, network, hardware, and other technical issues. There should be prompt access to a technical expert who either can answer the question or locate someone who can.

Some organizations have established information centers with formal user support staffs that provide all of these activities. The tendency is to reduce the size of these central staff groups and concentrate on low technical support within functional areas. The central staff can then be quite small and focus on standards, setup, and high technical support.

End user systems need some security and protection. They are more difficult to protect than large systems. They are not usually in locations that can receive any special physical protection. There is no special fire or water protection. However, there are still very useful and reasonably effective security and backup/recovery methods for small systems. These include:

- *Password protection.* Passwords can be used to deter unauthorized personnel from accessing confidential files and important software.
- *Backup and recovery software and procedures.* Every system, no matter how small, should have an established procedure for backup and recovery. There are software packages that facilitate the process, so it is not time consuming. For example, some packages use special procedures to backup very quickly; others keep track of files that have changed, so only those that have been altered are backed up.
- *Documentation and offsite storage of copies of critical data and programs.* The off-site storage need not be elaborate; the criterion is to protect the data, programs, and documentation from deliberate or accidental destruction.
- *Physical locks.* Simple precautions are possible using locks. Most personal computers can be locked. Cables can be attached to equipment to make it difficult to steal them. Documentation and some backup can be stored in locked cabinets.
- *Virus detection and removal software.* Installations can protect themselves from viruses by not using software of unknown origin and using a virus protection program to examine all diskettes brought into the installation.

THE INFORMATION SYSTEM MASTER PLAN

The primary coordination vehicle for information technology activities is the information system master plan. The master plan typically has two components—a long-range plan for three to five years (or longer) and a short-range plan for one year. The long-range portion provides general guidelines for direction; the short-range portion provides a basis for specific accountability as to operational and financial performance. It establishes a framework for all detailed information system planning. In general, it contains four major sections:
1. Information system goals, objectives, and architecture
2. Inventory of current capabilities
3. Forecast of developments affecting the plan
4. The specific plan

The plan is developed through the joint efforts of information system management and user management. An information system steering committee of key executives is often used to assist in the formulation of the plan and to review it for incorporation in the company plans.

Information System Goals, Objectives, and Architecture

This section of the plan might contain descriptions of the following:
1. Organization strategies and plans including considerations of the strategic effects of information technology.
2. External environment factors (e.g., related to industry, government regulations, customers, and suppliers) impacting information systems.
3. Internal organizational considerations such as management philosophy and assumptions about business risks impacting information systems.
4. Overall goals, objectives, and strategy for the information system.
5. Architecture of the information system.

The information system master plan provides a framework for detailed planning, especially for the design of databases and major applications.

Current Capabilities

This is a summary of the current status of the firm's information systems. It includes inventories of resources and analyses of how these have been used. The resources represent hardware, system software, database management systems, application systems, and personnel. There is an analysis of expense, utilization of hardware, software, and personnel, status of projects in progress, and assessment of strengths and weaknesses.

The purpose of the inventory is to clearly identify the current status of all systems. Applications may be classified by major functional systems (such as accounting, marketing, human resources), organizational strategies (e.g., provide online ordering by customers), and need for maintenance or revision.

In the case of personnel, useful classifications might include job classifications (programmer, operator, etc.), skill categories (COBOL programming, data communications, etc.), and functional area expertise (finance, accounting, manufacturing, etc.) In each case, the classification should reflect planning concerns.

Forecast of Developments Affecting the Plan

Planning is affected by current and anticipated technology. The impact of such developments should be reflected in the long-range plan. It is difficult to estimate technology far into the future, but most developments are announced one or more years before they become generally available. Broad technological changes can be perceived several years before they are implemented.

Software availability should also be forecast and the impact on future systems anticipated. Methodology changes such as automated development tools may also be forecast.

Environmental developments such as government regulations, tax laws, and competitor actions can also be included insofar as they affect information systems.

The Specific Plan

The plan should cover several years (say three to five) with the upcoming periods (say, the next one or two years) being reasonably specific. The next period should have sufficient detail to contain a budget. The plan should include:
1. Hardware acquisition schedule.
2. Purchased software schedule for system software and application software.
3. Application development schedule.
4. Software maintenance and conversion schedule.
5. Personnel resources required and schedule of hiring and training.
6. Financial resources required by object of expenditure (hardware, software, personnel, etc.) and by purpose (operations, maintenance, new development, etc.). Other classifications may also be useful.

> *Example.* Rather than creating a lengthy written master plan for information systems, the MIS manager of a division of Emerson Electric used the format of a master plan for a one-day presentation to the plant's management team. The format provoked lively discussion about information system goals, current capabilities, projected developments, and specific alternative plans. The discussion proved more valuable than a written document. It helped management understand tradeoffs in priorities, missing elements in integrated mission-critical applications, and their responsibilities to sponsor projects and allocate resources. Ongoing discussions between the MIS manager and members of the management team simultaneously shaped the specifics of their master plan and increased ownership of information systems.

Maintenance of the Master Plan

As each period passes, the information system plan requires updating. For example, the current status is updated with new equipment and changing personnel figures. Future plans are affected by changes in technology, experience with systems, competitor actions, and changes in the organization. Pressures for changes in plans may come from internal events such as changing financial constraints. The master plan is also updated to reflect the status of systems installed and the progress of new systems.

ALLOCATING SCARCE INFORMATION SYSTEM RESOURCES

A significant management task is the allocation of scarce resources. In the case of information systems, there are typically more demands for information resources than can be provided. There must be some mechanism for allocating them. This will often be a part of the information system planning process, but allocation often takes place outside of formal planning. The two major alternatives are a central authority method and a decentralized authority method.

Central Authority for Resource Allocation

The central authority approach to resource allocation assigns resource allocation to a central person or group. This may be the chief information systems executive who has a broad view of information resources. However, there are many political factors in such allocations, and the executive may not be able to act alone to resolve them.

The use of a central group that reflects the political environment of the organization is illustrated by a steering committee. It is made up of representatives from major users and therefore can take into account overall needs of the organization and yet operate within the political constraints.

The central authority approach helps ensure adherence to the information systems plan and facilitates integration. Final approvals of system development priorities are centrally controlled by the steering committee. Some central control is necessary for implementing an organizationwide database.

Decentralized Authority for Resource Allocation

Rather than a central authority trying to decide among competing projects, an alternative is to provide users with the basis for making such decisions. In many cases, this requires a chargeback system that gives users responsibility for their own information system costs. Under a chargeback system, users are charged full or partial costs for system operations and application development. The algorithms for establishing costs for services are complex and vary widely depending on the objectives of the chargeback system.

In order to serve decentralized planning and control, a chargeback system should be understandable to the users, so they can associate costs with specific activities. The user or user department receiving the bill for services should also receive (directly or indirectly) the benefits of those services.

The decentralized chargeback approach is consistent with a profit center concept for information systems in which the center operates in parallel with an outside competitive market. Prices for services must be competitive with alternative services external to the organization; users are free to "shop around" for a better price. One disadvantage of the profit center approach is the difficulty of accommodating corporate database or corporate telecommunications requirements.

INFORMATION MANAGEMENT OPERATIONS

The information management function runs a factory to process information and provide services to others in the organization who are using information technology. The operations of the information processing facility can be analyzed in terms of factory operations and how customers are serviced. Because of the rapid changes in patterns of technology use, capacity planning and technology acquisition are very important factors in operations. Information system security and related backup and recovery are vital elements with characteristics not usually found in factories.

Facility Operations

The traditional operations environment is associated with the batch mode of processing. In this mode, computer processing involves the execution of a series of discrete jobs submitted by users to the operations authority. Users normally have no knowledge or control over the precise timing or sequence of execution and normally remain unaware of technical or operational failures (e.g., those which can be corrected by re-runs) that are internal to the MIS operations department. In this mode, the role of the operations function is to control the flow of jobs through the processing cycle by tracking the receipt, execution and dispatch of jobs and by scheduling jobs in accordance with organizational priorities, task precedences, and production efficiencies. There are personnel who prepare jobs for execution (including data preparation where required) and maintain control of the jobs from acceptance to distribution of output. Operators schedule work, load jobs, monitor operations, and respond to errors or failures in equipment or software.

The traditional environment may be characterized as a job shop. The focus of operations management in this environment is on the workflow control and optimization of computer usage by scheduling. Operations performance is measured in terms of job throughput, i.e., the number of jobs processed during a defined time period.

In the online mode of operation, it is the user rather than the computer operator who initiates the execution of processing, and any failure (or degradation) of the processing resource is immediately visible to all active users. In addition, the online mode tends to increase the dependency of users on the continuous, smooth operation of the computer facility, since user work tasks and behaviors are determined by the response characteristics of the operation.

The online computer facility may be characterized as a processing utility. The role of operations is to maintain a defined level of capability. How and when the capability is used is determined by the aggregate actions of the entire community of users. The focus of operations management in the online mode is response time.

Most installations perform a mixture of the batch and online processing. The operations function must manage both input/output control and job scheduling for batch jobs and resource allocation and monitoring for online processing.

Various software packages are available to assist operations personnel in scheduling work and allocating resources. Many of these requirements are included in the features of operating systems. They also monitor a number of key operating characteristics such as utilization of devices and memory and existence of bottleneck facilities.

Performance monitoring uses monitoring hardware, software monitors, and operating system logs to measure system performance. The monitoring hardware measures hardware activity by the computer and input-output channels. The software monitor tracks patterns and trends in utilization levels, response times and other indicators which point to potential or actual problems. Network monitoring software is employed with data communications networks. It monitors communications traffic and identifies bottlenecks, overloads and failures.

A support function for operations is a library for software and data stored on magnetic tapes or other removable media. Librarian software is employed to aid in keeping track of the tapes, other media, and documents.

In installations doing substantial data preparation from documents, a separate data preparation function may perform these activities. This may involve keying data from documents or using various conversion devices to read data optically or magnetically.

Customer Service

Customer service levels are determined by the capacity of the processing resources to deal with both regular volumes and unexpected demands. From the user viewpoint, customer service for online processing is measured by system availability (uptime) and response time; for batch jobs, it is performance on schedule. Response time is the time taken by the computer system to process an individual transaction or command and send an output message on completion. It is measured from the time of the keystroke that sends the command to the receipt of the response.

Other factors in customer service are accuracy, consistency, and responsiveness. Accuracy in processing is a must for good customer service. Consistency is the maintenance of a steady level and amount of service without severe random fluctuations or erratic behavior. Responsiveness is reflected in personnel and procedures for accepting customer requests and complaints and acting on them promptly.

Capacity Planning and Technology Acquisition

Capacity planning is based on measurements that can be obtained from monitoring hardware and software. Comparisons of load to current available capacity can be used to project future needs. Making mistakes can have severe operational consequences.

> *Example.* A large food company had just installed a new sophisticated online order entry system. Estimates were that the new online system would use at peak times about 40 percent of capacity (the computer was at 30 percent of capacity), so that the system would still have enough capacity to deal with unusual surges in demand. The demand immediately increased to over 100 percent of capacity. A new computer had to be ordered, various jobs had to be rescheduled, and many activities were suspended temporarily. Even so, response time was poor until the new higher capacity system was installed. The problem was in estimating the demands of the new order entry system. The estimates were based on an analysis of an order clerk taking an order over the phone. The process was measured from start to finish. In practice, order entry often entered changes when customers called back or after the clerk performed followup activities. These and similar behaviors meant that a typical customer order required not one but an average of more than two transactions with the system. Also, others in the organization were accessing the system to obtain customer order information; their inquiries were much greater in number than anticipated.

> *Example.* A large data center of a major manufacturing firm was experiencing problems with inadequate disk storage space. An analyst was assigned to determine whether increases in volumes were more than anticipated and to project future disk storage needs. The analyst began by analyzing the file directories of the disk storage packs in use. He quickly discovered that, because of inadequate and careless procedures for assigning file space, only 35 percent of the available space was in actual use.

As part of capacity management, applications using large amounts of resources should be tuned for improvements in usage. Some remedies to be applied include changes in equipment, recoding of heavy-use program segments, redesign of disk storage files, and restructuring of access to disk storage records. The results from tuning of hardware-software systems have been significant. A 25 percent reduction in execution time for the jobs that normally take most of the processing capability is not unusual.

Because of the potential improvements, tuning should always be considered prior to making decisions on adding capacity. Although tuning can be done by in-house specialists, many organizations hire specialists for this activity.

Capacity planning can aid in selecting the most economical financing plan. Computers are often financed by a lease that has severe penalties for early termination. If capacity is estimated incorrectly, the computer lease may need to be ended in order to get a different machine.

The estimation of capacity needs is difficult, but software monitors provide data on historical trends. Vendors and consultants can assist in estimating capacities for future equipment.

Information System Security

A somewhat unique characteristic of information processing is the risk of having data or the system destroyed either accidentally or deliberately. There is also some risk from unauthorized access to data or unauthorized use of facilities.

Large computer installations can have physical security for equipment by locked doors, password entry, etc. They can be protected against fire, water, and other disasters. As a precaution, backup sites may be arranged by using vendors who provide the service, by using another site in the same company, or by a sharing arrangement with a similar company. Companies have disaster plans and have simulated the occurrence of disasters to ensure they can recover in a satisfactory time.

It is fairly easy to replace equipment; it is difficult or impossible to replace lost data and inhouse developed software. Because of this risk, companies follow backup and recovery procedures that involve copying of data and program files at specified intervals and after major batch processing runs. These are copied on magnetic tape and stored some distance from the computer center.

Unauthorized access to large computer systems is inhibited by security software packages that monitor password use, alert security personnel to possible violations, and so forth. Various levels of password protection are the most common protection method. This applies to programs as well as data.

MANAGING INFORMATION PROCESSING COSTS

Cost management is an ongoing process in the management of information services. New technologies and cost reductions for existing technologies provide ongoing opportunities. Some areas where cost reduction has been achieved illustrate the potential for management action.

Data Center Hardware Cost Management

The two major possibilities for cost reduction are downsizing the computers in the data centers and outsourcing of data center operations.

In place of a large data center with a number of mainframes, an organization may choose an alternative configuration with perhaps a single mainframe or one or two midrange computers with additional minicomputers and microcomputers dedicated to functional areas or special applications. The decrease in complexity of operations and reduction in cost may be substantial.

Another alternative is to outsource the data center operations. Instead of having company staff do all data center operations, an outside vendor takes over all responsibility. Economies of scale are realized by the vendor who can develop and apply proven management practices to the specialized problems of operations. The vendor can also manage the acquisition and disposal of equipment. A common option is to have the outsourcing vendors purchase existing data center computers. The vendor can then choose to continue use or to replace the existing hardware with a new configuration.

In the purchase of large mainframes, there are a small number of vendors, but in the purchase of microcomputers, it is possible to reduce costs by negotiating with resellers for equipment and maintenance.

Application Software Cost Management

Purchasing application packages for major systems can result in significant cost reductions. Use of common applications across business units is a similar strategy.

Outsourcing of application system development is also possible. Requirements can be developed and an outside contractor used for development. This may be especially appropriate for applications requiring specialized skills. Subcontractor development staff can also be used during overloaded periods in order to avoid significant increases in fulltime personnel.

Personnel Cost Reductions

Information system development and support are labor intensive. The personnel costs are very significant (say 30 to 40 percent of the budget). There are two broad strategies of cost reductions—either reduce need for staff or increase productivity of existing staff.

A variety of techniques can reduce the need for MIS staff. These include use of automation in the data center operations, end-user development approaches, use of standard methods, automation and high level development languages in development, and standard hardware and software (to reduce variety that staff must support). Outsourcing some activities reduces the need for internal staff. This is especially appropriate for activities that can be done more efficiently by external staff when the company itself does not have sufficient demand to justify performing the activities in house. Examples include data center operations staff, network management, and PC repair.

Productivity of information systems personnel may be increased by new tools and methods, high level languages, and methods of development that reduce rework.

Outsourcing

Why should a firm outsource? The major reasons are to obtain specialized or technical assistance, reduce costs, and eliminate the difficulties of organizing and supervising activities that require technical expertise. There may be improvements in service due to the discipline imposed by an external market for such services.

Why should a firm not outsource? Companies tend to outsource activities that are not central to the mission of the firm and do not threaten the factors that give the company a competitive advantage. In other words, if the information systems are central to an organization's competitive strategy, outsourcing may not be a good idea.

ASSESSMENT OF THE INFORMATION MANAGEMENT FUNCTION

The are two persistent questions from chief executive officers relative to the information systems in their organizations:

- How much should be spent for information systems? (Allocation of organizational resources to information systems.)
- How good are the information systems and the function that supports them? (Evaluation of organization, management, and services of the information systems function.)

Within industries, spending levels for information systems differ substantially between successful companies. Within the constraints of resource availability, how much should be spent depends on two factors: what the organization wants to achieve with information technology and how much it must spend to be competitive. Companies differ in culture, capabilities, and the way they use information technology, so what organizations wish to achieve will differ; industries differ in their use of information technology, so what organizations must spend to be competitive will differ by industry. This suggests that information systems can only be evaluated within their organizational and environmental context.

An in-context approach to information systems assessment provides the framework for investigating these key management questions.[1] The in-context

---

[1] Based on an upnpublished manuscript by Gordon B. Davis and Geoffrey Brooke, Carlson School of Management, University of Minnesota.

assessment framework is presented as a complete assessment approach. A company may wish to perform a complete, comprehensive assessment, but it is more likely that the assessment will be targeted at a high level evaluation or at a specific problem area. The value of the in-context assessment framework is in identifying factors to be included in assessment and in defining the overall context for targeted assessments.

The Context for Information Systems

The information systems for a company serve an organization that exists in an industry with a competitive environment, has a specific organizational structure, management style, and culture, and has specific information requirements. These define the overall context for assessment of the information management function and the portfolio of applications.

The existing industry context and competitive environment define what is expected of information systems at the current time; this can change as new applications and new information products (and other innovations) are used to change the industry structure and basis of competitive advantage. A critical assessment question is how information technology can help achieve competitive advantage by changing the way the organization or the industry operates.

An Overview of an Information Systems Assessment

A complete, comprehensive assessment of information systems can be divided into four stages, each of which is sub-divided into a series of assessment activities. The four stages represent a logical order of assessment in that there is a sequential dependency between the various stages. This suggests that assessment should proceed in a systematic fashion, since the activities within each stage build upon knowledge gained in prior stages.

In general, it may be possible to postpone or even omit a particular activity within a given stage, although it is probably inadvisable to omit a stage altogether. When an assessment is targeted or limited in scope, the stages provide a framework for doing enough work to establish an appropriate context for the area of assessment interest. For example, a targeted assessment of end-user computing should first establish some context consisting of relevant organizational context and the infrastructure context. For a limited assessment with a wide scope, the framework identifies the range of things to be considered, even though the depth of analysis may be limited.

The framework of four stages and the areas of assessment in each are summarized in Figure 11-4. The steps in the assessment framework are organized in a top down fashion: from the most general topic of competitive environment and company structure, to the overall structure of information systems and the service level being provided, to the management interface between information systems and the organization, then to the specific activities within the information systems function. The evaluation of the information management function is an organizational evaluation; it deals with processes more than outcomes.

Stage One: Analysis of the Organizational Context for Information Systems. At the conclusion of this stage of analysis, there should be a clear definition of competitive forces, major competitors, and key success factors in the market. There should be an understanding of the way the organization has responded to the competitive environment through its organization, policies, culture, etc. There should be an appreciation at a general level of the organization requirements for information and support services and how these relate to the context of the organization and its environment.

Stage Two: Assessment of the Information System Infrastructure. After establishing the organizational context in Stage One, Stage Two of the assessment analyzes the various components of the information systems infrastructure, i.e., the institutional structures and established processes that define the organization's information systems capability. The infrastructure is viewed in four dimensions: (1) an information dimension (the application systems and databases that provide information support); (2) an organizational dimension (the organization and management structure of the information systems function); (3) a technical dimension (the architecture of computer equipment, system or non-application software, and telecommunications facilities); (4) an economic dimension (the organization's investment in information systems).

Stage Three: Assessment of the Organizational Interface for Information Systems. Having assessed the institutional structures that represent the established information systems capability, the next stage is to evaluate the management processes that act as the essential interface between these structures and the rest of the organization. There is an assessment of information system planning and control to evaluate the existence of these processes and their quality. Assessment of information system use examines how effectively the organization manages the use of its information systems and meets the real needs of its users. This important part of assessment will be described further later in the chapter.

Stage Four: Assessment of Information System Activities. The last stage covers assessment of activities and management within the information systems function. There are six activities that encompass the assessment of individual functions contained within the information systems organization. Assessment of application development and maintenance is an evaluation of the methods and procedures for systems developed by professional programmers. The use of standard methods, methodologies, and development tools are included. Assessment of information system operations looks at the organization and management of operations. It includes an evaluation of facilities, use of operations software, and scheduling of work. Assessment of capacity plan-

FIGURE 11-4
Stages of In-Context Assessment of Information Systems and Activities within Stages

STAGE ONE:	**ANALYSIS OF THE ORGANIZATIONAL CONTEXT FOR INFORMATION SYSTEMS**
1.	Analysis of the industry and competitive environment for the organization
2.	Analysis of the historical development, culture, structure, and activities of the organization
3.	Analysis of the organization requirements for information and technology support
STAGE TWO:	**ASSESSMENT OF THE INFORMATION SYSTEM INFRASTRUCTURE**
4.	Assessment of information systems architecture of applications and databases
5.	Assessment of the technical architecture for information systems
6.	Assessment of organization and management structure for information systems
7.	Assessment of the investment in information systems
STAGE THREE:	**ASSESSMENT OF THE ORGANIZATIONAL INTERFACE FOR INFORMATION SYSTEMS**
8.	Assessment of information system planning and control
9.	Assessment of information system use
10.	Assessment of end-user computing
STAGE FOUR:	**ASSESSMENT OF INFORMATION SYSTEM ACTIVITIES**
11.	Assessment of application development and maintenance
12.	Assessment of information system operations
13.	Assessment of capacity planning and technology acquisition
14.	Assessment of information system support functions
15.	Assessment of information system safeguards
16.	Assessment of information system personnel management

ning and technology acquisition assesses the processes by which the information management function tracks utilization, forecasts needs, employs performance measurement tools, and evaluates alternatives. The step also evaluates the processes by which new technologies are identified and considered for use. Assessment of information system support functions is an evaluation of the way that the function deals with its customers, the users of applications and end-users who need support. Assessment of information system safeguards is a study of the security measures and backup and recovery provisions. It may focus on how well the organization has done in studying security issues and in providing for backup and recovery. Assessment of information system personnel management considers the current personnel policies and procedures and evaluates how they are working in terms of recruitment, upgrading, and retention.

ASSESSMENT OF INFORMATION SYSTEM EFFECTIVENESS

The assessment of information system effectiveness must take into account the underlying business processes. In other words, the assessment looks at existence of necessary business processes and how well they are being executed with information systems.

The process of information system effectiveness assessment can be illustrated with the systems for manufacturing resource planning. At two extremes, the most effective class A user of information systems has embedded information systems in the business processes for planning and control of the company, and continuous improvement is an ongoing process for employees, suppliers and customers. In the least effective class D company, the information systems are poorly understood, suffer from inaccurate data, and are used on a limited basis. They provide little help in running the business, and continuous improvement efforts have not been established.

An important set of processes to be evaluated are those in which the company uses information systems in planning and controlling the business. These processes include:

- The planning processes: strategic planning, financial planning, sales planning, capacity planning, and operations planning.
- The scheduling processes: production scheduling, manpower scheduling, materials scheduling, and supplier scheduling.
- The evaluation processes: performance measurement and comparison of planned and actual results.

The assessment should evaluate the effectiveness of data management. For example, the product design process can be evaluated in terms of data in bills of material, routing and related data, integration of data for planned changes, and data integrity.

LESSONS FOR MANAGERS

A new organizational function, information management, has emerged. The mission of the function is vital to the performance of specialized activities and coordination of information management activities performed by the organization, departments, and users. There are two basic organizational forms used in information systems: functional and matrix.

There are a number of different job positions in large installations. In small installations, there may be only a system administrator. End-user computing and personal computers support a trend to decentralization of information system operations and development. End users require support for facilities acquisition, training, use of applications, and technical issues.

There are a number of pressures in information technology and on organizational behavior for a decentralized information systems function; there are also pressures for a centralized function. An important consideration is making the information systems organization conform to the organization and culture of the organization it serves.

The information system functions that can be centralized or decentralized are operations and application development. Elements of system operation subject to centralization or decentralization are hardware location, processing control, and location of data. Systems development personnel may be centralized and organized functionally or decentralized to report directly to users. A hybrid approach is centralized development with analysts permanently assigned to certain user functions.

An important activity of the information system executive is development of a master plan for the function. The plan defines goals, inventories capabilities, forecasts developments, and establishes a specific plan of action for acquisition and use of resources. Allocating scarce information resources is a major management problem. One alternative is the use of a central authority such as the information system manager or a steering committee. A second alternative is the use of decentralized authority mechanisms such as chargeback for services. A chargeback system which decentralizes control to users must be understandable and controllable by the user.

Information management operations can be understood as a factory. There are facility operations, customer service issues, capacity planning and technology acquisition problems, and information system security. Some of these areas of operations are similar to a factory; others, such as security, have unique information system requirements.

One of the objectives of management and MIS is to control costs. Cost management can be applied to the data center, application software, and personnel. Outsourcing is used to obtain skills not available in house or to reduce costs.

Assessment of the information management function should be carried out periodically to evaluate how much is being spent and whether or not it is meeting organizational needs. A useful approach is to make an assessment of the function and its activities within the context of the organization and its strategies and plans. Information system effectiveness is analyzed within the context of existence of necessary business processes and how well they are being executed with information systems.

CHAPTER 12

INFORMATION SYSTEMS AND INTEGRATED RESOURCES MANAGEMENT

Information systems (MIS) is a support function. In an information age, it is one of the most powerful and pervasive influences in transforming the organization. The chapter explains the vital role of information systems as an integrative function for the organization and in reengineering of business processes. No organization can be world class without a first class information systems function, and no MIS function can be first class unless it enhances integration within the organization.

The information systems function performs important activities and integration at the corporate level; it also supports each individual function. It supports the functions dealing with customers and products, logistics, and manufacturing processes; it also provides services and support for human resources, accounting and finance, and quality management. The information systems function applies the integration capabilities of information technology to its own production, service, and management activities.

SOURCES OF CORPORATE INTEGRATION THROUGH THE INFORMATION SYSTEMS FUNCTION

Integrated resource management requires coordination and control of specialized activities toward organizational objectives. Coordination and control are dependent on the organization's ability to process and communicate information. If the flow of information is obstructed or too slow, or if the information cannot be processed and decisions made promptly, the business processes will fail to meet objectives. In a system sense, they will be out of control. Cross functional efforts will fail as each function performs its activities without considering (or knowing) the effects on other functions. The ability of an organization to process information and make and communicate timely decisions is dependent on two major factors: the structure of the organization (organizational structures differ in their ability to process information and communicate) and the information system (how the applications are embedded in business processes).

The information system function provides and manages the facilities that support corporate integration of business activities. Five ways in which this integration is supported are the information strategy and architecture, corporate data modeling and databases, communication and coordination technologies, information systems in business processes, and systems for analysis and decision making support. The five sources of corporate integration through information systems are shown in Figure 12-1 and explained briefly in the following pages.

Integration from an Information System Strategy and Architecture

A business strategy defines what the corporation does and how it competes. Using the business strategy as an anchor, an organization executes its strategy through business processes using information systems to communicate, coordinate, and control the activities.

Developing an information system strategy and architecture is an integrating process. Information architecture is not just an extension of business strategy execution. The information technology strategy can be used to change the organization's distinctive competencies and ultimately the business strategy. In doing so, the information architecture can require a transformation in the business architecture. Information technology can drive the organization structure, business processes, and strategies for production, customer service, and other areas of distinctive competence.

Whatever the driving strategy, the information technology strategy and business strategy must be aligned. The need for information, the flow of information, the flow of decisions, and the processing of business transactions should be reflected in the architecture of information system applications and databases. The infrastructure of hardware, software, communications facilities, and development and operating personnel should be designed to support the structure of the organization and its power and authority mechanisms.

Integration from Corporate Data Modeling and Corporate Databases

One of the major problems in coordination of different functions and activities within an enterprise is to share information. Prior to modern information processing, it was not possible to have a high level of information sharing. Many information systems still reflect the past and have islands of automation poorly linked together. Each part may operate well, but coordination and sharing of

FIGURE 12-1
Information Systems for Corporate Integration

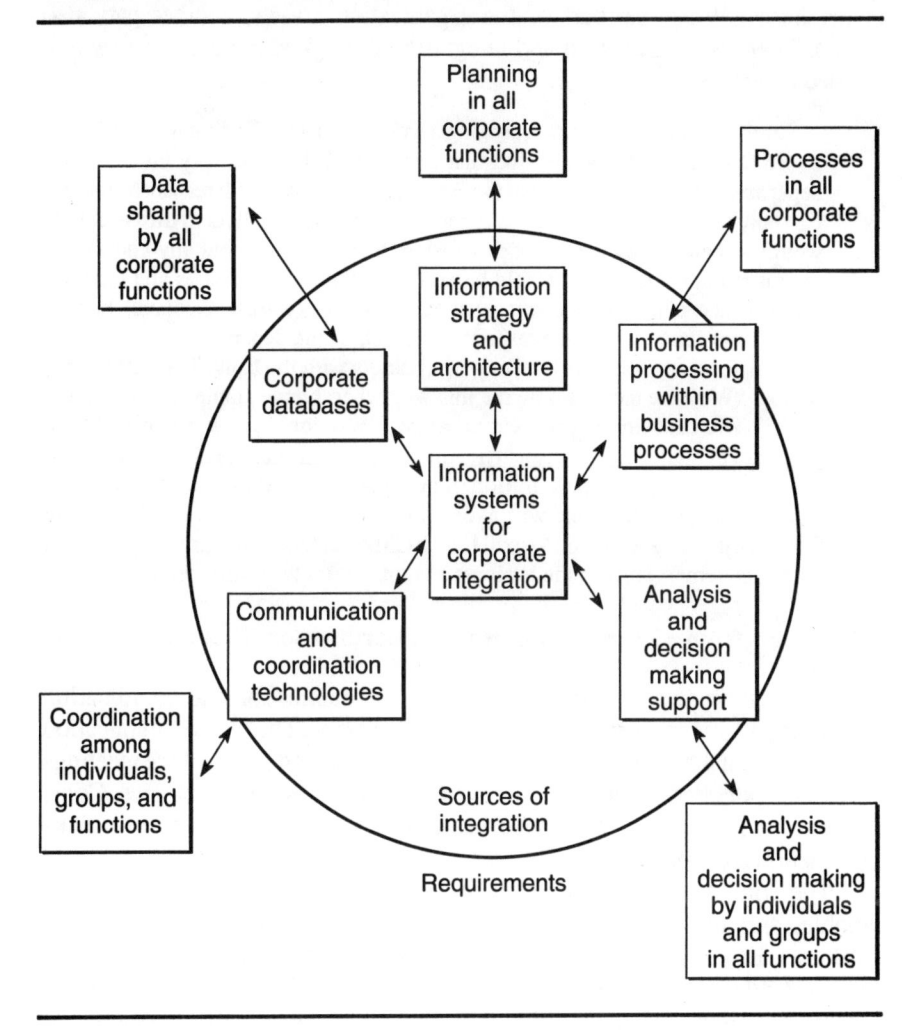

[Diagram: Information systems for corporate integration, showing a central circle with "Information systems for corporate integration" connected to "Information strategy and architecture," "Corporate databases," "Information processing within business processes," "Analysis and decision making support," and "Communication and coordination technologies." The circle represents "Sources of integration." Surrounding the circle are "Requirements" boxes: "Planning in all corporate functions," "Processes in all corporate functions," "Analysis and decision making by individuals and groups in all functions," "Coordination among individuals, groups, and functions," and "Data sharing by all corporate functions."]

information are poor. The solution is the design of integrative corporate databases.

Corporate data modeling addresses the issue of what objects of interest should be represented in the corporate databases and how information about them should be coded. The decisions about what is of interest and its coding are based on inputs and negotiation from the entire organization. The data models represent an integrated model of corporate data needs.

The physical databases result from the implementation of the logical data model. The conceptual integration of the organization is therefore represented in databases. What one part of the organization knows, another part also knows. There is coordination and integration through sharing of data (which has been consistently defined).

> *Example.* A bank customer, seeking service from a bank using uncoordinated information systems, would find that one part of the bank (say the checking department) will not know about the customer's activities with respect to another part (say trust department). A customer with millions of dollars in trust accounts would be handled by the check processing department without any knowledge of that relationship. There would be no coordination of activities and relationships. If the checking account customer (with large trust accounts) had an insufficient funds check, the response of the checking department would be the same as for a customer without any other assets with the bank. The customer is saying, "Why are they treating me this way when I have ample assets with the bank?" The checking department is saying, "We don't know anything about you except that you have insufficient funds for the check." An integrated system using a common definition of customer and maintaining all customer information in a database will avoid this error. The coordinated brokerage firm statements (such as the Merrill Lynch CMA account that reports all accounts on one statement) reflect the business advantage from information integration.

Integration from Communication and Coordination Technologies

The information systems function provides communication and coordination technologies to support group activities and decisions. The old communication technologies of the postal system, memos, telephone, and face-to-face meetings have been extended by new or improved communication technologies. Coordination by meetings or telephone has now been supplemented by various information technologies.

The communication options have increased. They provide faster, more reliable, and higher transfer rates to easily access and update corporate databases. Electronic communication of data, electronic mail and fax can be used instead of mail; digital communications makes telephone lines more reliable and more versatile. Worldwide communications make worldwide coordination and integration feasible.

Organizations use meetings extensively to integrate and coordinate activities and decisions. Information technologies that support coordination of group activities include group decision support systems (GDSS) or electronic meeting systems. These coordination technologies can be used by groups assembled in one location at the same time, groups with members located at different sites meeting at the same time, and groups with members interacting from different locations at different times.

Integration from Interaction of Business Processes and Information Processes

Integration in business processes occurs in system development and operation. System development is an integrative activity because, for processes that affect more than one part of the organization, representatives from different functions participate in the design and development effort. The information system programs and procedures cross functional boundaries in their effects on business processes. Information systems also require reengineering of business processes to improve productivity.

> *Example.* An insurance company reengineered its processes for dealing with customer requests. The former process took several days or even weeks because there was no integration within the process. Each person had to complete his or her work before it was passed on to the next person in the chain of activities. In reengineering, it was found that many of the activities could be done in parallel if the documents could be made available. The system reduced paper movement by having a single set of optically stored documents shared by everyone and available for concurrent activities. Also, many activities were combined to reduce the number of people handling the request.

Business processes and the information processing built into them serve to integrate the activities of business functions. The business process determines how work will be moved from one function to another and what information will move with the transaction.

Integration from Use of Analytical and Decision Making Tools

Information systems support integration across business functions through common use of analytical and decision making tools. Corporate models for planning are integrated with models for planning individual functions; an example is a corporate budget model. Analysis using spreadsheets and statistical packages can cross functional boundaries to include data found in the corporate database. Decision support systems may integrate the decisions and actions of more than one function in the model for decision making.

> *Example.* A software development company regularly had two-day meetings to come to agreement on projected sales revenue. Sales of each software module (the entire package consisted of 15 modules) directly affected sales of consulting services and education classes (with a time delay after each sale of a module). In addition, the software development schedule for a new module directly affected the software sales forecast for it (Figure 12-2).
>
> One of the managers developed four interrelated spreadsheets that reflected assumptions about each business process. For example, the model identified several types of sales (such as a small system, a large system, or add-on module sale) and had profiles for consulting time and education student-days for each

FIGURE 12-2
Company Relationships for Forecasting Model

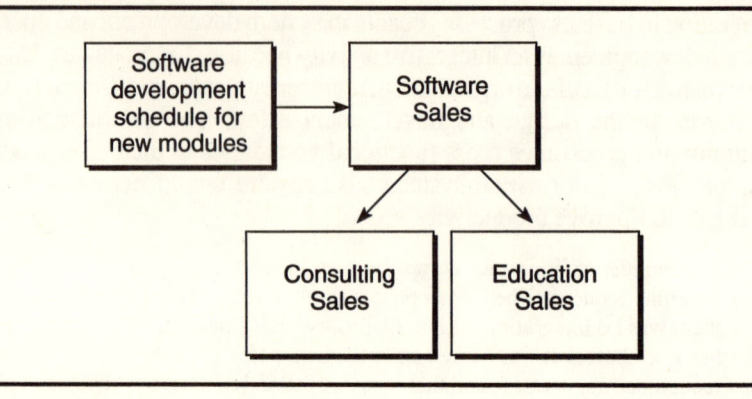

```
┌─────────────┐      ┌──────────┐
│  Software   │      │          │
│ development │─────▶│ Software │
│ schedule for│      │  Sales   │
│ new modules │      │          │
└─────────────┘      └──────────┘
                      │        │
                      ▼        ▼
               ┌──────────┐ ┌──────────┐
               │Consulting│ │Education │
               │  Sales   │ │  Sales   │
               └──────────┘ └──────────┘
```

type of sale.

As part of the forecasting meeting, the spreadsheet analysis was run interactively to test assumptions about availability of software modules, unit volume sales by type of sale, and the impacts on consulting and education revenues. The length of the meeting was reduced to two hours, and the analytical tool led to greater integration among the functional groups.

An executive information system (EIS) represents a high level integration of data and managerial applications of analytical tools. The perspective guiding the system is that of top management. The issue is not what one function is doing but the combined effect of all functions. Executive information systems typically allow executives to examine factors and relationships not provided by regular reports. An executive may, for example, ask for an analysis of the relationship between backorders and inventory levels.

Integration through Support to Business Functions

The above discussion has focused on the general integration effects of information systems; this next section will describe the effects of information technology on 13 functional areas involved in integrated resource management for organizations.

    CUSTOMERS AND PRODUCTS
        Marketing and Sales
        Field Service
        Product Design and Development

LOGISTICS

Production and Inventory Control
Procurement
Distribution

MANUFACTURING PROCESSES
Industrial Facilities Management
Process Design and Development
Manufacturing

SUPPORT FUNCTIONS
Human Resources
Accounting and Finance
Total Quality Management
Information Systems

For each of the functions, there are three ways to look at how information systems help integrate business processes. The three views, shown in Figure 12-3, are used to organize the descriptive text. The description starts with the integrated use of information by the functional area. Next, there is a discussion of expanded functional capabilities through the use of information systems in analysis and decision making. The third part describes how the function can use information technology in its products and services. The short descriptions for these three topics explain and illustrate uses but will not be a complete list of all uses.

MARKETING AND SALES AND INFORMATION SYSTEMS

The marketing and sales function is responsible for market research, competitive analysis, market planning, demand forecasting, promotion and advertising, pricing, and managing the distribution channels. These are information intensive activities requiring internal transaction data plus external data about customers, competitors, industry trends, and the economies of countries in which the company operates.

Integrated Use of Marketing and Sales Information

Marketing and sales manages information about customers and sales transactions (both actual and forecast). The information can be used to analyze sales and project sales force requirements. With an integrated information system, other functions can use this data to project resource requirements (such as material, labor, facilities and cash), develop production plans and business plans, and handle invoicing and accounts receivable.

FIGURE 12-3
Integration through Support to Business Functions

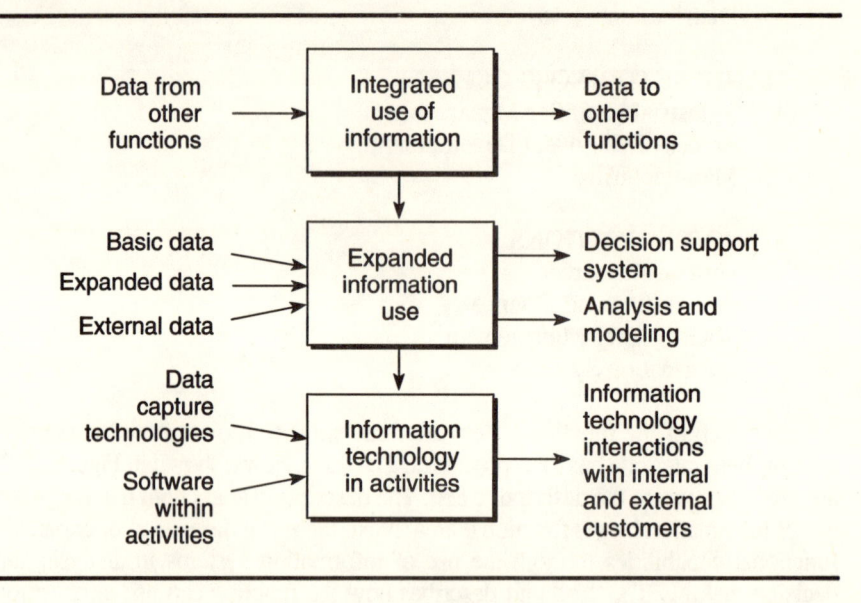

```
Data from ─────►  ┌─────────────┐  ─────► Data to
other             │ Integrated  │         other
functions         │ use of      │         functions
                  │ information │
                  └─────────────┘
                         │
                         ▼
Basic data ──────►┌─────────────┐ ─────► Decision support
Expanded data ───►│ Expanded    │        system
                  │ information │
External data ───►│ use         │ ─────► Analysis and
                  └─────────────┘        modeling
                         │
                         ▼
Data
capture                                  Information
technologies ────►┌─────────────┐        technology
                  │ Information │ ─────► interactions
                  │ technology  │        with internal
Software ────────►│ in activities│       and external
within            └─────────────┘        customers
activities
```

An integrated system assists marketing and sales by providing access to information from other functions. For example, the information on inventory and scheduled receipts facilitates availability checks to provide valid delivery promises. The sales function can also configure custom products, estimate job costs and completion dates, and check warranty information for handling customer returns.

Expanded Information Use by Marketing and Sales through Information Systems

Sales order processing applications capture information for subsequent processing and reports (e.g., for processing invoices, and for reports about taxes, commissions, reasons for lost sales, and so forth). Information systems can provide sales reports with comparisons between actual sales and forecasts and analyses by customer type, product type, distribution channel, and location. There are reports on sales force performance and commissions or other compensation.

Information technology has expanded the availability of external information useful in forecasting sales, identifying potential customers, and targeting markets. Much of the information is available from external databases with extensive information about the economy by geographic area, industries, and companies. Information systems can support more sophisticated integration of internal and external data in forecasting of demand and expected company sales.

The availability of data from both company databases and external databases, coupled with microcomputers and other end-user computing facilities, has substantially expanded marketing and sales analysis. Sophisticated market research (including sampling plans and analysis of data) is well supported by software packages. Generalized software packages such as spreadsheets are used often for market and sales analysis. Statistical analysis about the effects of promotions and advertising are routinely done with statistical software.

Applications of Information Technology to Marketing and Sales Activities

Information technology applications are widely used to support marketing and sales services. Examples are laptop computers for doing proposals and pricing during the sales presentation (such as insurance proposals), data entry devices for taking inventory by route sales personnel, and online credit authorization using simple card readers and data communications. Information technology is also used to provide customers with direct access to supplier applications, such as direct order placement into an order entry system with immediate response as to availability and delivery dates. Information technology has replaced personnel in some sales activities such as automated kiosks and automated teller machines for dispensing cash.

A direct application of information technology to marketing and sales is the combined use of a geographic database that has maps and a database containing economic data. The geographic data may range from very high level showing only broad features to detailed maps of houses, hills, etc. Key economic indicators for customers can be superimposed on geographic features to indicate marketing opportunities.

Expert systems for automated product configuration (driven by customer specifications) or validation of selected options as compatible are examples of using technology in sales order processing.

FIELD SERVICE AND INFORMATION SYSTEMS

The field service function is responsible for product installation and maintenance, product warranty and service contracts, repairs, customer training, and other activities related to customer service. Field service work draws on information initially defined through other activities and supplements it with task-specific information.

Integrated Use of Field Service Information

Field service requires information (e.g., about customers, sales orders and products) initially defined by other functions in order to perform field service activities. Field service also maintains information about problems and suggestions related to products and services that are valuable to other functional areas. For example, problems can be identified through telephone and field service support, customer training classes, and returns and repairs. Other functions can use this feedback information to improve product/process design, production and procurement, quality management, and training of personnel.

Field service information about specific product warranty and service contracts can be used by sales to handle return authorizations and credits and by accounting to handle billing for contracts and repairs.

Expanded Information Use by Field Service through Information Systems

Field service requires information to plan and control service parts inventories and tools, schedule and dispatch field service personnel, manage product warranties and service contracts, bill for field service, and coordinate customer training. In some cases, the information system must provide for product tracking (by lot/serial number) for proactive recalls or government reporting purposes.

The data from field service operations can be used in decision support systems and expert systems for diagnosing customer problems. Specialized software can be used in scheduling and routing field service personnel.

Applications of Information Technology to Field Service Activities

Examples of information technology to support field service personnel are remote diagnostics, help lines, and portable computers. Diagnostics are built into various machines such as elevators. When there is a failure, the diagnostic device provides information to guide the field service personnel. The device can usually be accessed through a telephone line. A help line for customers can provide assistance in diagnosing and fixing problems and reduce on-site visits by field service personnel.

> *Example.* A copier machine was not working. The display showed an error code. A built-in diagnostic routine guided the user through steps to identify and correct the problem. A help line was available if the diagnostic routine failed.

PRODUCT DESIGN AND DEVELOPMENT AND INFORMATION SYSTEMS

The product design and development function involves an interdisciplinary design team (from the engineering, marketing, manufacturing, field service and other functions, and possibly from customers and suppliers) to design new products and change existing products. Significant amounts of information are needed for design and the coordination of the design team.

Integrated Use of Product Design and Development Information

Product design and development produce a database of item and bill of material information. This is used for product costing, material planning, forecasting and production planning (via planning bills), custom product configuration during order entry (from a bill of options), and other purposes. In particular, the bill of material application must express how the product is manufactured (versus an engineering parts list), communicate relevant drawing information (e.g., find numbers or reference designators) and identify byproducts/ coproducts from the manufacturing process (such as controllable wastes and valuable secondary products). The bill of material also identifies the impact of engineering changes to the product structure, which may require detailed tracking of engineering change orders and product revision levels.

Expanded Information Use by Product Design and Development through Information Systems

Product design and development require information systems for the management of R&D projects, including schedules and capacity plans for each resource (such as design engineering and drafting) involved in product design, coordination of required materials (especially special purchase parts and operations), and tracking project costs and status.

The use of information systems for analysis and decision support in product design and development is illustrated by using cost estimation models and simulating the impact on costs of changing the product structure or component costs.

Simulation methods, based on software packages, are often used in product design and development. Instead of a physical prototype, the product is designed on the computer and different features examined.

Applications of Information Technology to Product Design and Development Activities

Information technology is used directly in product design and development through computer-aided design (CAD) applications, with possible integration to the bill of material application and computer-aided manufacturing (CAM) applications.

Information technology may be designed into the product. Examples are voice response to operator action, voice recognition, automatic diagnosis of operating conditions, and so forth.

PRODUCTION AND INVENTORY CONTROL AND INFORMATION SYSTEMS

The production and inventory control function is responsible for planning, scheduling, coordinating and controlling, the supply of materials to support sales and distribution requirements.

Integrated Use of Production and Inventory Control Information

The production and inventory control function maintains information about the production plan/master schedule and final assembly schedule. As an outgrowth of the sales and operations planning process, this information represents the manufacturing version of the overall plan that must be communicated throughout the organization.

Part of the production and inventory control responsibilities (typically embodied in a master scheduling function) is to maintain the planning bills. Planning bills facilitate forecasting, production and capacity planning, and sales order processing (e.g., in configuring custom products and checking available to promise) by synchronizing aggregate and detailed plans.

With an integrated system, the manufacturing plan can be communicated to production scheduling and purchasing for taking suggested actions, to sales for making valid delivery promises, and to other areas (such as accounting, human resources and field service) for assessing implications of the plan. The plan can also account for planned engineering changes to products and processes.

Expanded Information Use by Production and Inventory Control through Information Systems

The production and inventory control function also maintains information about scheduled production, inventory balances and item master planning parameters (such as lead times and replenishment logic). In order to keep information accurate and up-to-date, information systems can be used to monitor completion status of scheduled production, to plan and report cycle counting and physical inventory activities, and to review/modify item master planning parameters (e.g., through leadtime analysis).

Measurements of actual results against plans help provide feedback information to the sales and operations planning process. On a monthly basis, for example, actual results are compared to the production plan, inventory and/or backlog plan, and shipment plan.

Decision support applications are used to formulate the production plan and master schedule. For example, these applications may support capacity planning simulations using various sets of demand data and production plans. Other applications include mixed model and rate-based scheduling, schedule sequencing to optimize production, and calculation of optimal inventory balances in visible scheduling systems.

Applications of Information Technology to Production and Inventory Control Activities

Innovative applications of information technology have been employed in automated material handling systems and storage/retrieval systems. Data collection applications use a variety of devices (such as bar code readers) to minimize data entry efforts in recording material receipts, movements, and shipments.

As part of just in time manufacturing efforts, visible scheduling systems can employ electronic replenishment signals (e.g., to notify stockroom personnel to replenish floor stock inventory).

PROCUREMENT AND INFORMATION SYSTEMS

The procurement or purchasing function is responsible for sourcing, negotiating, supplier relationships, order placement, followup and receiving, and other procurement activities.

Integrated Use of Procurement Information

Procurement manages information about suppliers and purchases (both contracts and specific delivery schedules). Joint efforts between the procurement, product design and quality functions help identify approved vendors. Purchasing information is used by accounting; information about vendors, receipts and returns is used in accounts payable processing; information about planned deliveries is used in cash planning.

Expanded Information Use by Procurement through Information Systems

Using the projected material requirements from MRP calculations, procurement can project demand in units and dollars for a group of similar parts to assist product family sourcing and negotiation efforts. Sourcing decisions can also be based on vendor performance information (in terms of price, quality and delivery against promised delivery dates) collected as part of the receiving activities.

Vendor schedule information helps coordinate supplier activities with production and distribution plans. In communicating the impact of the production plan/master schedule and final assembly schedule to procurement, the information system can recommend specific purchasing actions (such as order release, followup, reschedule, cancel, and close). This exception-oriented approach to communicating plans applies to normal purchased material, subcontract manufacturing, and one time purchases. Procurement of expense items and capital expenditure items can also utilize the purchasing information system.

Dispatch reports for receiving inspection help coordinate disposition of material that is in quarantine, waiting for inspection, or requiring a return to vendor.

Applications of Information Technology to Procurement Activities

Information technology can be used to electronically communicate delivery schedules to suppliers. In addition, electronic replenishment signals may be transmitted to suppliers as part of just in time manufacturing efforts. Information technology is also used to obtain direct access to supplier applications, such as direct purchase order placement with immediate response as to availability and delivery dates.

The receiving function can use a variety of information technologies (such as bar code readers) to minimize data entry efforts and reduce errors in transaction processing, such as transactions to record purchase receipts and returns and to record disposition of materials in inspection.

DISTRIBUTION AND INFORMATION SYSTEMS

The distribution function is responsible for receiving, storing and transporting materials and products to meet customer requirements.

Integrated Use of Distribution Information

The distribution function draws on information about customers, items, and sales orders to coordinate delivery of products to meet customer requirements. The distribution function may be responsible for maintaining some item master information, such as weights, dimensions, and freight codes, that will be used in generating bills of lading.

In multiple site operations (consisting of more than one distribution and/or manufacturing site), the distribution function is responsible for distribution requirements planning (DRP). The DRP information is used in sales order processing, inventory control of finished goods, intersite material transfers, and production planning at manufacturing sites.

Expanded Information Use by Distribution through Information Systems

By communicating sales order requirements to distribution, the information system can recommend shipping actions to deliver orders as promised and generate required paperwork. Consolidated picklists, for example, identify needed materials for a selected subset of sales orders (e.g., a shipment going on a particular carrier, to a particular geographic area, or to a specified customer). The distribution function records packing and shipping information for each shipment, and generates paperwork such as packing lists, box labels, and bills of lading.

The distribution function can use management reports to measure performance, such as fill rates, percentage of on-time deliveries, response time and inventory accuracy (based on cycle counting procedures).

In multisite operations, the distribution function is responsible for maintaining information about the distribution network, such as source/destination, transportation modes, lead times and effectivity dates for each link. Distribution may also be responsible for maintaining calendar information about available shipping and receiving days, and other information about routes and carriers.

The distribution function can use transportation management applications to plan, route and track shipments to customers (and shipments among sites in multisite operations). These may include decision support applications to minimize transportation costs (e.g., via transportation mode selection, container optimization or routing optimization).

Applications of Information Technology to Distribution Activities

Information technology can be used in distribution to support automated material handling and automated storage and retrieval. The shipping function can use a variety of information technologies (such as bar code readers) to record shipments and customer returns.

Information technology can be used to electronically communicate shipment information to customers (or other sites in multisite operations).

INDUSTRIAL FACILITIES MANAGEMENT

The facilities management function is responsible for planning, installing and maintaining the plant facilities and equipment required to produce the products and services.

Integrated Use of Industrial Facilities Management Information

The facilities management function maintains information about plant facilities and equipment. This information may be shared with (or replicated by) accounting for managing fixed assets and with production for scheduling equipment. Facilities management uses capacity planning information from production control to project needed equipment purchases/upgrades. It also uses employee information maintained by human resources for managing maintenance personnel.

Expanded Information Use by Industrial Facilities through Information Systems

The facilities management function can be viewed as a job shop operation that uses information systems to plan and control maintenance activities. Maintenance tasks represent jobs requiring repair parts, labor, tools and documentation. In this sense, the information systems for facilities management are very similar to a job shop manufacturer. For example, the information systems need to handle forecasting (of preventive and emergency maintenance tasks), inventory control and purchasing of repair parts and tools, labor scheduling (by skill level) and capacity planning, manufacturing (rework) of repairable parts, management of subcontracted services, and tracking job costs.

Information systems can be used to report on facilities management performance, such as downtime, maintenance costs versus budget, and safety records. Expert systems can be used as part of maintenance diagnostic procedures.

Applications of Information Technology to Facilities Management Activities

Examples of information technology to support facilities management include automatic controls in equipment to monitor the need for maintenance or identify reasons for failures and electronic access to vendor-supported maintenance and repair information.

PROCESS DESIGN AND DEVELOPMENT AND INFORMATION SYSTEMS

The process design function involves an interdisciplinary design team and preferably works in parallel with the product design efforts. The process design function identifies the type of manufacturing process, layout, and type of work force, equipment, control devices and tooling to produce and deliver products.

Integrated Use of Process Design and Development Information

The process design and development function is responsible for maintaining information about resources (workcenters, equipment, people), tools, operations and routings. Engineering changes to the process design must also be incorporated into the database. This information is used by other functional areas for product costing, forecasting and production planning (via planning bills), custom product configuration during order entry (from a bill of options), lead time calculations, capacity planning and dispatching, production activity control/tracking and other purposes.

Expanded Information Use by Process Design and Development through Information Systems

In conjunction with product design efforts, the process design and development function requires information systems to support the management of R&D projects, including schedules and capacity plans for each resource (such as design engineering and drafting) involved in process design, and tracking project costs and status.

The process design function may use decision support applications for planning plant layout. Using simulations, they can assess the impact on cycle times and material movement distances of changing layouts and equipment.

Applications of Information Technology to Process Design and Development Activities

Information technology can be embedded in the production process, possibly using programmable logic controllers to monitor product quality, process reliability, and scrap/yield.

MANUFACTURING AND INFORMATION SYSTEMS

The manufacturing function is responsible for planning and managing production resources such as people and equipment to meet the manufacturing plan and satisfy customer expectations for delivery, quality, and cost.

Integrated Use of Manufacturing Information

The manufacturing function uses information provided by other functional areas to make the manufacturing plan happen. This includes information about schedule and material availability from production and inventory control, custom product configurations from sales, product and process definitions from engineering, work force capabilities from human resources, and equipment capabilities and availability from facilities management.

When manufacturing cannot produce to schedule, the exceptions must be communicated to affected areas. For example, sales may have to change promised delivery dates, distribution may send partial shipments, and the master schedule may be changed.

Manufacturing reports information that can be used by other functional areas. Examples are consumption of material and resources (e.g., to update inventory status and calculate costs and variances) and completion status (e.g., to update capacity requirements and support job status inquiries).

Expanded Information Use by Manufacturing through Information Systems

Manufacturing uses information systems for detailed scheduling and tracking of production activities. Dispatch lists can be used to provide daily (and hourly) scheduling priorities for each workcenter, although visible scheduling systems (as part of just in time manufacturing efforts) may provide a superior alternative for managing execution of the manufacturing plan.

Decision support and expert system applications can be used. Examples of DSS applications are assignment of employees or equipment to specific jobs (based on skill attributes) and selection of optimal schedule of jobs and alternate routings based on maximum utilization, sequencing requirements, or shortest throughput times. An example of an expert system is one employed by a large computer chip manufacturer to diagnose reasons for defects in chips being manufactured. The diagnostic system is useful because of the scarcity of personnel with diagnostic skills and because of the number of factors to be considered.

Applications of Information Technology to Manufacturing Activities

Manufacturing can use information technology in many production activities. These applications include computer-aided manufacturing (CAM) systems that download design data to computers that control machines producing parts; flexible manufacturing systems (FMS) that make an entire family of parts in any sequence or quantity; robotics for material movement and value-added processing; automated test equipment to monitor and adjust the manufacturing process; and shop floor data collection devices for recording material movements, labor expended, and quality management data. Efforts to link these technologies are the focus of computer integrated manufacturing (CIM) strategies.

HUMAN RESOURCES AND INFORMATION SYSTEMS

The human resource management (HRM) function is responsible for recruiting and selecting personnel, career planning, training, performance appraisal and ongoing job design. The HRM responsibilities include programs for compensation, benefits, training, government reporting, and other areas.

Integrated Use of Human Resources Information

The human resource function maintains information about employees and current/projected positions, which can be used by other functions for purposes such as budgeting and manpower planning. Accounting uses the compensation information for payroll processing. Managers require employee (and possibly applicant) information to match task requirements with the skill levels and availability of personnel.

Expanded Information Use by Human Resources through Information Systems

In addition to information about current status of employees, human resource information systems can provide historical tracking data (e.g., previous positions, pay rates, and performance ratings of current and previous employees).

An information system for managing employment applicants helps identify internal and external applicants who possess the needed skills.

Specialized applications help meet government reporting requirements, such as the preparation of equal opportunity employment plans and reports using internal statistical data and external census data.

Applications of Information Technology to Human Resources Activities

Information technology has been effectively employed in computer-aided instruction (CAI) to train personnel at their own pace and convenience. The developments in specialized authoring languages have increased productivity in designing computer-aided instructional materials. User training on information systems has been enhanced with hands-on exercises, self-paced tutorials, and online access to documentation.

Training efforts have also taken advantage of online optical disk technology to display images (such as technical drawings or other graphics). For example, one company made their drawing information accessible online by almost all employees; order entry and field service personnel frequently checked the drawings to verify they clearly understood what a customer was ordering when the part was described in lay language (the small doo-dad on the back).

ACCOUNTING AND FINANCE AND INFORMATION SYSTEMS

The finance and accounting function is responsible for acquiring and managing the firm's financial resources and providing financial information in internal and external purposes.

Integrated Use of Accounting and Finance Information

The accounting and finance function is responsible for maintaining budget information and tracking the financial impact of all activities in the organization. With respect to cost data (for valuing inventory and costs of goods sold), they use information from product/process design to develop product costs. Information from the sales function about custom product configurations is used to develop job costs. As actual manufacturing activities are reported, actual costs can be tracked against these planned (or standard) costs.

General accounting applications (such as accounts payable, accounts receivable, payroll, fixed assets and general ledger) require integration with other business functions to reflect manufacturing activities (such as purchase receipts, labor reporting, shipments, and costed manufacturing transactions). Consolidation of financial statements from different companies is an integrating activity requiring exchange of data and rules for reporting purposes.

Expanded Information Use by Accounting and Finance through Information Systems

The accounting and finance function uses financial report writer capabilities, especially for generating internal and external reports (such as a profit and loss statement and balance sheet).

As an illustration of a decision support application, finance can project and manage cash more effectively by using information about projected sales and purchases in addition to information about existing payables, receivables and payroll.

Information systems can help manage the complex issues of currency conversion, where sales orders/receivables and purchase orders/payables must be expressed in multiple currencies. One issue, for example, is identifying the currency gains/losses as the conversion rates change over time (from order placement to shipment to invoice to payment). Companies that purchase foreign exchange to hedge against losses from foreign exchange may use a decision support system (and external information on foreign exchange rates) to support hedging decisions.

Applications of Information Technology to Accounting and Finance Activities

Accounting departments use information technology directly in accessing external databases of accounting principles and rulings, accounting reports, and similar financial reporting data. They employ audit software for internal audit examination of records. Internal audit may also employ software to collect data during processing of critical applications and to test controls in selected applications. The tax department may use external databases of tax regulations and internal revenue service rulings in tax research. Tax preparation software is used for preparation of both individual and corporate returns. The payroll operations may employ information technology to make direct payroll deposit transactions for employees. The company prepares the payroll information in a standard format; the file is transferred to a bank that processes the deposits.

The finance function employs information technology in monitoring credit worthiness of customers and suppliers and in methods of payment. External credit reporting services provide corporations access to data on credit worthiness; various online external databanks with financial reporting data support text searches for articles, reports, analyses, and financial reports of selected customers. Methods of payment frequently involve electronic funds transfer systems. When transfers are made among USA corporations that have accounts at major money center banks, the transfers are made using the Clearing House Interbank Payments System (CHIPS); if not, the Federal Reserve FedWire system is used. If the transfer involves corporations in foreign countries, the transfer may use SWIFT (Society for Worldwide Interbank Financial Telecommunication). A finance function that must oversee significant cash management may have a terminal inhouse to track funds in different accounts and electronically move funds among banks and other institutions.

QUALITY MANAGEMENT AND INFORMATION SYSTEMS

The quality management function is responsible for ensuring the delivery and support of quality products/services and other activities related to quality processes.

Integrated Use of Quality Management Information

The quality management function maintains information about process and product performance, such as information about customer returns, customer satisfaction, defect and error rates, scrap and yield rates, mean time to repair and mean time between failures. This information provides valuable feedback to other parts of the organization. For example, other functions use this information to improve product/process design, change practices, or improve training to improve quality.

Quality management functions, such as measuring of process variability (via control charts), are being performed by personnel throughout the organization. Quality management personnel participate (with procurement and engineering) in the process of qualifying approved vendors. Quality management also participates in product/process design to identify specifications regarding products, tests and tolerances.

Expanded Information Use by Quality Management through Information Systems

Quality management uses decision support applications to perform failure analysis, diagnose test results and field performance data, and suggest corrective action (possibly with expert systems).

Decision support applications have also been used to calculate the cost of quality in terms of prevention, detection and correction.

Quality management requires information about lot traceability on materials and processes. Lot control information may specify quarantine periods, expiration and retest requirements, potency measures, and records of other lot attributes.

Applications of Information Technology to Quality Management Activities

Examples of information technology to support quality management personnel include diagnostics built into manufacturing processes. When there is a failure, the diagnostic device provides information to guide quality control personnel to the source of the problem.

INFORMATION TECHNOLOGY APPLIED TO THE INFORMATION SYSTEMS FUNCTION

The information systems function is responsible for managing the corporate database and information technology resources, developing applications, supporting end-user utilization of information technology and other activities related to information processing.

Integrated Use of Information Systems Information

The corporate database provides an integrating role across the organization. Information about its availability, integrity, security and access is maintained by the information systems function. In firms employing chargeback mechanisms, the information systems function measures the costs of providing database access and information technology applications and handles chargeback to users.

In firms employing information technology in products and services, the information systems function may provide significant contributions to product/process design and development, manufacturing, marketing and sales, and field service.

Expanded Information Use by Information Systems through Information Systems

Extended information use by the information systems function focuses on analysis and modeling of operations and analysis and modeling of development activities. The MIS operations can make use of software to model the hardware/software configuration and analyze bottlenecks and compare alternative approaches to capacity management.

Project management software is used to plan and control development activities and project costs. Software estimation packages are available for estimating the cost and time to develop large applications.

Chargeback systems are frequently used by MIS to charge out the costs of information processing. Analytical software is used to model the behavior of the system and evaluate alternative chargeout methods.

The function usually collects and reports data on error rates, downtime, productivity, project status, and so forth. Extended analyses to detect cause and effect relationships for these data use statistical analysis packages.

Applications of Information Technology to Information System Activities

The information systems function uses information technology in its operations for obtaining data on use of hardware and software and security performance. Both hardware and software monitors measure use of hardware; software monitors measure use of software. These systems provide data for analyzing bottlenecks and tuning hardware or software and for identifying the need to replace hardware or software. Security sensors are used on doors and on some equipment to restrict access and to record those who gain authorized use. Security software monitors online access to the system and to various critical resources; passwords are checked and potential security violations are recorded for followup. Files of programs and data, including backup files, are maintained by librarian software. Operations are scheduled and monitored by software.

The function employs computer-aided system engineering (CASE) technology in application development. These tools provide automated support for many development activities. There are also a variety of software tools for assisting programmers in writing and testing code.

LESSONS FOR MANAGERS

A critical resource in integrated resource management is information. Communication of the company plan helps each functional area and individual work toward common goals. Information helps coordinate activities within and between functional areas. In order to achieve quick response operating strategies, information must be communicated efficiently and effectively. Delays in communication affect flexibility and competitiveness. Time-based competition requires that an organization communicate information in a seamless fashion so that all parts of the organization are informed and aware.

As a critical resource, the corporate databases must be managed. The information systems function is responsible for managing them. This involves database administration and the development/operation of applications software to support business processes using the corporate databases.

In designing information systems, it is critical to examine and redesign the business processes and infrastructure. Changes to organizational structure, for example, can eliminate obstructive relationships and barriers to communication (e.g., the cross functional flow of information), streamline decision making through reductions in bureaucracy, and improve teamwork. Changes to the business process can simplify procedures and information requirements, thereby eliminating the need to replicate unnecessary complexity in the design of information systems.

Applications software helps integrate business processes. The sales and operations planning process, for example, translates the firm's strategic goals and plans into action plans that require coordination of activities and measurement of performance. Information systems provide critical support for this integrated management process, as they communicate information with which to make decisions and measure performance against the plan.

Information systems are integrative mechanisms for each function. In addition to integration through information systems, each function can innovate in its use of information technology and can incorporate the technology in its products and services.

The chapter demonstrates the importance of information systems both to individual functions and to integration of activities and resources. Without high quality information systems, it is virtually impossible to achieve the goals of integrated resources management.

INDEX

A

Acceptance testing, 166
Access path, 117
Access times, 217
Accounting, 59, 61
    effect of information systems, 272-73
    impact of manufacturing resource planning, 30, 35-36
    information flows, 52
Accounts receivable, 61
    impact of manufacturing resource planning, 33-34
ADA, 145
AD/Cycle (Application Development Cycle), 174-75
Adhocracies, 78
Algorithmic programming languages, 144, 152, 154
American National Standards Institute (ANSI) standard X.12, 127
American Standard Code for Information Interchange (ASCII), 100
Analytical software, 275
Annual Statement Studies, 34
APL (A Programming Language), 154
Application development
    centralization versus decentralization, 235
    cycle, 156-57
    for end-user computing, 158-59, 172-74
    methodology, 157-58
    programming process, 142-51
    prototyping approach, 158-59, 167-70
    selection methods, 174-75
    sociotechnical approach, 176-77
    software package approach; *see* Applications software packages
    strategies, 157-58
    system testing, 165

Application development—*Cont.*
    tools, 135-36
    traditional approach, 158-67
Application development cycle (AD/Cycle), 174-75
Application programmers, 231
Applications
    categories, 65-69
    defined, 65
    development; *see* Application development
    evaluation, 177-78
    types, 65-69
Applications software packages; *see also by type*
    adoption methodology, 170-72
    adoption strategy, 158-59
    advantages, 8-9, 136-37
    application generators, 139-40
    business process redesign for, 7-9, 138
    buy versus build analysis, 137-38
    centralized versus decentralized, 54
    conversion features, 141
    coordination costs, 141
    cost management, 246
    customizing, 138-39
    decision support systems, 76-77
    demonstration copies, 142
    difference from systems software, 132-34
    disadvantages, 137
    domain-based, 44
    impact, 19-20
    implementation, 172
    just-in-time strategy, 16
    local area networks, 119
    maintenance, 172
    PC-based, 10
    portability, 140-41
    post audit, 172

278 Index

Applications software packages—*Cont.*
  as prototypes, 169
  site licenses, 141-42
  training programs, 141, 172
  universal toolkit, 41
  volume discounts, 141
Arithmetic logic unit (ALU), 93
ASCII (American Standard Code for Information Interchange), 100
Assemblers, 136, 143
Assembly language, 144
Asynchronous transmission, 112
Attributes, 201
Authorization levels, 108
Automated product configuration, 261

B

Backup and recovery procedures, 238, 245
Backup units, 106
Balance sheet, impact of manufacturing resource planning, 30-31
Bandwidth, 114
Bar code scanners, 102-3, 265-66
Baseband networks, 119
BASIC, 145, 154
Batch systems, 107
Baud rates, 111
Berstein, Don, 48n
Bills of lading, 266-67
Bills of material, 263
  standardized, 59-60
Binary arithmetic, 101
Binary code, 100-101
Binary digits, 99
Bitnet, 125
Bits, 99
Booting, 108
Bowman, B., 193n
Brainstorming, 186
Broadband networks, 119
Brooke, Geoffrey, 27n, 248n
Brooks, F., 147
Buffers, 117
Bulletin boards, 42, 125
Buses, 89-90
Business architecture
  elements, 46-48

Business architecture—*Cont.*
  trends, 55
Business integration, 54
Business operations, 49-53
Business planning, 49
Business processes
  information requirements, 187-88
  information technology, 6-9
  integration, 54, 257
  reengineering, 7, 19-21, 54, 138, 257
  software packages, 7-9
Business strategy, 1-5, 254
Business Systems Planning (BSP) method, 187
Buy versus build analysis, 137-38
Bytes, 89

C

Cache memory, 93
CAD (computer-aided design) applications, 263
CAI (computer-aided instruction), 271
Caller identification, 128-29
CAM (computer-aided manufacturing), 264, 270
Capacity planning, 51
Card entry, 102
Carlson, M., 48n
Carrier-sense multiple-access collision detection (CSMA/CD), 119
CASE tools, 175, 275
  data models, 210
Cash management, 61
CD-ROM (compact disk read-only memory), 95-96, 107
Central processing unit (CPU), 93
Chargeback systems, 241, 274-75
Chief Information Officer (CIO), 226
CISC (complex instruction set computer), 91
C language, 151
C++ language, 151-52
Clearing House Interbank Payments System (CHIPS), 273
Client server systems, 122-24
  advantages, 58
  distributed approach, 57-58

Client server systems—*Cont.*
  limitations, 58
  local area networks, 58
  nature, 57-58
  software, 141-42
Clock speed, 94
COBOL, 145, 152-53
Collaborative work
  electronic mail systems, 80
  software, 41, 43
Collaborative work systems
  elements, 77
  organizational changes, 77-78
Commands
  internal versus external, 98
  versus menus, 196
  natural language, 197
  text search, 221
Communication applications, 124-30
Communication networks
  basic facilities, 110
  concept, 117-18
  configuration, 117
  uses, 115-17
Communications software, 135
Communications systems
  channels, 113-14
  conceptual model, 110
Competitive advantage, 5-6
Compilers, 136, 143
Complex instruction set computer (CISC), 91
Computer-aided design (CAD)
  applications, 263
Computer-aided instruction (CAI), 271
Computer-aided manufacturing (CAM), 264, 270
Computer-aided system engineering (CASE) tools, 175, 210, 275
Computer chips, 88
Computer integrated manufacturing, 3, 17, 270
  elements, 17
  information technology, 17
  relationship to manufacturing resource planning, 17
Computer literacy, 37-40
Computer systems, 96-97

COMSERVE, 125
Concentrators, 115
Conceptual design, 161-62
Conceptual machines, 91-92
Conditioned lines, 114
Control unit, 93
Corporate databases, 219-20, 254-56, 274
Cost control, 60
Cost reductions, 10
  through manufacturing resource planning, 29-30
  personnel, 246
Credit card transactions, 102
Critical factors analysis methods, 187
Critical Success Factors (CSF) method, 187
Customer call-in systems, 104
Customer Resource Life Cycle, 11-14
Customer service
  through information technology, 11-15, 28
  through just-in-time strategy, 15
  through manufacturing resource planning, 30
Custom product manufacturing, 53
Cycle time reduction, 20-21, 78

D

Daisy wheels, 96
Data
  basic concepts, 200-202
  centralization versus decentralization, 235
  defined, 66
  encoding, 111
  narrowband versus broadband, 114
  representation, 99-101
  sequencing, 203
  voice band, 114
Database administrators, 204, 231
Data-based neural networks, 85
Database management system (DBMS)
  decision support, 216
  defined, 204-5
  elements, 205
  high performance, 216

Database management system—*Cont.*
  host language, 145
  packages, 81
  program development facilities, 133, 135
  report generators, 136
Database managers, 139
Databases
  access methods, 217-19
  centralized versus decentralized, 54, 58
  conceptual organizations, 211-26
  corporate, 254-56, 274
  enterprise, 219-20, 254-56
  geographic, 261
  graphics, 220-21
  hierarchical model, 211-12
  implementation, 67
  indexes, 218-19
  information requirements, 181
  logical concept, 204
  of models, 221
  multimedia data, 220-21
  network model, 212-13
  object-oriented model, 214-15
  online, 221-22
  operation types, 217
  physical model, 215-16, 256
  physical organization, 216-19
  public access, 128, 130
  relational model, 213-14, 216
  sales function support, 260-61
  sequential organization, 217-18
  text, 220-21
  voice messages, 220-21
Data communications, 92
Data communications specialists, 231
Data control clerks, 232
Data dictionary, 205
Data entry clerks, 232
Data entry devices, 101, 261, 265-66
Dataflow diagram, 163
Data independence, 206
Data models
  CASE tools, 210
  elements, 206
  major schemas, 207
  preparation, 209
  types, 206

Data processing languages, 144
Data representation, 99-101
Davis, Gordon B., 193n, 248n
Decentralization, 9-11, 54, 57-58, 233-35
Decision support systems, 216
  applications, 265
  corporate integration function, 257
  elements, 68
  financial, 272-73
  functions, 68-69, 75-76
  for job scheduling, 270
  software packages, 76-77
  for total quality management, 274
  transportation applications, 167
Dedicated lines, 114
Delphi techniques, 186
Detail file, 203-4
Device drivers, 99
Diagnostic devices, 262
Dialing software, 128-29
Dial-up lines, 114
Direct access storage device, 104-6
Direct manipulation systems, 197
Disaster plans, 245
Disk drives, 217
Distributed systems
  advantages, 121-22
  defined, 121
  disadvantages, 122
  organization, 121-22
  types, 121
Distribution function, effect of information systems, 266-67
Distribution requirements planning, 61-62, 266-67
Document images, 104
Domains, 202
Dot matrix printing, 96
Downsizing, information technology during, 9-11
Dynamic correlation analysis, 85

E

EBCDIC (Extended Binary Coded Decimal Interchange Code), 100
EDIFACT, 127

Edunet, 125
800 numbers, 128
Electronic data interchange (EDI), 53, 127-28
Electronic mail software, 41-42
Electronic mail systems, 125-26, 256
 for collaborative work, 80
Electronic meeting support, 43, 256
Electronic meeting systems
 coordination technology, 256
 effect on cycle time, 78
 meeting room support, 79
 parallel processing, 78
 software, 79
E-Mail; *see* Electronic mail systems
Encoding methods, 102-3
Ends-means analysis, 187-88
End-user computing, 158-59, 172-74
 organization, 236-37
 security, 238
 technical support, 237
Enterprise analysis, 181
Enterprise databases, 219-20
Enterprise integration, 253-59
Entities, 71, 200-201
E-R (Entity-Relationship) modeling, 208
Error checking, 115
Error control, 182
Error detection, 196
Exception-oriented approach, 266
Executive information systems
 corporate integration function, 258
 costs, 75
 databases, 75
 design, 75
 elements, 68-69, 72-74
Executive support systems; *see* Executive information systems
Expert systems
 features, 82-85
 self-modifying, 85
Expert system shell, 43
Extended Binary Coded Decimal Interchange Code (EBCDIC), 100

F

Falkenberg, E. D., 45n

Fax boards, 127
Fax machines, 126-27, 256
Feasibility assessment, 160-61
Federal Reserve FedWire system, 273
Feedback, 273
Fields, 202
Field service function, effect of information systems, 261-62
File building, 166
Files
 defined, 202
 types, 203-4
File server systems, 123
Financial information consolidation, 59
Financial modeling software, 41, 43
Financial ratios, impact of manufacturing resource planning, 32-35
Financial report writers, 272-73
Flexible manufacturing systems, 270
Floppy disks, 95, 105
Flowcharts, 149
FOCUS, 146
Forecasting software, 41, 43
Forms-based interface design, 197
FORTRAN, 145, 152, 154
4-bit coding sets, 100
Fourth generation languages, 145-46
Freeware, 142
Front-end processors, 115-16
Full-duplex mode, 115

G

Geographic databases, 261
Graphical user interfaces, 135
Graphics, 96
Graphics databases, 220-21
Graphics output devices, 104
Graph plotters, 96
Group decision support systems, 43
 coordination technology, 256
 meeting room support, 79
 role, 68-69
 software, 79
Groupware
 advantages, 78
 defined, 77-78
 effect on organization, 78

H

Hagelstein, J., 157n
Half-duplex mode, 115
Hard disks, 95, 105
Hardware
  basic equipment, 92
  centralized versus decentralized, 54, 57-58, 235
  for the central processing unit, 93-95
  cost management, 245-46
  direct entry, 93
  distributed approach, 57-58
  instruction processing, 94
  output, 96
  secondary storage, 95-96
Hardware/software platform, 132-34
Hashed access method, 218
Help facilities, 196
Hierarchical database model, 211-12
Human-machine systems, 132
Human resources management, effect of information systems, 271

I

Icons, 197
Identifiers, 201, 217
Income sheet, impact of manufacturing resource planning, 31-32
In-context assessment framework, 247-51
Indexed access method, 218
Industrial facilities management, effect of information systems, 267-68
Information analysts, 231
Information center analysts, 232
Information centers, 237
Information defined, 66
Information flows, 49
Information management
  defined, 22
  individual competence, 37-40
Information management function
  activities, 228
  assessment, 247-51
  capacity planning, 244-45
  centralization versus decentralization, 233-35

Information management function—*Cont.*
  cost management, 245-47
  customer service, 243
  facility operations, 242-43
  large organizations, 224-26
  matrix versus functional form, 228-30
  organization structure, 228
  performance monitoring, 243, 275
  role, 227, 274-75
  small organizations, 226
  software, 275
  staff, 231-33, 246-47
  system security, 245
Information requirements
  analysis, 161
  application-level, 181, 194-97
  business processes, 187-88
  database, 181
  determination pitfalls, 182-84
  determination strategies, 184-91
  levels, 180-82
  organization-level, 181, 191-94
  sociotechnical approach, 195
Information technology
  business processes, 6-9
  competitive advantage, 5-6, 27
  computer integrated manufacturing, 17
  critical applications, 6
  customer service, 11-15
  defined, 21, 65
  during downsizing, 9-11
  effect on business strategy, 1-5, 254
  impact, 18-19
  in just-in-time strategy, 15-16
  organizational benefits, 27-35
  productivity improvements, 18
  societal benefits, 25-27
  strategic uses, 181
Input devices, 93, 101-3
Input/output device control, 99
Input-output interface chips, 89
Input-process-output analysis, 188
Input versus entry, 93
Integrated circuit chips, 88-89
Integrated Services Digital Networks (ISDN), 127-28
Integrated systems, 67

Interaction theory of user resistance, 176
Interblock gap, 106
Interface software, 134-35
International business, 53
Inventory control, 264-65, 269
    through manufacturing resource planning, 29, 32-33
Inverted index, 218-19
Invoicing, 61
ISDN (Integrated services digital network), 127-28

J

Jenkins, A. Milton, 168
Just-in-time strategy, 3, 265
    applications software packages, 16
    benefits, 29
    changes wrought, 15-16
    in corporate culture, 15
    customer benefits, 15
    goal, 15
    information technology, 15-16

K

Keyboards, 101
King, W. R., 193n
Knowledge-based systems
    design, 82
    rule-based versus frame-based, 82, 84
Knowledge work, 40
Knowledge work software
    design, 81
    difference from clerical applications, 80-81
    individual competence, 40-44
    programming facilities, 82
    toolkit, 40-41, 141
    types, 81

L

Laptop computers, 261
Laser beams, 96
Laser printers, 104
Leadtime analysis, 264

Leased lines, 114
Librarian software, 243
Lindgreen, P., 45n
Local area networks, 117-19
    advantages, 10
    for client server systems, 58
    communication methods, 123
    communications software, 135
    for electronic meeting support, 79
    management products, 123
    software packages, 119, 135
Logical data models
    elements, 206-7
    formalisms, 208
    goals, 208
Long haul networks, 117
Loops, 149

M

Macdonald, I. G., 157n
Machine language, 90-91
Machine operations codes, 144
Macro instruction, 149
Macro language, 139
Magnetic ink character readers, 102-3
Magnetic media, 95, 106
Mainframe computers, 96
Maintenance programmers, 231
Management information systems; *see also* Information management function
    architecture, 46-48, 239, 254
    chargeback system, 241
    corporate integration through, 253-59
    cost reduction, 10
    decentralization, 9-11
    defined, 22, 65-67
    development priorities, 18-21, 241
    effectiveness, 251
    goals, 239
    impact of manufacturing resource planning, 37
    implementation, 175-77
    integrated, 54, 57-58
    large organizations, 224-26
    master plan, 238-40
    non-integrated, 55-57

Management information systems—*Cont.*
  objectives, 67, 239
  PC-based applications, 10; *see also* End-user computing
  planning model, 71, 191-92
  profit center approach, 241
  resource allocation, 240-41
  as a separate function, 227
  small organizations, 226
  structure, 67-69
  subsystems, 68
  system strategy, 254
  trends, 55
Management reporting applications, 71-72
Manufacturing equation, 49
Manufacturing function, effect of information systems, 269-70
Manufacturing resource planning
  accounting controls, 30
  balance sheet benefits, 30-31
  cost reductions through, 29-30
  customer service, 30
  decentralized PC/LAN-based, 10
  financial ratios impact, 32-35
  impact on accounting, 35-36
  impact on management information systems, 37
  impact on materials management, 36
  impact on product design, 36
  impact on production management, 36
  impact on receivables, 33-34
  impact on return on assets (ROA), 34
  impact on sales, 37
  impact on stock appreciation, 35
  income sheet benefits, 31-32
  integrative effects, 35-37
  inventory control, 29, 32-33
  organizational benefits, 28-35
  relationship to computer integrated manufacturing, 17
Maps, 221
March, Salvatore, 210n
Marketing, effect of information systems, 259-61
Markus, M. L., 176n

Master file, 203
Materials management, impact of manufacturing resource planning, 36
Materials planning, 51-52
Megahertz (MHz), 94
Memory chips, 89
Memory management, 99
Menus, 196
Microcode, 88, 90-91
Microcomputers, 97
Microprocessor chips
  capabilities, 89
  data paths, 90
  internal architecture, 90
  types, 89
Minicomputers, 97
Modelbases, 221
Modems, 111-12
Modules, 148
Motherboards, 90
Mouse, 101
Multiattribute access method, 218-19
Multicomputer configurations, 97
Multicomputer minisystems, 97
Multimedia databases, 220-21
Multimedia output, 96
Multiple business unit integration, 58-62
Multiplexor, 115-16

N

Narrowband data, 114
Natural language commands, 197
Network basic input/output system (NetBIOS), 123
Network database model, 212-13
Network monitoring software, 243
900 numbers, 128, 130
Node, 117
Normative analysis methods, 187
Notebook computers, 97
Numerical database management software, 41-42

O

Object codes, 139, 144
Object-oriented database model, 214-15
Object-oriented languages, 147
Object programs, 144
Office automation coordinators, 232
Offline defined, 92
Olle, W. T., 157n
Online credit authorization, 261
Online databases, 221-22
Online data sources, 42
Online defined, 92
Online processing, 108
Operating systems, 97-99, 132
  basic functions, 134
  logs, 243
Operators, 232
Optical character readers, 102-3
Optical disk storage, 220
Optical storage, 107
Order entry, 61
Organizational inertia, 20
Output, 92
Output devices, 96, 103-4
Outsourcing, 246-47

P

PABX (Private Automatic Branch Exchange), 119
Packed decimal approach, 100
Packet switching networks, 120
PASCAL, 154
Password protection, 108, 238, 245
Payables, 61
Pen entry, 102
People-oriented theory of user resistance, 176
Performance evaluation, ratio analysis, 34
Personal computer management software, 41-42
Personal computers; *see also* End-user computing
  applications software packages, 10
  management information systems, 10
  in manufacturing resource planning, 10

Personal computers—*Cont.*
  memory, 89
  user responsibilities, 109
Personnel
  cost reductions, 246
  job descriptions, 231-33
  outsourcing, 246-47
Photographs, 221
Physical database design, 164
Physical database model, 215-16
Physical system design, 162, 164
Picklists, 267
Pipelining, 94
Pirate software, 142
Pixels, 95, 101
Pointer, 217
Portability of software, 140-41
Presentation graphics software, 41-42
Primary storage, 93
Printers, 96
  laser, 104
Problem-oriented programming facilities, 145
Procedure development, 165
Procedure-oriented languages, 144-45
Process analysis, 187
Process design function, effect of information systems, 268-69
Procurement function, 52
  effect of information systems, 265-66
Product design
  effect of information systems, 263-64
  impact of manufacturing resource planning, 36
Production activity control
  defined, 52
  effect of information systems, 264-65
Production management, impact of manufacturing resource planning, 36
Production planning/master scheduling, 51
Productivity
  defined, 25
  improvement through information technology, 19
  measurement, 25
Products
  cost control, 60

Products—*Cont.*
  customization, 26
  tracking, 53
Program generators, 135
Program librarian, 231
Programmers
  application, 231
  maintenance, 231
  systems, 231
Programming languages, 90-91
  algorithmic, 152, 154
  levels, 143
  standard, 140
  types, 144-47, 151-54
Programming process, 143-44
Programs
  coding, 149
  defined, 148
  development, 164-65
  flowchart, 149
  loops, 149
  paths, 149
  structure, 147-51
Project management software, 275
PROMs (programmable read-only memories), 89
Proposal definition, 160
Protocols, 119
  layers, 120-21
  types, 120
Prototype development model, 168
Pseudocode, 92
Public database access, 128, 130
Purchasing, 60-61, 265-66

R

RAM chips, 89
Random access devices, 105
Realtime processing, 105
Realtime programming, 145
Record key, 217
Records, 202
Reduced instruction set computer (RISC), 91
Reengineering of business processes, 7, 19-21, 54, 138, 257
Registers, 93

Relational database model, 213-14, 216
Relationships, 201
Repetitive manufacturing, 53
Report file, 204
Report generators, 136
Reports
  applications, 71-72, 272-73
  financial, 272-73
  soft, 72
Request for proposal, 171
Response time, 182, 196
Return on assets (ROA), impact of manufacturing resource planning, 34
Reusability, 149
RISC (reduced instruction set computers), 91
Robotics, 270
Rocckhart, J. F., 187n
Rolland, C., 157n
ROM chips, 89
Rotational delay, 105
Routines, 148, 150
RS-232 cables, 120

S

Sales
  effect of information systems, 259-61
  impact of manufacturing resource planning, 37
  order processing, 51, 260-61
  planning, 50-51
Schedulers, 99
Scheduling and project management software, 41, 43, 51, 60, 265, 270
Schema, 207
Screens
  color, 197
  design, 182, 196
  touch sensitive, 102
SDLC (Synchronous Data Link Control), 121
Secondary storage, 92
  hardware, 95-96
Security, 238, 245
  coordinators, 232
  software, 275
Semantic data model, 207

Sequential access method, 217
Serial access devices, 106
Shareware, 142
Silicon chips, 88-89
Single business units
   integrated systems, 57-58
   non-integrated systems, 55-57
Site licenses, 141-42
SNA (System Network Architecture), 121
Sociotechnical design, 176-77, 195
Soft reports, 72
Software; *see also* Applications software packages
   analytical, 275
   backup and recovery, 238
   client server systems, 141-42
   communications, 135
   cooperative work, 41, 43
   decision support systems, 76-77
   defined, 131
   development tools, 133
   dialing, 128-29
   electronic mail, 41-42
   electronic meeting systems, 79
   engineering, 147
   financial modeling, 41, 43
   forecasting, 41, 43
   group decision support systems, 79
   information management, 275
   interface, 134-35
   knowledge work toolkit, 40-41, 81
   librarian, 243
   local area networks, 119, 135
   network monitoring, 243
   numerical database management, 41-42
   PC management, 41-42
   pirated, 142
   portability, 140-41
   presentation graphics, 41-42
   project management, 275
   role, 131-32
   scheduling and project management, 41, 43, 51, 60, 265, 270
   security, 275
   spreadsheet, 41-42
   statistical, 41-42
   system, 97-99, 132-34

Software—*Cont.*
   text database, 41-42
   types, 132
   user interface, 134-35
   word processing, 41-42
Software estimation packages, 275
Software monitors, 243, 275
Sol, H. G., 157n
Sorting, 203
Source codes, 139, 143
Source programs, 143
Spreadsheet processors, 139
Spreadsheet software, 41-42
SQL (Structured Query Language), 146, 154
Statistical software, 41-42
Stock appreciation, impact of manufacturing resource planning, 35
Storage devices, 104-7
Strategy set transformation, 193
Streaming tape, 106
Structured query language (SQL), 146, 154
Stylus, 102
Subprograms, 148
Subroutines, 148, 150
Supercomputers, 94, 96
Super-minicomputers, 97
SWIFT (Society for Worldwide Interbank Financial Telecommunication), 273
Symbolic operation codes, 144
Synchronous transmission, 112
System designers, 231
System development life cycle (SDLC)
   definition stage, 160-62
   development stage, 162-65
   elements, 157
   installation, 166-67
   maintenance activities, 167
   post audit, 167
System network architecture (SNA), 121
System operations organization, 234-36
System-oriented theory of user resistance, 176
System prompting, 196
Systems analysts, 231
Systems programmers, 231
Systems software, 97-99
   difference from applications software packages, 132-34

T

Tape unit designs, 106
Telephone services, 128-30
Text databases
  retrieval, 220
  software, 41-42
  storage, 220
Text search commands, 221
Thimbles, 96
32-bit string, 101
Token ring design, 119
Total quality management
  defined, 15
  effect of information systems, 273-74
Touch sensitive screens, 102
Touchtone direct inquiry systems, 128-29
Trackball, 102
Training programs, effect of information systems, 271
Transaction file, 203-4
Transaction processing applications, 69-71
Transmitters, 110
Transparent operations, 92
Tuples, 213
Turnkey systems, 226
Twisted pair cable, 119
Typewriter terminals, 96

U

Units, 202
Universal product codes (UPC), 102-3
User-developed systems, 173-74; *see also* End-user computing
User interface design, 195-97
User interface software, 134-35
User liaisons, 232, 236
Users
  resistance, 176
  training, 166

V

Van Assche, F. J. M., 157n
Van der Poel, P., 45n
Van Waes, R., 45n
Vector processing, 94
Vendor information, 61, 266
Verrijn-Stuart, A. A., 157n
Very high level programming languages, 145-46
Virtual machines, 91-92
Virtual storage, 92
Viruses, 142
  detection, 238
Visible scheduling systems, 265
Visual display units (VDU), 96-97
VLSI (very large scale integration), 89
Voice band data, 114
Voice entry, 102
Voice mail, 123-25
Voice message databases, 220-21
Voice synthesizers, 104

W

Wafers, 88-89
Waveform, 111-12
Wetherbe, J. C., 193n
"What if" analyses, 43
Wide area networks, 117, 120
Word processing
  software, 41-42
  text search commands, 221
Workflow streamlining, 20
Workstations, 97
WORM (write-once-read-many), 107
Write ring, 106

X

X.25 open systems interconnect model, 120-21

Z

Zachman, J. A., 45n